# THE
# CAR
# BIBLE

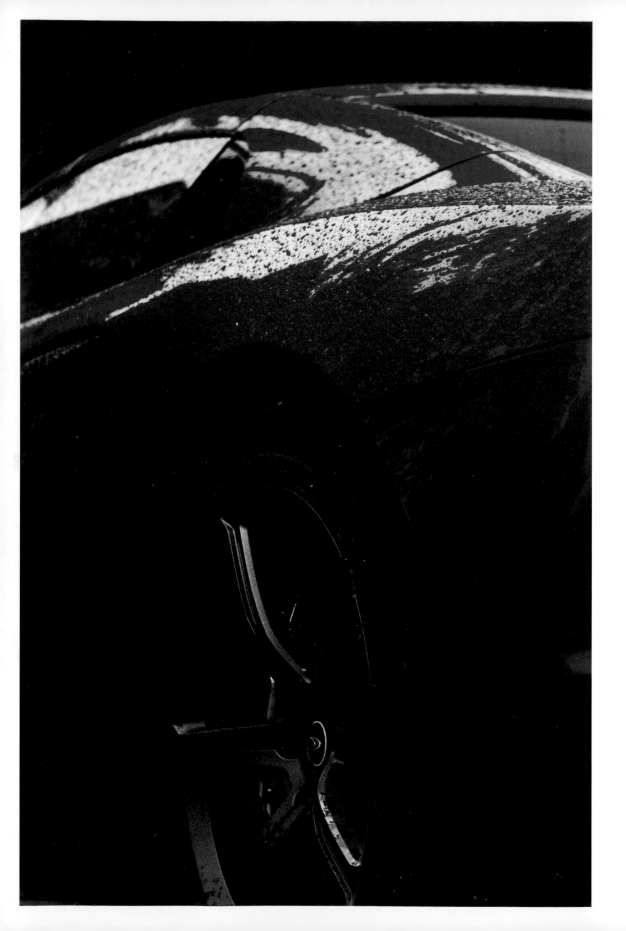

# THE
# CAR
# BIBLE

## 100 YEARS OF
## CLASSIC, CONCEPT &
## CONVENTIONAL CARS

An Hachette UK Company
www.hachette.co.uk

First published in Great Britain in 2018 by Pyramid,
an imprint of Octopus Publishing Group Ltd
Carmelite House, 50 Victoria Embankment, London EC4Y 0DZ
www.octopusbooks.co.uk

ISBN 978-0-7537-3336-3

A CIP catalogue record for this book is available from the British Library

Printed and bound in China

10 9 8 7 6 5 4 3 2

Publisher: Lucy Pessell
Designer: Lisa Layton
Editor: Sarah Vaughan
Contributing Editor: Sian Parkhouse
Production Controller: Katie Jarvis

Some of this material previously appeared in *501 Must-Drive Cars*.

# CONTENTS

# INTRODUCTION

**Within these pages, you'll find cars from all over the world, of all sorts, shapes and sizes – from tiny microcars to gigantic behemoths, from stately sedans to death-defying racers, 1920s classics to post-modern concept prototypes, almost unobtainable rarities like the exotic Bugatti Royale to models manufactured in their millions like the Fiat 124, gallant failures like the Cord 810 to runaway successes like the Triumph TR6.**

It is extraordinary to think that scarcely more than one hundred years ago Queen Victoria's long reign was drawing to a close, at the end of an era that saw the dramatic unfolding of a world-changing Industrial Revolution in Western Europe and the beginnings of serious industrialization in the USA, a superpower in waiting. History doesn't record what the elderly Queen thought of those new-fangled horseless carriages that started appearing on Britain's streets – but in 1896 the law that required road-going 'locomotives' to be led by a pedestrian carrying a red flag was repealed, allowing 'light locomotives' to proceed at a dizzying 14 mph (22 km/h). 'The Century of the Automobile' had dawned.

In due course, the building of cars would become the world's single most important manufacturing sector, both in its own right and – more significantly – by generating massive spin-off economic growth. Nowhere was this truer than in the USA. That vast young country acquired its first coast-to-coast motor route, the Lincoln Highway, in 1913 and the way in which economic activity and prosperity spread along its entire length like wildfire was a blueprint for things to come, as the automobile rapidly opened up a continent. Meanwhile, oil production to fuel those burgeoning internal combustion engines became a boom industry.

In those early years car manufacture attracted a host of clever engineers, eager entrepreneurs and downright chancers who started operating in almost every country of the developed world. The decade before World War I saw rapid technological advance, and by the dawn of the Roaring Twenties foundations for the modern automobile had been well and truly laid. This book tells the fascinating story of the motorcar's extraordinary evolution since then, by highlighting some of the most iconic vehicles ever produced. These are the ones that we'd all love to drive if we were lucky enough to get the chance, for they encompass the most important, interesting, exciting or desirable cars ever built – often with all four qualities represented in one car.

The reason that the car is deeply entrenched in the affections of so many – and remains an unflagging object of desire – is that it represents the ultimate expression of personal freedom. Once that basic motivation is established, the car is capable of stirring all sorts of other emotions. Cars can be beautiful works of automotive art or thrilling driving machines, status symbols or vital workhorses . . . even a serious investment proposition. It is no accident that many of the cars featured in these pages come with price tags bearing lots of zeros, as competition to own these very special classics from the annals of motoring history drives prices to dizzy heights.

Of course, the automobile's very success has created problems. With the people of emerging nations keen to share motoring freedoms long enjoyed in the industrialized world – China is now challenging the USA as the largest single automobile market – the problem of vehicle emissions contributing to the rapid advance of global warming can only become more severe. At the same time, the very things that make the car so desirable in the first place – fast, convenient and flexible personal transport coupled with the freedom of the open road – are slowly being smothered by the sheer volume of traffic.

Realistically, there's no way that drivers will be persuaded to give up cars en masse, nor any possibility that people around the world will abandon their dreams of joining the empowered motoring fraternity. It may seem like a recipe for ultimate disaster, but this book's closing chapter contains tantalizing hints that car-makers are close to perfecting the alternative technologies that may well make this 'The Century of the Green Machine'.

For now though, whether your fantasy is to roar off behind the wheel of a Lamborghini, be swept off in a chauffeur driven Mercedes-Benz, take to the highway in a Ford pickup, go for a Sunday drive down country lanes in a Morris Minor or even just spend your days tinkering with your old MG, *The Car Bible* is a book to linger over and to dream on.

1900s, 1920s & 1930s

# ALFA ROMEO 8C 2300

The 8C (for eight-cylinder) engine was designed by Vittorio Jano and introduced by Alfa Romeo in 1931. In various forms this brilliant power plant with its finned aluminium casing was destined to propel the company's sought-after cars throughout the 1930s and become synonymous with triumph on the racetrack and prestige on the street.

The 8C's first incarnation was in the 8C 2300, which came in long (lungo) or short (corto) versions, plus a shorter-still Spider Corsa racing chassis. Road cars were mostly created by outside coachbuilders who added bodywork to a rolling chassis. However, Alfa did build their own bodies – occasionally even converting redundant race cars for road use.

This meant that – like many vehicles produced in the 1930s – the 8C 2300 Series road cars ended up with a plethora of body styles. Indeed, there were no two the same in the production run of 188 cars, with an assortment created by talented design-and-build companies such as Zagato, Farina, Figoni, Brianza, Carlton, Castagna and Touring. But they all had one thing in common – graceful lines that make these exclusive vehicles as sought after today as they were in the 1930s. The lungo chassis was used for elegant four-seater bodies and the corto chassis for more sporty open-top or coupe coachwork.

In fact, racing remained the name of the game and the three versions of the 8C 2300 are generally known by their competition designations – Le Mans for long-chassis versions (as the 24-hour race specified a four-seater), Mille Miglia for the short-chassis cars and Monza for the racing version. The reason behind the enduring success of the Alfa Romeo 8C 2300 was both simple and complex – it simply had the best build quality and was the most technically advanced, competitive car of its era.

**COUNTRY OF ORIGIN:**
Italy

**FIRST MANUFACTURED:**
1931 (until 1935)

**ENGINE:**
2,336 cc Straight Eight

**PERFORMANCE:**
The boat-tailed Monza racing version was capable of 140 mph (225 km/h)

**YOU SHOULD KNOW:**
If you can't find one to drive, at least try to listen to one – the throaty roar of Jano's 8C engine is unmistakable, having been described by one over-enthusiastic fan as 'a symphony in which each gear tooth and roll bearing plays a note'.

# ALFA ROMEO 8C 2900B

**COUNTRY OF ORIGIN:**
Italy

**FIRST MANUFACTURED:**
1935 (until 1939)

**ENGINE:**
2,905 cc DOHC Straight
Eight

**PERFORMANCE:**
Top speed of around
120 mph (175 km/h),
depending on bodywork.

**YOU SHOULD KNOW:**
Finding an 8C 2900B
Spider for that thrilling
'must drive' moment
won't be easy – only
30 were ever made (20
short wheelbase, 10 long
wheelbase) and anyone
lucky (and rich) enough
to own one guards it like
the Crown Jewels.

In the 1930s, Europe's dictators saw motor-racing success as excellent publicity for their countries, and German–Italian rivalry saw the production of some very seductive racing cars. Italy's contributions were impressive. The Alfa Romeo P3 – the world's first single-seater Grand Prix car – was one of the 8C Series. Its successor was the 8C 2900A, powered by a bored-out version of Vittorio Jano's 8C engine. This advanced flying machine was soon winning races, and Alfa Romeo decided to cash in on its supercar status by producing a road-going version.

Thus was the 8C 2900B conceived and born, a sibling of the Grand Prix car with a road body and slightly detuned engine. There were two versions – long and short chassis – and such was the cost of these magnificent machines that only a few were ever made, making them incredibly rare, with some two-thirds of the run being open-topped Spiders and the rest being sports coupes. Although one or two 8C 2900Bs had factory bodywork, most were supplied to external coachbuilders in rolling chassis form for finishing.

The results were stunning – as all those enthusiasts who regard the 8C 2900B as one of the very best prewar passenger sports cars will testify. They are true masterpieces of elegance with a beauty and charm that make them irresistible, always gathering an admiring crowd when they appear at classic car shows. Most of the bodies were made by the Touring company, who used an innovatory lightweight metal framework developed by Zagato. Their long-wheelbase convertibles are the crème de la crème visually, but every single 8C 2900B is a masterpiece, including one or two special racing versions. The varying body styles are invariably slender and elegant, introducing the *ala spessa* concept that incorporated previously separate elements like mudguards and lights into streamlined bodywork.

# ALVIS SPEED 25

**One car every dashing man about town coveted in the 1930s was the gorgeous Alvis Speed 25 – a sleek machine that would never fail to look super-stylish arriving outside a stately home ahead of that discreetly decadent country-house weekend. Opinions haven't changed. Many classic car aficionados consider the beautifully proportioned Speed 25 to be one of the finest vehicles produced in the 1930s – not only for its stunning appearance, but also for advanced technical features that characterized all Alvis cars and make them a pleasure to drive today.**

The marque produced its first vehicles in 1920 and continued in business until the 1960s. Although Alvis built various saloons, the company's real forte was the sports tourer. The powerful Speed 25's immediate predecessor, the racy Speed 20 series, was introduced by Alvis after a brief foray into front-wheel drive with the pretty, innovative but not-very-successful 4/15s and 8/15s of the late 1920s.

Capitalizing on their sporty reputation, Alvis produced the popular Silver Eagle in 1928 with the option of a two-seater, coupe, drophead coupe or saloon body. The Speed 20 Series followed in 1932, ushering in the spectacular flowering that Alvis enjoyed in the 1930s. This came to a climax with the introduction of the Speed 25 in 1936, and who can say how far the company would have developed this superb model if World War II had not intervened.

Three types of Speed 25 were manufactured – a two-door sports tourer, a two-door drophead coupe and a two-door sports saloon. Today, these sought-after classics command top prices, and their quality build has ensured that over half the production run has survived. Anyone lucky enough to slip behind the wheel of a Speed 25 (over 200 are out there somewhere) will be effortlessly transported back to the Golden Era of Alvis.

**COUNTRY OF ORIGIN:**
UK

**FIRST MANUFACTURED:**
1936 (until 1940)

**ENGINE:**
3,571 cc OHV Straight Six

**PERFORMANCE:**
Top speed of around 90 mph (145 km/h)

**YOU SHOULD KNOW:**
The end of the line for the Speed 25 came in late 1940, production ceasing abruptly when the Luftwaffe bombed the Alvis factory in Coventry – and when the company resumed car manufacture in 1946 it was with the solid but much-less-glamorous TA-14.

# AUBURN SPEEDSTER 851

**COUNTRY OF ORIGIN:**
USA

**FIRST MANUFACTURED:**
1935 (until 1937)

**ENGINE:**
4.6 l (280 cid) Flathead
Straight Eight

**PERFORMANCE:**
Top speed of 103 mph
(166 km/h); 0–60 mph
(97 km/h) in 15 secs

**YOU SHOULD KNOW:**
The Auburn company's
art deco former
headquarters building
in Auburn, Indiana, is
now a National Historic
Landmark that houses the
Auburn Cord Duesenberg
Automobile Museum.

**Several thousand Auburn 851s in various body styles were sold by entrepreneur Errett Lobban Cord at the height of the Great Depression – no mean feat. The star was the Speedster 851 – developed from earlier Speedsters that had been produced since 1929 with enough fresh features to justify a new-model tag in fixed-head and convertible coupe form. Improvements designed by ex-Duesenberg maestro Gordon Buehrig included a raked radiator, sinuous front bumpers, teardrop headlamps and flowing lines ending in a characteristic boat tail.**

After decades of unremarkable life in the automobile business, making an assortment of worthy cars without really capturing the public's imagination, Auburn finally earned a place in the motoring hall of fame with one of the few sports cars produced in America before World War II – a powerful, stylish machine that helped to establish the American trend towards size coupled with tremendous straight-line performance, with the added bonus of a reasonable price tag. This was because the Speedster 851 was offered as a loss-leader in the hope that admirers lured into the showroom by its delicious looks would actually buy a cheaper but more profitable model – a ploy that worked so well that only a few hundred Speedsters were manufactured.

Following a New Year's Day launch in 1935, the Speedster 851 was duly promoted on the grounds of . . . speed. A top-of-the-range supercharged SC model with its four external exhaust pipes and no additional modifications did an amazing 12-hour endurance run during which it averaged over 100 mph (160 km/h) in the hands of land-speed record holder Ab Jenkins, who went on to set many other records. Although there was little or no change, 1936 cars were given an 852 designation. When sales collapsed, production ended and the Auburn company folded in 1937.

# AUSTIN 7

**COUNTRY OF ORIGIN:**
UK

**FIRST MANUFACTURED:**
1922 (until 1939)

**ENGINE:**
3,571 cc OHV Straight Six

**PERFORMANCE:**
Top speed of around 90
mph (145 km/h)

**YOU SHOULD KNOW:**
Many Austin 7s were
repurposed after World
War II, including the first
race car built by Bruce
McLaren, and the first
Lotus. The name was also
used for early versions of
the Austin A30 in 1951
and Mini in 1959.

If there's one quintessential British prewar car it must surely be the Austin 7, one of the most popular small cars ever produced. After a slow start in 1922 with barely two thousand 'Sevens' sold, progress was spectacular. Before the outbreak of World War II abruptly ended production in 1939, over 290,000 had rolled off the line in Britain. Overseas manufacture was licensed in France, Germany and the USA, whilst Japan's reputation for copying others' technology was partially established when Nissan used the Austin 7 as the template for its first cars.

This iconic 'people's car' owed its inception to Sir Herbert Austin, who bulldozed his board of directors into sanctioning a 'big saloon in miniature' and personally designed it in conjunction with Stanley Edge, who was responsible for the engine. The first production model was the AB Tourer. With a wheelbase of just 6 ft 3 in (1.9 m) and weighing in at a mere 794 lb (360 kg) it used a small, economical engine mounted on an A-frame chassis. This may be one of the easiest 'must-drive' cars to find, but double-declutching should be mastered before taking to the road.

There were six types produced over time – tourers, saloons, cabriolets, sports, coupes and vans – most with many variants as technical advances were regularly introduced. In addition, the distinctive two-tone Austin 7 Swallow was coachbuilt by William Lyons of the Swallow Sidecar Company. A Swallow open tourer was introduced in 1927 with a saloon following in 1928. Some 3500 Swallows were produced in various body styles before Lyons started making his own SS (later Jaguar) cars in 1932. He backed a good pony. By the end of the 1920s the runaway success of the Austin 7 had effectively wiped out most other small British cars and cyclecars.

# BENTLEY 8L

It was the last of the line – and the most impressive. The 8 litre Bentley made its debut at the Olympia Motor Show in 1930 and caused a sensation. It was the largest car hitherto made in Britain and a serious competitor for the Rolls-Royce Phantom II. This was W O Bentley's shot at producing a headline-stealer that would catapult him to the top of the luxury car league, thus stealing Rolls-Royce's mantle and rescuing Bentley from financial difficulty.

The ploy was a gallant failure. Only one hundred 8Ls were produced and by mid-1931 Bentley Motors was bankrupt. W O Bentley thought the receiver's sale would see Napiers of Acton emerge with the assets and was already planning a Napier-Bentley with his new partner. But Rolls-Royce, slyly acting through an intermediary, outbid Napier and promptly killed off the 8L.

It was a clever move. The 8L was a formidable challenger for anything Rolls-Royce made. A state-of-the-art engine offered innovatory features like twin-spark ignition and four valves per cylinder, plus a sturdy chassis with servo-assisted brakes all round, making this an exclusive but expensive vehicle. Bentley Motors supplied a rolling chassis (in short or long wheelbase) and the customer was required to employ a coachbuilder to add bodywork.

Famous names like H J Mulliner, Gurney Nutting and Barker duly obliged, creating a variety of body styles. Most were built on the long chassis, with relatively few buyers choosing the short version. Although the idea was to compete with the luxury saloons of the era, around 20 8Ls were finished with stunning open-topped bodies and even the limousines tended to have racy lines. Whatever bodywork was chosen, the package offered incomparable smoothness and quietness of ride and these magnificent machines are a pleasure to drive, now as then.

**COUNTRY OF ORIGIN:**
UK

**FIRST MANUFACTURED:**
1930 (until 1931)

**ENGINE:**
7,983 cc Straight Six

**PERFORMANCE:**
Over 100 mph (161 km/h) with the heaviest limousine coachwork

**YOU SHOULD KNOW:**
With their exemplary build quality, many of the Bentley 8Ls that were manufactured are still around, but such is their cachet that well-restored examples sell at auction for up to $1.5 million . . . and beyond.

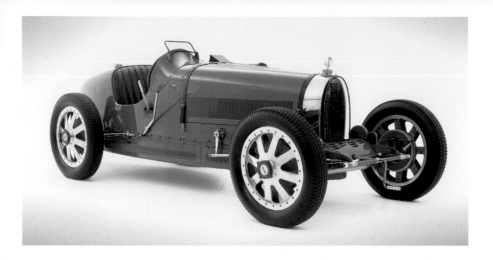

# BUGATTI TYPE 35

**COUNTRY OF ORIGIN:**
France

**FIRST MANUFACTURED:**
1924 (until 1931)

**ENGINE:**
1,991 cc or 2,262 cc
Straight Eight

**PERFORMANCE:**
Varied according to
model, with around 90
mph (145 km/h) being
the norm

**YOU SHOULD KNOW:**
When a customer had
the temerity to complain
that the brakes on his
Type 35 left something
to be desired it is said
that Ettore Bugatti
disdainfully replied 'I
make my cars to go, not
to stop'.

Conceived by a brilliant Italian and built in France, this is the ultimate vintage racing car. The two-seater Bugatti Type 35 was certainly the most successful racer of all time, various models winning over two thousand races and establishing the marque's mythical status. This blue bombshell with its superb handling and reliable engine was the first Bugatti to feature that iconic arched radiator and remains an all-time favourite with classic car aficionados. With nearly 350 Type 35s made, plenty survive to thrill weekend drivers.

The original Type 35 of 1924 had a new engine with five main bearings and a unique ball-bearing system that allowed this potent power plant to rev at an impressive 6000 rpm and produce 90 hp. This state-of-the-art machine was expensive and complicated, so the Type 35A of 1925 addressed the problem. The public swiftly nicknamed this simplified model 'The Tecla' after a maker of cheap jewellery, but it was nonetheless hugely successful.

Although Ettore Bugatti claimed to dislike forced induction, he allowed Type 36C cars to be fitted with a supercharger that boosted power output by a third and brought two French Grand Prix victories (1928 and 1930). Type 35T with a bored-out engine was created for Sicily's famous endurance race and swiftly christened the Bugatti Targa Florio – justifying the nickname with straight victories between 1925 and 1929. Its successor – the final Type 35 – was the 35B (originally 35TC) of 1927. It was the same as the 35T with the addition of a large supercharger. A 35B won the French Grand Prix of 1929. The Bugatti Type 37 was an extension of the 35 series. This sports car reused the chassis and body of the 35 but had a smaller 1,496 cc engine – supercharged in the Type 37A. Type 39 was visually identical to the Type 35, but with a smaller engine.

# BUGATTI ROYALE

**The simple 'Bugatti Type 41' designation hardly hints at the grandeur it represents, for this is one of the most impressive automobiles ever created. No wonder the Type 41 was swiftly nicknamed 'The Royale', for it was intended as luxurious transport for monarchs and heads of state.**

Measuring in at an impressive 6.4 m (21 ft) in length, each Royale was treated to a different body created by a leading coachbuilder. Sadly for the visionary Ettore Bugatti, his grand design was conceived in the extravagant 1920s, with the prototype completed in 1927. But it was launched as the world tumbled into recession and only half a dozen Royales were built, of which three were sold. One went to France, another to Germany and the third to England.

Ettore's plan to build 25 of these magnificent machines sank beneath the weight of economic adversity, and after failing to sell half the limited production run the dream was over. All six Royales still exist, though not all in original form – two have been rebodied more than once. In chassis number order there's the Coupe Napoleon (Ettore's own car that has had five different bodies), the Binder Coupe de Ville (two bodies), the Weinberger (original roadster body), the Park Ward (original limousine body), the racy Kelner coupe (original grand tourer body) and finally (though possibly the first made) the Double Berline de Voyage (original body).

Whilst driving one of these beauties is not a realistic ambition, seeing one most certainly is – the Coupe Napoleon is in France's Mulhouse National Automobile Museum, together with an authentic replica of No 2 with original roadster body. The Weinberger cabriolet now resides in The Henry Ford, that impressive museum in Dearborn, Michigan created by someone who operated at the diametrically opposite end of the automotive spectrum.

**COUNTRY OF ORIGIN:**
France

**FIRST MANUFACTURED:**
1927 (until 1933)

**ENGINE:**
12,763 cc Straight Eight

**PERFORMANCE:**
Capable of 100 mph
(161 km/h)

**YOU SHOULD KNOW:**
Economic disaster eventually turned to a modest triumph when Ettore Bugatti cannily recycled unused 'Royale' engines to power a new line of railcars.

# BUICK ROADMASTER

**COUNTRY OF ORIGIN:**
USA

**FIRST MANUFACTURED:**
1936 (until 1958)

**ENGINE:**
5.2 l (320 cid) OHV
Straight Eight

**PERFORMANCE:**
Top speed of 90 mph
(145 km/h)

**YOU SHOULD KNOW:**
In the GM 'family',
carefully structured to
appeal to all levels of
buyer, Buick occupied
the Number Three slot
behind Cadillac and
La Salle, but ahead of
Oldsmobile, Pontiac and
Chevrolet.

**This is a respected name in US automotive history, for when Buick revamped its model range in 1936 as America started to emerge from the Great Depression, 'Roadmaster' was the title chosen for newcomers designed to replace the company's former Series 80 model. The name lasted until 1958 and badged a number of evolution models that were quintessentially American, before being revived briefly in the 1990s.**

From 1936 to 1948 General Motors' Roadmaster range consisted of a sedan, coupe, convertible phaeton and station wagon. These imposing long-wheelbase vehicles shared a basic structure with top-of-the-range Oldsmobile stablemates and remain a pleasure to drive today, giving a wonderful sense of stately progress on soft suspension. Innovative features included GM's all-steel 'turret top' body, bullet-shaped headlights and a raked windscreen. The Roadmaster also incorporated technical advances like independent front suspension and hydraulic brakes.

The very name conjured up an image of supremacy – exactly as GM intended – and these highway cruisers were an instant success, with a competitive price tag ensuring that 17,000 Roadmasters were snapped up in the first year of production. The sportiest option was the four-door soft-top phaeton, though the car-buying public much preferred the sturdy sedan.

As sales slowly declined, cosmetic modifications took place, including a slight reduction in size and fitting (in 1941) of the powerful Fireball Eight engine with twin carburettors. Changes were small, but visually enhanced these handsome vehicles. New styling was finally introduced for 1942, but production was suspended as a result of wartime stringency and the new models would serve as the basis of the first Buicks produced after World War II. From 1946 until they were superseded after 1958, the Roadmaster became Buick's top-of-the-range offering and variants included the last wood-bodied station wagon to be produced in the USA, the 1953 Model 79-R.

# CADILLAC SIXTY-SPECIAL

**In the period when American automotive design was evolving from stuck-in-the-Depression-era styles towards the very different cars of the late 1940s, no vehicle was more influential in setting a new agenda than the Cadillac Sixty-Special. This derivative of the Series 60 entry-level Caddie was designed by Bill Mitchell, newly appointed head of styling at Cadillac and LaSalle.**

GM bosses were sceptical about his creation, so radical was its understated styling in a notoriously conservative marketplace. This daring yet elegant four-door sedan without running boards looked like a convertible with a low ride height, built-in trunk, large windows with narrow frames, no belt-line trim and little chrome embellishment. But Mitchell proved to be a man of vision when the Sixty-Special outsold every other Cadillac in its debut year.

In 1939 there was some cosmetic updating, plus new options like a sunroof and sliding glass panel to separate driver and passengers. There was major evolution in the final two years of the Sixty-Special's first incarnation (the name would return on later models) when Cadillac's Fleetwood operation started building the bodies, allowing four styles to be offered – the basic touring sedan, an Imperial sedan and two formal Town cars with different finishes that allowed the roof above the driver to be removed and a glass partition raised to protect passengers and guarantee their privacy.

It is generally agreed that the 1941 Sixty-Specials – with a revised front-end design and skirted fenders – were the most attractive of all, before being superseded by a completely new model for 1942. Nearly 18,000 Specials were manufactured before this change, making it a huge commercial success. It may have started as an innovative low-end product, but as the years rolled by the Sixty-Special steadily climbed the Cadillac pecking order and has become a coveted drive for 1930s car enthusiasts.

**COUNTRY OF ORIGIN:**
USA

**FIRST MANUFACTURED:**
1938 (until 1941)

**ENGINE:**
5.67 l (346 cid) V8

**PERFORMANCE:**
Top speed around 90 mph (145 km/h)

**YOU SHOULD KNOW:**
The rarest Sixty-Specials were three one-offs dating from 1938 – two four-door convertibles owned by General Motors executives and a lone coupe. It is thought that there were no more than a dozen custom bodies fitted between 1938 and 1941.

# CITROËN TRACTION AVANT

The name of the game for Citroën in the mid-1930s was 'frontal traction', for the phenomenally successful Traction Avant was launched in 1934 and over three-quarters of a million would be sold before eventual discontinuation in 1957. As with many French cars over the years, both technology and design were innovative. The Traction Avant's looks were rakish and it had an arc-welded monocoque body – abandoning the traditional 'chassis with separate bodywork bolted on' approach in favour of an integrated unit…thus popularizing a method of car construction that became almost universal. Another advanced feature was the Traction Avant's independent front suspension.

This novel low-slung machine was daring indeed compared to its contemporaries. But unfortunately its high development costs bankrupted Citroën, which was taken over by Michelin – thus enabling production to continue, with the added benefit for the new owner that Traction Avants could be used to pre-test Michelin tyres. The original 7A model was a saloon with a small engine. This was quickly superseded by the 7B and 7C, each in turn having a slightly larger engine.

Later models were introduced with still larger engines, but the design hardly changed over two decades (though there was a rear-end tweak in 1952). Two-door coupes and four-door saloons were augmented with imaginative variants like the Commerciale, a clever hatchback with split tailgate. There was also a pleasing convertible and 'long' model with an extra row of seats, though plans for automatic transmission and a luxury V8-engined limousine version never came to fruition.

Traction Avants were not only built at the main Paris plant, but also in Belgium, Germany and England. These robust vehicles survive in large numbers, with owner-drivers regularly holding rallies all over the world and quite a few still in use as regular road cars.

**COUNTRY OF ORIGIN:**
France

**FIRST MANUFACTURED:**
1934 (until 1957)

**ENGINE:**
1,303 cc, 1,529 cc, 1,628 cc, 1,911 cc Straight Four; 2,867 cc Straight Six

**PERFORMANCE:**
A mid-range engine could reach 70 mph (112 km/h)

**YOU SHOULD KNOW:**
The new monocoque body was treated with widespread suspicion when the Traction Avant was launched, with traditionalists believing it lacked strength – so to confound doubters Citroën arranged an impressive crash test in which the new vehicle remained in one piece after being pushed over a cliff.

# CHRYSLER CL CUSTOM IMPERIAL

**COUNTRY OF ORIGIN:**
USA

**FIRST MANUFACTURED:**
1933

**ENGINE:**
6.3 l (385 cid) Straight
Eight

**PERFORMANCE:**
Up to 100 mph (161 km/h)

**YOU SHOULD KNOW:**
This will be a really tough
nut for 'must drivers' to
crack – only eight of the
superb LeBaron Custom
Imperial phaetons are
known to survive.

Wow! The Chrysler CL Custom Imperial must surely be one of the most impressive classic American car series ever, with the phaetons in particular being breathtakingly beautiful. Chrysler's luxury Imperial line was introduced in 1926 to challenge Cadillac and Lincoln at the top end of the market, and remained around in various shapes and forms for years. But enthusiasts are truly thankful for the 1931 revamp, which saw the second generation 'Imperial 8' with its new engine produced in four delightful standard body styles – a four-door limousine, a four-door sedan, a two-door roadster and a two-door coupe, all with signature wire wheels.

But four-door CL Custom Phaetons of 1933 with bodywork by LeBaron are the unchallenged Imperial superstars – and like all superstars they are certainly precious, as just 36 phaetons with bodies commissioned from the prestigious New York design-and-build company were included in the total of 151 Custom Imperials manufactured in 1933. With its endless hood and rounded trunk, this is a truly eye-catching vehicle. It was technically advanced, too, with Chrysler's 'Floating Power' system (added to the Imperial range in 1932) coupled with near-perfect weight distribution making a smooth ride even smoother, and ensuring that this large vehicle was a pleasure to drive.

However, a glass partition could be raised to separate front and back seats for those who preferred to let a chauffeur have the fun. Unfortunately, with the Great Depression in full swing, there weren't too many of these around to support continued production. So the flowing lines of the Imperial would soon be banished by Chrysler's more advanced, commercially successful but infinitely less appealing Airflow. Given the choice, today's classic car driver would choose the Imperial every time . . . hoping against hope that the magnificent machine would be an ultra-desirable Custom Phaeton.

# FORD MODEL B/18

**The first Ford Model B appeared in 1904 – one of the company's earliest products. The second coming of the Model B was in 1932, when Ford produced and sold around 118,000 of these typical Bonnie-and-Clydemobiles, developed from the Model A. The lesson of lingering with the Model T for too long – and relying for success on a single car – had finally been learned by Henry Ford.**

The Model B made history by being the first to run alongside a concurrent model – the visually identical Model 18 (aka Ford V8) that differed only in that its engine was the awesome V8 destined to serve the company (and its customers) so well over the years ahead – though not before initial teething troubles were ironed out. But – despite relying totally on his trusty four-cylinder motor for decades – Henry Ford had become obsessed with his new engine and the Model 18 V8 was potentially so superior to its sibling (selling 224,000 in its launch year) that the four cylinder Model B was phased out by 1934 (when the V8 was redesignated Model 40A).

In the meantime a mighty impressive selection included 18 different models, each with the option of a four- or eight-cylinder engine, making a total of 36 tempting choices for the buyer. The full range included two basic roadsters, three basic coupes, convertible sedan, cabriolet, Tudor sedan (two doors, get it?), Fordor sedan (you got it, four doors), DeLuxe roadster, DeLuxe coupe, DeLuxe phaeton, Victoria coupe, DeLuxe Tudor sedan, DeLuxe Fordor sedan and station wagon.

This serves as a reminder that Ford's 'one model' policy actually concealed a wealth of choice for car buyers. The number produced and availability of spares makes the B/18 an attractive option for restorers, and a large number are still enjoyed by weekend drivers.

**COUNTRY OF ORIGIN:**
USA

**FIRST MANUFACTURED:**
1932 (until 1934)

**ENGINE:**
3.3 l (201 cid) Straight Four (B); 3.6 l (221 cid) Flathead V8 (Model 18)

**PERFORMANCE:**
The Model 18 could reach 80 mph (129 km/h)

**YOU SHOULD KNOW:**
From the 1940s the Model B/18 became the most popular vehicle in a fashion that swept through America's testosterone-charged young men like wildfire – hot rodding – and the one customizers coveted above all others was the stylish 'Deuce coupe'.

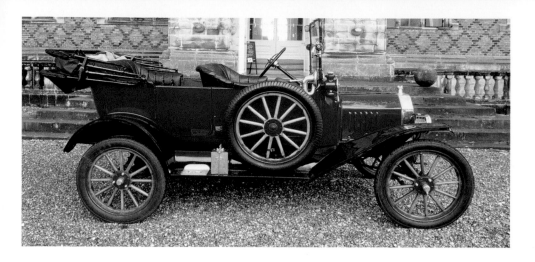

# FORD
# MODEL T

**COUNTRY OF ORIGIN:**
USA

**FIRST MANUFACTURED:**
1908 (until 1927)

**ENGINE:**
2.9 l (177 cid) Straight
Four

**PERFORMANCE:**
Top speed was a stately
45 mph (72 km/h)

**YOU SHOULD KNOW:**
'Must drivers' should
know that the throttle is
the lever on the steering
wheel, the left foot pedal
engages two forward
gears, the middle pedal
engages reverse and
the right-hand pedal is
the brake, whilst the
lever beside the driver's
seat is the parking and
emergency brake, also
being used to put the car
into neutral. Simple!

**Cheerfully dubbed 'Tin Lizzie' or 'Flivver', the foundation of the Ford Motor Company's mighty automotive empire was the Model T, introduced in 1908. The world's first affordable automobile changed the face of America, kick-starting an industry that generated rapid economic growth in the USA (and beyond, for the Model T was manufactured in 11 other countries).**

This phenomenal machine continued in production for nearly two decades, with each new car assembled in just 93 minutes. Over time the Model T did evolve, though Henry Ford was so fond of his soar-away success that he was reluctant to sanction too much development and allowed relatively few innovations. He had reason to believe in his baby – by 1918 half the cars in America were Model Ts and, though they were unsophisticated, with a throttle hand lever for acceleration and hand crank starting, the low prices achieved as a result of Ford's advanced production-line manufacturing techniques undercut the competition and ensured enduring success.

But when other companies started matching Ford on price, whilst offering better comfort and styling, Henry stubbornly refused to abandon the Model T and it lingered stoutly on through the 1920s, now with electric starter and coming in an assortment of body styles that included two-door tourers, roadsters, convertibles, coupes, pickups, trucks and wagons. Henry Ford may have famously said that customers could have any colour 'as long as it's black', but actually the Model T came in various colours before 1914 and again in 1926 and 1927.

Production ended on 26 May 1927, after 15,007,034 had been built (yes, someone was counting). The last innovation was to make wire wheels standard, with wooden wheels finally being discontinued. To service existing Model Ts the trusty engine was still manufactured until 1941, during which time another 170,000 were made.

# HISPANO-SUIZA J12

This beautiful beast was a luxurious marriage of Swiss precision design, Spanish capital and French engineering expertise – a polyglot relationship that actually produced one of the finest cars ever made, well able to challenge top marques like Rolls-Royce on build quality and style. The J12 engine married to the Type 68 chassis succeeded the long-lived H6 model, launched in 1919 and so highly regarded that it lasted for a dozen years.

Unfortunately, it's hard to find a J12 Type 68 to drool over as they belong to that unique class of prewar vehicle inhabited by the likes of Duesenberg and the Bugatti Royale – luxurious custom-built automobiles for the super-rich that were therefore manufactured in very limited numbers. In fact, only 120 Hispano-Suiza J12s were created in eight years, fitted with a striking assortment of saloon, coupe, cabriolet and roadster bodies by leading coachbuilders of the day. Customers had a choice of four wheelbase sizes to ensure that there was one suited to the preferred body configuration.

There was no shortage of power for these weighty vehicles – the engine was developed from those the company had produced for fighter aircraft a decade earlier, and an even larger engine was offered alongside the massive incumbent from 1935, increasing fuel consumption that was already thirsty in the extreme.

Such was the prestige of Paris-based Hispano-Suiza under founder Mark Birkigt that the company never had to employ sales staff, for the company's reputation for producing the finest automobiles ensured that the orders kept on coming from European connoisseurs of luxury motor cars, keeping Hispano-Suiza's dedicated band of craftsmen busy even in the depths of recession. Anyone lucky enough to take to the road in a J12 today will enjoy the ultimate experience available only to the wealthiest of 1930s motorists.

**COUNTRY OF ORIGIN:**
France

**FIRST MANUFACTURED:**
1931 (until 1938)

**ENGINE:**
9,424 cc or 11,310 cc OHV V12

**PERFORMANCE:**
Up to 120 mph (180 km/h) depending on body style

**YOU SHOULD KNOW:**
It was no idle boast when Hispano-Suiza J12s were compared favourably with Rolls-Royces, as contemporary Rollers incorporated patented Hispano-Suiza technology – notably the advanced braking system.

# LANCIA APRILIA

**COUNTRY OF ORIGIN:**
Italy

**FIRST MANUFACTURED:**
1937 (until 1949)

**ENGINE:**
1,352 cc V4

**PERFORMANCE:**
Top speed of 80 mph
(129 km/h)

**YOU SHOULD KNOW:**
The Aprilia followed the
prewar convention of
producing steering on the
right for countries where
driving on the right-hand
side of the road made
left-hand drive a more
natural configuration
– though demand for
the latter option grew
as traffic increased on
the roads, necessitating
frequent overtaking.

**The last project undertaken by company founder Vincenzo Lancia before his sudden death in 1937 showed that he had lost none of his forward-thinking prowess. The Aprilia Berlinetta Aerodinamica was a final masterpiece. It was designed with the help of a wind tunnel and no production car had achieved such a low drag coefficient. The neat Berlinetta (saloon) body featured four pillarless doors and Lancia's all-new V4 engine, offering a perfect vehicle for an increasingly prosperous middle class as the 1930s recession slowly receded. It offered speed combined with economy and was easy to drive with a crisp gearbox, superb suspension, precise steering and great roadholding.**

Although the Aprilia was a quality saloon for the family market, the second series from 1939 offered a lusso (luxury) option and later a stretched version was introduced. The advent of World War II saw the end of many 1930s cars, but the Aprilia soldiered on – literally, with production switching mainly to a militarised version, the Italian army's Torpedo Militare; the manufacture of civilian versions did not resume until 1946.

Lancia had learned the lesson that coachbuilders must be catered for back in the 1920s, when their introduction of unitary bodies closed off the lucrative custom market. So a rolling chassis was offered throughout the production run and about a quarter of all Aprilias came in this form. This guaranteed the appearance of many interesting body types, including tourers, cabriolets and some spectacular coupes that showed Italian stylists had lost none of their adventurous flair and love of dashing design. Striking 'specials' included a Carrozzeria touring convertible and a beautiful red Mille Miglia racing car.

The Aprilia was a great success, with some 28,000 produced in all. It was a fitting tribute to Vincenzo Lancia, who contributed so much to the formative years of automotive technology.

# LAGONDA V12

When his company went bust in the early 1930s, W O Bentley soon bounced back, joining Lagonda to head the tech team after the company was rescued from bankruptcy in 1935. Ringing in his ears were the words of new Lagonda boss Alan P Good: 'We have to produce the best car in the world and have only two years'. This demanding ask was achieved, and if the Lagonda V12 wasn't the world's finest it was certainly one of the most interesting cars produced in the 1930s.

Bentley's team designed an innovative V12 power plant that delivered more horsepower than any comparable non-supercharged engine. The chassis was also special, with an advanced suspension system that delivered an ultra-smooth ride, always a major consideration with wealthy clients. Equally important was the fact that the chassis was available in three sizes – short, medium and long.

This enabled a discerning customer to choose any body style, with the long chassis perfect for grand limousine bodies and the shortest for speedy roadsters. Fabulous shapes were created in-house by Frank Feeley, reflecting the decline of independent coachbuilders, though some striking bodies were still constructed outside. Varieties included limousines, saloons, tourers, coupes and dropheads.

Two of the most attractive V12s were a pair hastily prepared to compete in the 1939 Le Mans 24 race. They performed brilliantly, finishing third and fourth overall with 'The Old Number Five' winning its class. Another lightweight version beat the lap record at the famous Brooklands circuit – setting a mark of 120 mph (190 km/h), ironically beating a Bentley in the process. Sadly, the outbreak of World War II saw an end to the brilliant Lagonda V12, which would surely have become an all-time great if W O Bentley had been able to continue its development.

**COUNTRY OF ORIGIN:**
UK

**FIRST MANUFACTURED:**
1938 (until 1939)

**ENGINE:**
4,480 cc V12

**PERFORMANCE:**
Top speed around 105 mph

**YOU SHOULD KNOW:**
These supreme machines are very exclusive, and still reserved for the wealthiest of drivers today – fewer than 200 Lagonda V12s were hand-built and they top many a classic-car wish list.

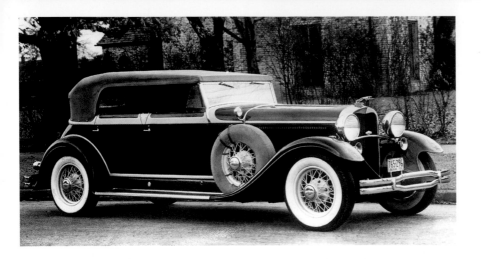

# LINCOLN K-SERIES

**COUNTRY OF ORIGIN:**
USA

**FIRST MANUFACTURED:**
Launched as the KA in
1931 (until 1939)

**ENGINE:**
The KB could reach 100
mph (160 km/h)

**PERFORMANCE:**
6.3 l (385 cid) V8; 7.3 l
(448 cid), 6.3 l (382 cid),
6.8 l (414 cid) V12

**YOU SHOULD KNOW:**
One final – and
impressive – Model
K built in 1939
(subsequently updated in
1942) was the singular
'Sunshine Special'
convertible limousine
created especially for
President Franklin D
Roosevelt.

Henry Ford relished his acquisition of the bankrupt Lincoln Motor Company in 1922, for he had been forced out of his own Henry Ford Company in 1902 by Henry M Leland – the now-ruined boss of Lincoln. Leland had renamed the original Ford company Cadillac . . . ironically Lincoln's main competitor. The Lincoln was pitched at the luxury end of the spectrum and new ownership didn't change much.

Assorted body shapes were introduced in 1923 but the first real advance was the Lincoln K-series. Launched in 1931, it initially had a V8 engine, though this was swiftly upgraded to a V12 for added power and refinement. Further evolutions of this motor were introduced over time but failed to catapult the K-series to commercial glory. It never really caught the public's imagination and only two thousand were produced before the series was discontinued in 1939, finally being finished off by the introduction of its own stablemates – two phenomenally successful Lincolns – the Zephyr (1936) and Continental (1938).

This is unfortunate, as the hand-built K-series was very good indeed, especially after the introduction of the KB with the first V12 engine in 1932, though the KA line continued. These big machines came with different wheelbases allowing for a variety of interesting body styles produced both by the factory and external coachbuilders, including leading luminaries like Brunn and LeBaron. Amongst the favourites were formal town cars, four-door sedans, phaetons, convertible sedans, touring cabriolets and two-door convertibles.

In 1935 the KA and KB lines merged as the Model K, with a smaller but more efficient V12 power plant, but this failed to halt the sales slide. These handsome cars appeal mightily to the modern eye and they drive beautifully, so the problem can only have been price sensitivity during the Depression years.

# ROLLS-ROYCE SILVER GHOST

**Ford wasn't the only company that clung to a model that served the company well, and – whilst it couldn't be further away on the automotive spectrum – the signature Rolls-Royce Silver Ghost was contemporaneous with Ford's famous Model T. There was a slight difference in numbers, with over fifteen million Model Ts sold as opposed to just 7,874 Silver Ghosts, but each defined its own market section and set a benchmark for others to chase.**

As the Roaring Twenties got under way, the Silver Ghost was still the car of choice for most really wealthy buyers on both sides of the Atlantic, having been around for 15 years and established an enviable reputation for quality build, absolute reliability and a comfortable ride in the process. In fact, Rolls-Royce prosaically described this enduring icon as the 40/50 hp (horse power) series, and only one car initially had the name 'Silver Ghost' – which press and public soon attached to the whole series.

This was an aluminium-painted 40/50 with silver-plated fittings and open-top body by Barker that took part in the Scottish reliability trials of 1907 and then – packed with journalists – set endurance record after endurance record in the course of a punishing 15,000 mile (24,000 km) test over Britain's rough roads. Don't expect to drive that one – it's owned by Bentley Motors and insured for $35 million.

Reputation made, the series duly dominated the embryonic luxury car market, finally being officially named 'Silver Ghost' in 1925. In pioneering times when cars were unreliable, the Rolls-Royce 40/50 stood out as the exception to the rule. Its robust engine and sturdy chassis ensured enduring success, with no more than periodic technical updates. Its appearance never dated – buyers were able to select custom-built contemporary bodies in the style of their choice.

**COUNTRY OF ORIGIN:**
UK

**FIRST MANUFACTURED:**
1907 (until 1926)

**ENGINE:**
7,036 cc or 7,428 cc
Straight Six

**PERFORMANCE:**
Late models with
lightweight bodies
reached 85 mph
(137 km/h)

**YOU SHOULD KNOW:**
To take full advantage of the world's most important car-buying market, over 1,700 Silver Ghosts were produced at the Rolls-Royce company's American factory in Springfield, Massachusetts between 1921 and 1926.

# STUDEBAKER CHAMPION

**COUNTRY OF ORIGIN:**
USA

**FIRST MANUFACTURED:**
1939 (until 1958)

**ENGINE:**
2.7 l (165 cid) Straight Six

**PERFORMANCE:**
Early models were capable of 78 mph (125 km/h)

**YOU SHOULD KNOW:**
So good was the Straight Six engine first used in 1939 Champions that it was fitted to the wartime Studebaker M29 Weasel cargo/personnel carrier and was still in use for the 1964 model year (after an OHV makeover in 1961).

**If one car finally restored Studebaker's fortunes after the disastrous bankruptcy of 1933 it was the sensational Champion, introduced just as one decade was coming to its end and providing solid foundations for the next. This cleanly styled and well-engineered vehicle was offered as an economy business coupe, club sedan and four-door cruising saloon, immediately capturing the car-buying public's imagination.**

Part of the Champion's appeal lay in the fact that it was an entirely new project (engineered by Roy Cole and Eugene Hardig) that allowed blue-sky thinking untrammelled by the need to use existing design features or components. The inspired result was achieved by putting particular emphasis on trimming down weight. This meant that a very economical small engine could deliver performance comparable with the larger Studebaker Commanders and Presidents, but at a bargain price. There had been a nationwide slump in 1938, leading to significant losses at Studebaker, but the Champ's buoyant reception the following year soon repaired the damage, with 34,000 units sold.

The next year small cosmetic changes were made, like Custom DeLuxe trim options and sealed-beam headlights, and a second coupe with rear 'opera seat' was introduced. Sales nearly doubled, to over 66,000, and further success followed a revamp by someone who had become very important to Studebaker – external industrial design consultant Raymond Loewy.

The Champ certainly lived up to its name, attracting 85,000 buyers in 1941 to become Studebaker's best-seller ever. Thanks to their outstanding fuel economy, Champions swiftly vanished from showrooms after all car production was suspended for the duration of World War II in February 1942, whilst used examples were like gold dust when gas rationing started to bite. Just as soon as hostilities ended, the Studebaker Champion was back – in the form of an all-new bullet-nosed beauty.

# TALBOT-LAGO T150C SS

**For slinky, streamlined looks that can more than hold their own against the Bugatti Type 57 Atlantic and Mercedes-Benz 540K Autobahnkurier, it would be hard to beat the Talbot-Lago T150C SS. This splendid French speedster emerged from the wreckage of the Depression-hit Anglo-French Sunbeam-Talbot-Darracq combine, which imploded in 1935, and is one of the most eye-catching production cars ever to hit the street.**

The French end of the collapsed company was taken over by Anthony Lago. The new outfit changed its name to Talbot-Lago and introduced models designed by Walter Becchia. These featured independent suspension and included the two litre T11, three litre T17 and four litre T23. Lago was a clever engineer and developed the existing six-cylinder engine considerably. The resulting T150 served as the ideal power plant for the larger cars and acquired racing pedigree mounted on the T150C (for 'competition') chassis. This combo enjoyed great success on the track and spawned Talbot-Lago's SS (for Super Sport) road cars.

Bodies for these were made by leading coachbuilders like Saoutchik and Figoni & Falaschi . . . and the star was undoubtedly the latter's T150C SS coupe. This sensational machine was nothing less than mobile sculpture and was nicknamed the Goutte d'Eau (Teardrop) for its sensual curves. But this was no posturing dandy, for sensational looks were combined with terrific performance.

Two versions were made, though the sky-high price ensured exclusivity – five Teardrops with the so-called 'Jeancart' body (after the first owner) were made on the longer chassis, while eleven in New York Style were built on the short chassis. Although the overall look was the same, each car had exclusive design details specified by the wealthy purchaser. Teardrops had slightly heavy steering, but were still a dream drive – and high in the league table of desirable classic cars.

**COUNTRY OF ORIGIN:**
France

**FIRST MANUFACTURED:**
1937 (until 1939)

**ENGINE:**
3,966 cc Straight Six

**PERFORMANCE:**
Top speed around 115 mph (185 km/h)

**YOU SHOULD KNOW:**
The Teardrop's competition potential was dramatically proved when a car straight from the showroom was placed third in the 1938 Le Mans 24 race – a huge achievement.

# VOLKSWAGEN BEETLE

**COUNTRY OF ORIGIN:**
Germany (later also manufactured in Brazil)

**FIRST MANUFACTURED:**
1938

**ENGINE:**
985 cc eventually uprated to 1,303 cc (four sizes in between) Flat Four

**PERFORMANCE:**
The early Type 1s could reach 71 mph (115 km/h)

**YOU SHOULD KNOW:**
After World War II the Volkswagen factory was offered (free!) to American, British and French motor manufacturers. They all turned it down, Ford dismissing the car as 'not worth a damn' . . . hindsight, anyone?

**After coming to power in 1933, the Nazi dictator Adolf Hitler wanted to produce a 'People's Car' (Volkswagen). Hitler told brilliant engineer Ferdinand Porsche to create this affordable vehicle – in an echo of Henry Ford's 'any colour as long as it's black' remark telling Porsche that the price could be anything he liked 'as long as it's under a thousand Marks'. This was impossibly low and, despite Porsche's efforts, little progress was made until the German state threw its weight behind the project in 1936. American technicians were hired and mass-production know-how imported.**

But in truth the People's Car, or Type 1 (nicknamed 'Beetle' for its shape, though the title was not used officially by Volkswagen until the New Beetle was launched in 1998) was merely a propaganda tool to impress the German people. No Beetles were delivered to the German citizens who had joined a savings scheme to purchase one, though Hitler was presented with a Type 1 cabriolet on his 49th birthday in 1938. As World War II loomed production at the purpose-built Wolfsberg factory (complete with new town for the workers) switched to an open-topped military version called the Kübelwagen (Bucket Car).

One of the world's great automobile success stories really started after the war, when the British occupation forces reopened the damaged factory in 1946. It finally ended in 2003, when production of Beetles was stopped in Brazil after 21,529,464 had been built over half a century. Along the way the Beetle hardly changed visually, retaining its unmistakable shape and trademark rear-mounted air-cooled engine – though there were plenty of technical modifications and a commercial version (including the famous camper van beloved by hippies and Aussies touring Europe) was introduced. So the Beetle is surely the easiest-to-find 'must-drive' car in the world, wherever you may be.

# BUICK Y-JOB

## CONCEPT CAR

From the earliest years of the car industry, manufacturers had been producing elegant custom coachwork designs for wealthy patrons, but mass-market autos were an entirely different matter – functional, unimaginative wagon bodies were cobbled on to whatever chassis happened to be rolling off the production line and aesthetic appeal was low on the agenda. The Buick Y-Job broke the mould. It was the first-ever concept car – that is, a prototype designed specifically for the purpose of gauging consumer reaction.

Alfred Sloan, the far-sighted head of GM, realizing that style and mass-market production were not mutually exclusive, set up the Art and Color Section of GM (later to morph into the Styling Department) with Harley J Earl at its helm. Earl was the son of a wagon builder who had branched out into custom-built car bodies for the Hollywood film industry. He had made a name for himself by designing the hugely successful La Salle for Cadillac in 1927. Having been invited to join the GM team as designer-in-chief, he went on to become a vice-president of the company.

The Y-Job was Earl's first design for GM. Based on a stretched version of a standard Buick chassis, it was a streamlined two-seater sports car with numerous trend-setting features: electric windows, power-operated hidden headlamps and recessed tail lights; power-operated soft top; wraparound bumpers, flush door handles and seamless hood and fenders; the horizontal grille that was to become such a distinctive feature of Buick autos. After the Y-Job had been shown around America to widespread acclaim, Earl used it as his own daily car and could regularly be seen driving it through the streets of Detroit.

The Buick Y-Job is a truly iconic 20th-century American design. It is on display at GM's Design Centre in Warren, Michigan as part of the GM heritage collection.

**COUNTRY OF ORIGIN:**
USA

**FIRST MANUFACTURED:**
1938

**ENGINE:**
5.2 l (320 cid) Straight Eight

**PERFORMANCE:**
N/A

**YOU SHOULD KNOW:**
Harley Earl supposedly called his car Y-Job because experimental cars were habitually designated with an X; he simply went to the next letter of the alphabet.

1940s

# ARMSTRONG SIDDELEY HURRICANE

**COUNTRY OF ORIGIN:**
UK

**FIRST MANUFACTURED:**
1945 (until 1953)

**ENGINE:**
1,991 cc or 2,309 cc
Straight Six

**PERFORMANCE:**
Top speed of 70 mph
(120 km/h); 0–60 mph
(97 km/h) in 29.7 secs

**YOU SHOULD KNOW:**
Those driving Hurricanes
on today's roads often
use cars with retro-fitted
overdrive gearboxes, as
the low-geared originals
are not ideal for high-
speed cruising on dual
carriageways and
motorways.

After a succession of mergers, the Hawker Siddeley group emerged as the producer of Armstrong Siddeley cars – and when World War II ended one of the first models announced was the slinky two-door, four-seater Hurricane drophead coupe. The name shamelessly appealed to patriotic feelings generated by the exploits of the group's wartime Hurricane fighter planes (a companion saloon car was named after the Lancaster bomber).

So the stylish two litre Hurricane 16 appeared in 1945, with the Hurricane 18 following in 1949 – a similar model but fitted with a larger engine. The related Typhoon sports saloon (named after another Hawker fighter plane) was essentially a Hurricane with fixed hard top. The reason Armstrong Siddeley was the first British manufacturer able to resume postwar car production was that the company promised to put the emphasis on exports – and indeed the first two Hurricanes built were sent to America, where they completed an impressive coast-to-coast drive from New York to Los Angeles to generate favourable publicity.

One interesting feature of the Hurricane was the optional Wilson gearbox. This allowed gears to be preselected with a hand lever, and subsequently engaged with a 'change' pedal that replaced a conventional clutch. This made for smooth, fast gear changes and versions of this innovative system were used on buses, military vehicles and racing cars produced by other companies.

Just over 2,600 Hurricanes were built, but despite generally robust build quality only a few hundred survive – the chassis did tend to rust where it passed under the rear axle and the Hurricane had yet to acquire classic status when the Ministry of Transport (MOT) roadworthiness test was introduced in 1960. Sadly, as time passed plenty of Hurricanes went to the scrapyard – along with many other fine cars that their owners wish they still had today.

# CADILLAC SERIES SIXTY-TWO

Although Cadillac's entry-level Series Sixty-Two was manufactured for many years – from 1941 until 1958 – 1948 saw a distinct change of style for third generation Sixty-Twos, with the long wheelbase enjoyed by previous generations reduced to a shorter model that was virtually identical to that of the junior Series Sixty-One. This heralded the forthcoming demise of the latter (in 1951) and the consequent emergence of the Sixty-Two as Cadillac's sole 'budget' model. Budget or not, it was still an awful lot of motor for the money – and late 1940s examples are keenly sought as drivable classics.

There was little to distinguish the merging Sixty-One and Sixty-Two lines visually, though the Sixty-Two sported more chrome and was offered in convertible form (an option the Sixty-One lacked) as well as in two-door club coupe and four-door sedan style. This was the year that marked the start of Cadillac's inexorable drift towards the pronounced stylistic features that became the hallmark of late 1940s to late 1950s American cars – including huge tailfins and wrap-around windscreens. Cadillac brought the craze to a soaring climax in 1959 with a tailfin display that was never bettered, but initially 1948 models acquired more modest fins (albeit ambitiously inspired by the twin-boom tail assembly of the Lockheed P-38 Lightning fighter bomber aircraft).

Just two years on, Sixty-Twos from General Motors' Fisher body shop got back a longer wheelbase and acquired the much-hyped new Cadillac OHV V8 engine and a more luxurious interior. New body options that year included a Coupe De Ville 'convertible hardtop', and soon there would be a top-of-the-line Eldorado luxury convertible, too. The fourth generation appeared in 1954, and in 1959 (though the cars remained the same) the designation changed to Series 6200, marking the end of the Sixty-Two, one of Cadillac's most successful lines.

**COUNTRY OF ORIGIN:**
USA

**FIRST MANUFACTURED:**
1941 (until 1958)

**ENGINE:**
5.7 l (346 cid) sidevalve V8 or 5.4 l (331cid) OHV V8

**PERFORMANCE:**
Top speed was up to 95 mph (153 km/h), depending on model

**YOU SHOULD KNOW:**
During 1948 two fabulous custom-built Saoutchik drophead coupes were created in Paris costing $70,000 apiece (when the standard model sold for $2,837) – a black-and-violet beauty for a New York furrier and a glitzy white-and-violet number for Hollywood star Dolores del Rio.

# BRISTOL 400

**COUNTRY OF ORIGIN:**
UK

**FIRST MANUFACTURED:**
1947 (until 1950)

**ENGINE:**
1,971 cc Straight Six

**PERFORMANCE:**
Top speed of 82 mph (132 km/h); 0–60 mph (97 km/h) in 19.7 secs

**YOU SHOULD KNOW:**
One or two custom examples were also built, including an extraordinary 'woodie' estate car by Hyde. The long, sloping boot had a characteristic raised circular housing for the spare wheel.

**When is a Bristol not a Bristol? In the case of the Bristol car company, which started production after World War II, the answer is 'when it's really a BMW'. For though the sinuous Bristol 400 touring car did indeed bear a Bristol badge, it borrowed heavily from the prewar BMW 328, which the German company had actually exported as a rolling chassis to Britain, where it was bodied and sold by Frazer Nash.**

In 1945 Frazer Nash formed a joint venture with the Bristol Aircraft Company (maker of wartime Blenheim and Beaufighter aircraft) to explore the possibility of manufacturing luxury cars. Representatives of the new consortium visited the wrecked BMW factory in Munich during 1945, 'liberating' plans and engines before the Americans managed to ship the remains of the factory's contents and machinery Stateside. BMW chief engineer Fritz Friedel was swiftly recruited to continue developing the 328 engine and a prototype was constructed in 1946. BAC gained complete control of the venture in 1947, registered the name Bristol Cars and started production of the first series Bristol 400, which was replaced by the refined second series in 1948.

The BMW heritage was significant indeed. The rear suspension replicated that of the BMW 326, the body echoed the BMW 327 and the engine and front suspension came from the BMW 328, and even the distinctive BMW twin radiator grille was incorporated. The Bristol 400's appealing aerodynamic body came in various styles. The standard saloon had bodies designed by Touring and Zagato, whilst there was a drophead styled by Farina and built at Bristol.

# HEALEY SPORTSMOBILE

**In the immediate aftermath of World War II Donald Healey trod the path that also attracted fellow travellers like Colin Chapman in Britain and Frank Kurtis in America – the journey from successful race driver (and accomplished automobile engineer) to manufacturer of sporty road cars. The Donald Healey Motor Company obtained a factory in Warwick and set about marrying proprietary components like Riley's proven twin cam 2.4 litre four-cylinder engine and Lockheed hydraulic brakes with a light steel box-section chassis and suspension designed and built by Healey.**

Production was never prolific – the best-seller among eight different models was the 200-unit Healey Tickford Saloon of the early 1950s, whilst the Healey Elliott Saloon was the success story of the 1940s with 101 produced – but Healey's innovative cars punched far above their commercial weight by establishing a great reputation for advanced engineering, thus influencing a generation of car designers. They were all variations on the same basic mechanical package, though there were two different versions of the chassis.

The third Healey off the line was the long, low Sportsmobile, first seen in 1948 and produced until 1950, during which time very few were actually made. This four-seater drophead coupe with winding windows was built on the B chassis and is sturdy rather than handsome – with its replacement, the Abbott Drophead, definitely being more attractive to look at. Nonetheless, the Sportsmobile was a prestigious four-seater tourer that was ahead of its time, offering outstanding performance in its class.

Unfortunately, it was held back and denied the success it deserved by the British Government's imposition of punitive purchase tax on all luxury cars costing more than £1,000 (when the Sportsmobile was more than double that), which badly affected Healey's sales and profitability.

**COUNTRY OF ORIGIN:**
UK

**FIRST MANUFACTURED:**
1948 (until 1950)

**ENGINE:**
2,443 cc Straight Four

**PERFORMANCE:**
Top speed of 105 mph
(164 km/h)

**YOU SHOULD KNOW:**
Bearing in mind that only 23 were ever made, the Healey advertising campaign for the Sportsmobile rather disingenuously stated that 'in spite of the demands of the export market a limited number of these superb cars is now available for home delivery.'

# HUDSON COMMODORE EIGHT

**COUNTRY OF ORIGIN:**
USA

**FIRST MANUFACTURED:**
1941 (until 1952)

**ENGINE:**
4.1 l (254 cid) Straight Eight

**PERFORMANCE:**
Top speed of 91 mph (146 km/h)

**YOU SHOULD KNOW:**
Those third generation 'step-down' Commodores were very well built and still drive beautifully today, representing great value for money as drivable classics with good original examples available for well under $50,000.

**The luxurious Hudson Commodore was the Detroit outfit's top-of-the-range model from 1941 to 1952, with the inevitable production break during World War II. The debut line consisted of two wheelbases – short for coupes and convertibles, long for the sedan. There was also a choice between the Straight Six and Straight Eight engines, though the 'Eight' was always the star. The convertible was particularly impressive with its bold bonnet, V-shaped grille and fancy chrome bumpers, and is highly prized today.**

In common with most US manufacturers, postwar offerings were tweaked versions of the 1941 line and second generation Hudsons weren't very different from the first. But the choice of coupe styles was reduced to one (club), with the sedan and convertible also remaining in production. To their credit, Commodores were better fitted than the competition, with neat features like sealed-beam headlights, twin air horns, double wipers, stop lights, arm rests, lockable glove box and pile carpeting.

In 1948, everything changed with the arrival of the third generation. If a picky film director ordered a classic late-1940s sedan from Central Casting, he would have been ecstatic if a road-hugging Commodore arrived. Hudson introduced an aerodynamic 'step-down' body that placed the passenger compartment within the chassis, so there was no need for the running boards that helped people step up into a raised compartment, allowing for stunning low styling and great roadholding. The Commodore again came with a host of features that others only fitted as extras, and had a fabulous dashboard.

Unfortunately, the simple step-down styling of the Commodore was quickly overtaken by the dash for flash as soaring wings and chrome in Wurlitzer quantities started to appear. Despite selling 60,000 units in two years, the 1951–52 model proved to be the last, as Hudson disastrously abandoned class and switched to compacts.

# HUMBER HAWK

**The Humber car company had an illustrious history, being one of the manufacturers who produced horseless carriages in the late 19th century. By World War I, Humber was the second largest carmaker in Britain and afterwards expanded into commercial vehicle production with the acquisition of Commer. Hillman was taken over in 1928 but in 1931 Humber itself became a takeover victim as it was swallowed by the Rootes Group.**

Still, Humber continued to operate at the smart end of the Rootes spectrum throughout the 1930s, and with the advent of war switched to sturdy staff cars, sturdier armoured cars and military utility vehicles. But Humber was ready to resume car production when the war ended and – in keeping with lean times – introduced the new four-cylinder Humber Hawk rather than immediately relaunching the six-cylinder Super Snipe. Despite its name, the Hawk lacked either the grace or speed of a stooping raptor – and had the dubious advantage of being a typical British car of the immediate postwar period. In truth the snazzy name fooled nobody. The new Humber was an old prewar Hillman 14 by any other name, with a lame sidevalve engine dating back to the early 1930s.

No matter. Rationing and a general shortage of cash ensured that few consumers could afford a new car, but Humber's reputation for nicely appointed interiors and good build quality ensured that plenty of bureaucrats and businessmen were happy to splash out other people's cash for this solid four-door saloon with three window lights on each side and a sunshine roof as standard. The Mk I became the Mk II in 1947, but the only noticeable difference was that the gear lever migrated from the floor to become a column change. By 1948 Humber was able to introduce the Mk III, a genuinely fresh model.

**COUNTRY OF ORIGIN:**
UK

**FIRST MANUFACTURED:**
1945 (until 1949)

**ENGINE:**
1,944 cc Sidevalve
Straight Four

**PERFORMANCE:**
Top speed of 65 mph
(105 km/h)

**YOU SHOULD KNOW:**
The Hawk went on to better things after humble beginnings, continuing to evolve as a genuine premium brand within the Rootes stable – the last big revamp coming in 1957, with Series I to IVA Hawks continuing until Rootes finally abandoned luxury car production a decade later.

# LAND ROVER SERIES 1

**From sturdy acorns mighty oaks may grow – and that's certainly what happened in the case of Land Rover. For the inspired Series 1 was the forerunner of a vehicle type that would reach its zenith half a century later when the SUV (Sports Utility Vehicle) became the transport of choice for millions.**

Back in the aftermath of World War II the British economy was wrecked and rationing ruled, Rover's Coventry factory had been bombed and materials for consumer goods (especially cars) were in short supply. But dispensation was available for useful products, especially anything with export potential, and chief designer Maurice Wilkes used that to advantage. A surplus wartime Willys Jeep chassis and Rover P3 car engine went into a prototype that was a cross between light truck and tractor, with the PTO (power take off) feature that allowed it to drive farm machinery.

This satisfied the 'useful' requirement and production began in 1948. Better still, buyers paid no purchase tax as this was a 'commercial' – even though the machine launched at the Amsterdam Motor Show had become less tractor-like. The clever four-wheel drive stopgap before normal car manufacture resumed was so well received that the proposed two-year production run never ended, with the Land Rover outselling revived Rover road cars.

The original Series I was so basic that window panels and a roof of metal or canvas were optional extras, but various improvements were made before the major revamp that saw the introduction of the Series II a decade later. Larger engines were fitted (including a diesel) and long- and short-wheelbase variants appeared. But the essential character remained the same and it's not hard to find a Series I for some off-road fun – nearly three-quarters of these robust workers are still chugging on.

**COUNTRY OF ORIGIN:**
UK

**FIRST MANUFACTURED:**
1948 (until 1958)

**ENGINE:**
1,595 or 1,997 cc Straight Four petrol; 1,997 cc Straight Four diesel

**PERFORMANCE:**
Up to 65 mph (104 km/h) for the 2 litre models

**YOU SHOULD KNOW:**
Nobody at Rover ever actually said it, but the message must have been glaringly obvious to buyers of early Series 1 Land Rovers – you can have any colour you like as long as it's Army-surplus green.

# MASERATI A6

**COUNTRY OF ORIGIN:**
Italy

**FIRST MANUFACTURED:**
1947 (until 1953)

**ENGINE:**
1,488 cc (A6 1500), 1,980 cc (A6GCS) Straight Six

**PERFORMANCE:**
Top speed of 95 mph (153 km/h)

**YOU SHOULD KNOW:**
During World War II an unseemly race developed between Maserati and Volkswagen to develop the first prestigious V16 town car for their respective dictators, Benito Mussolini and Adolf Hitler – but neither succeeded.

**After the Maserati family sold out to Adolfo Orsi and the factory moved from Bologna to Modena, World War II intervened and car production was suspended. But Maserati returned vigorously to the postwar fray with exclusive cars that were built around the company's powerful Straight Six engines.**

The A6 Sport (also known rather more laboriously as the Tipo 6CS/46) was a barchetta (open-top two-seater racing car) prototype by Ernesto Maserati and Albert Massimino. This was transformed into the A6 1500 two-door berlinetta (coupe) by Pininfarina first shown at the Geneva Motor Show in 1947. Only 59 of these low-slung, stylish machines were ever built, along with just two of the spider convertible versions shown at the 1948 Turin Motor Show. The line was discontinued in 1950.

A further development was the introduction of the two-seater A6GCS, with a larger two-litre engine. The company's real emphasis was on producing engines and chassis that would succeed on Europe's racing circuits, and various manifestations of the CGS (including single-seaters and cycle-wing versions) duly obliged, becoming one of the great race cars and laying firm foundations for Maserati's track success that continued through the 1950s, with the heroic red-trident badged machines repeatedly being driven to victory by such luminaries as Juan-Manuel Fangio. A typical CGS racing car was capable of 130 mph (205 km/h) with blistering acceleration to match. Just 16 of these cars were produced before they were superseded by the iconic A6GCS/53.

But a sideline in road cars was maintained, and the early 1950s saw the basic A6G rolling chassis with alloy engine being supplied to the likes of Pininfarina, Zagato, Bertone, Pietro Frua, Vignale and Carrozzeria Allemano, who created a few stylish coupes and roadsters to maintain the Maserati A6's road-going credentials.

# MERCURY 1949

**Edsel Ford created Mercury in 1939, to fill the gap between Ford's regular models and the company's Lincoln luxmobiles. The two divisions were merged after World War II to create the Lincoln-Mercury Division, to stress the fact that the Mercury should be seen as a 'junior Lincoln' rather than 'senior Ford'. The Mercury's soaraway decade would be the 1950s, with a succession of big winners, but the trend started in 1949 when the Mercury new-look integrated body was introduced, updating a tired line that had mainly been styled in the early 1940s.**

The rounded number newcomer with its flush wings became known as the 'inverted bathtub', echoing the modish styling of contemporary Hudsons and Packards. The well-built Mercury had a solid presence, yet appeared streamlined with clean, pleasing lines. Four body styles were offered – a four-door sport sedan, coupe, convertible and a two-door station wagon with much less wood than its predecessor.

Along with the Mercury 1949's attractive looks came a beefed-up engine sitting on a new chassis with independent front suspension and longitudinal leaf springs at the rear that (at last) superseded old Henry Ford's beloved but somewhat insensitive single transverse leaf system. The result was a fast, comfortable machine that did indeed establish Mercury's luxury credentials and even offered Touch-O-Matic overdrive as a tempting option. Other tasty possibilities included power windows (standard on the convertible), power seats, a heater, two-tone paintwork and whitewall tyres.

There were new models added to the line-up in 1950 (a starter coupe and limited edition Monterey coupe), whilst the eagerly awaited Merc-O-Matic automatic transmission arrived in 1951. Impressive all-new styling appeared in 1952 to oust the classic Bathtub Mercurys and capitalize fully on the marque's proven appeal in a new decade, but not before over 900,000 1949–51 units had been sold.

**COUNTRY OF ORIGIN:**
USA

**FIRST MANUFACTURED:**
1949 (until 1951)

**ENGINE:**
4.2 l (256 cid) V8

**PERFORMANCE:**
Top speed of 105 mph (169 km/h)

**YOU SHOULD KNOW:**
From the start, one of the chief selling points of Mercury cars was their high performance, echoing the model name (Mercury was the speedy winged messenger of Greek mythology) and easily outrunning Fords V8s with the same motor, as a result of Mercury's careful engine-tuning programme.

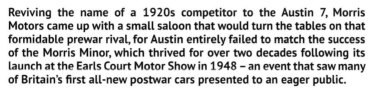

# MORRIS MINOR

Reviving the name of a 1920s competitor to the Austin 7, Morris Motors came up with a small saloon that would turn the tables on that formidable prewar rival, for Austin entirely failed to match the success of the Morris Minor, which thrived for over two decades following its launch at the Earls Court Motor Show in 1948 – an event that saw many of Britain's first all-new postwar cars presented to an eager public.

Later to become famous for creating the Mini, Alec Issigonis was responsible for the Minor's innovative design. It was conceived as a vehicle for the mass market at a very reasonable price for the build quality. There were three versions in Series I – two- and four-door saloons and a convertible tourer. Plans to use a Flat Four motor were scrapped late in the day and a Straight Four sidevalve was substituted. Around a quarter-of-a-million Minors were built in under four years, with the convertible taking a third of sales.

Series II in 1952 saw the fitting of a smaller but more powerful OHV engine (from the competing Austin A30, as Austin and Morris had merged to form the British Motor Corporation). Three new body styles appeared, too – the van, pickup and Traveller with its signature wooden frame. Series II lasted until 1956.

Cosmetic modifications were made for Series III, including a further uprating of the engine and in 1961 the Morris Minor became the first British car to sell more than one million units. An even larger engine was introduced the following year but it was the beginning of the end. The 1960s saw a steadily declining sales graph until the convertible went in 1969 and the saloon in 1970. The last of the line were Travellers made in 1971. Sadly, the Minor's replacement was the eminently forgettable Marina.

**COUNTRY OF ORIGIN:**
UK

**FIRST MANUFACTURED:**
1948 (until 1971)

**ENGINE:**
918 cc Straight Four
(Series I)

**PERFORMANCE:**
Series 1 had a top speed
of 60 mph (97km/h)

**YOU SHOULD KNOW:**
The names Morris Minor (and later Minor Thousand) undoubtedly have a familiar ring but they might well have sounded strange to modern ears had the original name been kept – the prototype was known as the 'Morris Mosquito', though this was wisely dropped.

# ROVER P4 75 'CYCLOPS'

**COUNTRY OF ORIGIN:**
UK

**FIRST MANUFACTURED:**
1949 (until 1954)

**ENGINE:**
2,106 cc Straight Six

**PERFORMANCE:**
Top speed of 85 mph (137 km/h); 0–60 mph (97 km/h) in 21.6 secs

**YOU SHOULD KNOW:**
The Rover P4 75 chassis and engine were used by two ex-Rover engineers to create the two-seater Marauder sports car – but they failed to make a success of it and only 15 roadsters and coupes were actually produced in two years from 1950 before the chastened would-be entrepreneurs rejoined Rover.

The maker of the Victorian Rover Safety bicycle started producing motor cars at the dawn of the 20th century and became one of the most famous – and enduring – names in the pantheon of British motor manufacturers. Rover moved up market in the 1930s, and maintained its appeal to middle-class motorists after World War II. But in common with many cars on both sides of the Atlantic, the old-fashioned Rover P3 of 1948 was very much a prewar revival that filled the gap before new models could be introduced.

When it came, the Rover P4 four-door saloon was mould-breaking. The modern styling had more than a hint of new-fangled American streamlining about it. Indeed, the P4 owed more than a little something to the contemporary Studebaker Champion, two examples of which had been studied closely at the Rover works. This audacious piracy was not to everyone's taste but time would tell – the ongoing P4 series lasted for 15 years and became a firm favourite with the conservative target market.

The 'P4' was actually a factory designation not in popular use. Owners would normally have referred to their 'Rover 75', but the P4 75 quickly acquired the nickname 'Cyclops' for a fog lamp mounted on the radiator grille (ironically, this feature was soon dropped as it interfered with cooling). The engine came from the Rover P3, but the addition of twin carburettors improved performance.

Around 33,000 original P4 75s were sold, though when the evolution 60s, 75 Mk IIs, 80s, 90s, 95/110s, 100s and 105R/105Ss were added the grand total for the P4 series was over 130,000 units. With all those different models, it might be assumed that there was considerable change during the life of the evolving P4, but in fact that iconic design remained virtually unaltered to the end.

# SAAB 92

For a car powered with a transversely mounted, water-cooled, thermo-syphon, two-cylinder, two-stroke engine of modest proportions, the Saab 92 was influential beyond any reasonable expectation. It was not the sort of offering anticipated from a Scandinavian company that had never made a car before and was developing jet fighters for the Swedish Air Force – although the 92 certainly had a slithery shape, with an aerodynamic coefficient that was better than that of (to name but one) a Ferrari F40. Although it looked futuristic in its day, this eye-catching machine can be claimed by the 1940s – production began in December 1949.

It proved to be an immediate winner (not quite literally) when finishing second in its Swedish Rally class weeks later. This was the starting point for several years of competition success, albeit with the help of a highly tuned engine. This compact two-door coupe was also a huge hit with the Swedish car-buying public. Just 1,246 were produced in the first year, all offered with no choice of colour (dark green it had to be). But there was a waiting list of 30,000 because these sturdy machines were solid, reliable and capable of dealing with the harsh Swedish winters for which they had been designed.

There were various mechanical enhancements and the 92B arrived in 1953 with a larger rear window and increased luggage space – plus a choice of colours, a box that converted the car into a small van and a bed kit that transformed the interior into a double bed. Buoyed by continued demand, production built up and laid the foundations for the most successful car company to start from scratch after World War II. The Saab 93 arrived to supersede the 92B in 1955, but the two models were produced side by side until early 1957.

**COUNTRY OF ORIGIN:**
Sweden

**FIRST MANUFACTURED:**
1949 (until 1957)

**ENGINE:**
764 cc Flat Twin

**PERFORMANCE:**
Top speed of 65 mph (105 km/h); 0–60 mph (97 km/h) in 26.6 secs

**YOU SHOULD KNOW:**
When America's mighty General Motors made a list of their all-time great cars in 2008 the humble Saab 92 finished (wait for it) . . . in first place.

# AUSTIN-HEALEY 100

**COUNTRY OF ORIGIN:**
UK

**FIRST MANUFACTURED:**
1953 (until 1957)

**ENGINE:**
2,660 cc Straight Four

**PERFORMANCE:**
Top speed of 106 mph
(171 km/h); 0–60 mph (97
km/h) in 11.2 secs

**YOU SHOULD KNOW:**
The final '100' models
became 100-6s with
the fitting of a smaller
Straight Six engine and
were the 2+2 BN4 of
1956 and the two-seater
BN6 of 1958. These were
marginally slower than
the original four-cylinder
100s but offered better
acceleration.

**The quirky Austin A90 Atlantic gave birth to a rather attractive child, though not without a lot of help from midwife Donald Healey. For he it was who took an A90 engine and chassis as the basis for his prototype Healey 100 (that seductive figure representing the car's ability to top the 'ton') which he proudly showed at the Earls Court Motor Show in 1952. The owner of the parent Austin Atlantic, BMC, was so impressed with Healey's streamlined roadster that it decided to sponsor a production run.**

The BN1 model that resulted was built by Jensen Motors at West Bromwich and finished at BMC's Longbridge plant in Birmingham. The BN1 had a well-tuned A90 engine and drivetrain with modified manual transmission – a three-speed box with overdrive on second and top gears. There was independent front suspension and Girling drum brakes were fitted all round. These classics with their fold-flat windscreens and clean-cut lines with few embellishments hit the market in the summer of '53 and proved to be a popular buy, vindicating BMC's decision to back Donald Healey's vision. Better still, the Austin-Healey 100 sold well in America, establishing the marque as a serious contender in the international sports car market.

The BN2 appeared in 1955, offering a four-speed gearbox, new rear axle and a choice of natty paint jobs – for the first time including a two-tone option. To satisfy those sporty buyers who wanted extra performance, a modified 100M version was created. This could be distinguished by its louvred bonnet (complete with strap). A small number of aluminium-bodied 100S (for Sebring) cars were also made. These lightweight speedsters were the most powerful 100s of all, and the first production cars in the world to have disc brakes front and back.

# AUSTIN-HEALEY SPRITE

**Buoyed by the success of the Austin-Healey 100, partners BMC and Donald Healey came up with a clever new concept. The innovative 1958 Austin-Healey Sprite was designed to appeal to increasing numbers of youngsters with good incomes who were excited by the idea of open-top motoring but couldn't afford the expensive roadsters driven by their well-heeled elders. It proved to be an inspired thought.**

This time the Sprite's major 'donor' was Austin's well-proven A35, with help from the Morris 1000. The engine acquired twin carburettors and the body was simplicity itself, with no external boot access or door handles. Trim was minimal and the one fancy element – pop-up headlights set into the bonnet lid – was soon abandoned as too complicated. However, fixed headlights substituted, giving this neat little sports car its characteristic appearance and quickly earning the nickname 'Frogeye Sprite' ('Bugeye' in America). The front end, wings and all, was hinged to fold forward and give access to the engine compartment. This was also the first production sports car to use integrated construction where body panels provide the vehicle's structural strength.

These nippy little cars were ideal competition material and were campaigned by the BMC Competition Department, almost immediately securing a class win at the 1958 Alpine Rally. Many privateers appreciated the Sprite's competitive qualities and the ultimate development was the Sebring Sprite built by Williams & Pritchard under the direction of rally champion John Sprinzel. This was accepted by the FIA (Fédération Internationale de l'Automobile) as a separate model in its own right.

Many Sprites are still driven for pleasure or in competition today, maintaining that early intention that they should be the most accessible of sports cars. The early 'Frogeyes' are considered more desirable than later Mk II, III and IV evolutions with more conventional styling.

**COUNTRY OF ORIGIN:**
UK

**FIRST MANUFACTURED:**
1958 (until 1961)

**ENGINE:**
948 cc Straight Four

**PERFORMANCE:**
Top speed of 83 mph (133 km/h); 0–60 mph (97 km/h) in 20.5 secs

**YOU SHOULD KNOW:**
MG with their Midget subsequently imitated the 'junior sports car' idea and the two junior sports cars are referred to collectively as 'Spridgets' (both were built at the MG factory in Abingdon). Triumph also jumped on the bandwagon with their 1962 Spitfire.

# BMW 507

**COUNTRY OF ORIGIN:**
Germany

**FIRST MANUFACTURED:**
1956 (until 1959)

**ENGINE:**
3,168 cc OHV V8

**PERFORMANCE:**
BMW claimed a top
speed of 140 mph
(225 km/h) and 0–60
mph (97 km/h) in around
10 secs

**YOU SHOULD KNOW:**
Elvis Presley bought a
white 507 TS whilst on
Army service in Germany,
but rather crassly
replaced the engine with
a Ford V8 after returning
to the States – he later
gave the car to actress
Ursula Andress.

After nearly going bust in the late 1950s, BMW recovered to become a giant of the international automobile industry, but it was a close-run thing. The car that did the damage and pushed the Bavarian outfit to the brink was the BMW 507. It all started innocently enough in 1954. American importer Max Hoffman saw a niche for a $5,000 sports car and was confident he could sell several thousand a year in the USA.

This ambitious project was duly undertaken by BMW, with the prototype 507 TS (for Touring Sport) making its debut at New York's Waldorf-Astoria Hotel in the summer of 1955. The idea was to produce a high-performance two-door roadster that could compete with Mercedes-Benz and Jaguar on the race track, thus reminding everyone of BMW's racing pedigree and gaining valuable publicity for mass-market road cars.

With its inward-slanting grille and curvaceous lines, the 507 TS was almost shark-like. It was based on a modified platform from the BMW 503, the handsome 2+2 coupe and cabriolet model also introduced in 1955. Albrecht von Goertz designed both sporty models and each was powered by the company's lightweight OHV V8 engine, as borrowed from the BMW 502, and fitted with twin Solex Zenith carburettors.

The 507's body was hand-crafted in aluminium, with the result that no two cars were identical. There was a removable hardtop available, but if ordered it was made to fit the car in question and these hardtops are not interchangeable. The result of all this detailed work was a price tag double that originally envisaged by Max Hoffman, a virtually unsaleable car, massive accumulated losses for BMW and discontinuation of both loss-making sports cars in 1959. Only 252 507s and 414 503s were built – making these rare 1950s BMWs ultra-collectable.

# CITROËN DS

**COUNTRY OF ORIGIN:**
France

**FIRST MANUFACTURED:**
1955 (until 1975)

**ENGINE:**
1,911 cc OHV Straight
Four

**PERFORMANCE:**
Top speed of 98 mph
(158 km/h); 0–60 mph
(97 km/h) in 21.2 secs

**YOU SHOULD KNOW:**
A junior (more
affordable) look-alike
version of the DS was
introduced in 1957,
without many of the
DS's advanced features
– though it too had a
punning model name in
ID (as in idée for idea).

The debut of the Citroën DS series at the Paris Salon in 1955 was sensational. Some humorously suggested Flaminio Bertoni's design was so futuristic that aliens must have invaded his drawing office and sketched out a 23rd-century machine, but the point was well made. No other car before or since has provoked so much comment, for this was truly unlike any other car seen before or since. The European reaction was replicated when the DS 19 appeared in New York, billed as 'the dream car of tomorrow, on the road today'. This aerodynamic marvel boasted a 'Citro-Matic' hydraulic system that controlled the suspension, steering, brakes, clutch and gear change.

It followed a grand tradition of French cars that broke the mould, and would go on to enjoy two successful decades of automotive life. Throughout that period it remained the world's most technically advanced car, packed with amazing innovations. The DS was a machine that divided opinion into 'love it' and 'hate it' camps and whilst technical wizardry delighted supporters, detractors seized upon the car's complexity as a disadvantage.

But some even worshipped this slinky car – its DS designation denoted Desiree Speciale, but these letters are pronounced the same way as the French déesse, which means goddess. So 'Goddess' the DS became, and remained. Even those who disliked the car had to admit that roadholding, ride quality, handling and braking were exceptional. A station wagon and rare convertible were introduced, and further enhancements throughout the production run ensured that the DS remained at the cutting edge with styling updates in 1962 and 1967, plus the introduction of features like electronic fuel injection, five gears, automatic transmission and headlights that turned with the steering. Though relatively few sold in America (just 38,000) nearly 1.5 million DS models were produced.

# CHEVROLET BEL AIR

**The Bel Air name appeared in 1950 but did not become a distinct series until 1953, when it was designated as Chevrolet's premium offering, pitched at growing numbers of middle-class buyers who were migrating to leafy suburbs. Lavish trim and heavy chromework distinguished spanking new Bel Airs from lesser Chevys, with two- and four-door sedans, a sports coupe and convertible offered to eager buyers.**

Dealers were delighted to find (with over half a million sold) that demand was brisk. An eight-seat Townsman station wagon was added for 1954, whilst the following year saw an all-new contemporary look for six Bel Air body styles, plus strikingly colour-coordinated interiors and the chance to select the fabulous new V8 Turbo-Fire engine. Other optional extras included air conditioning, power steering and electric windows. Although the stylish Nomad station wagon was nominally part of the Bel Air family, the wagon that did serious business was the Townsman four-door model.

In 1956 a new four-door Sport Sedan was introduced and the Bel Air range had a facelift. This saw a reworked grille, revised wheel apertures and two-tone paint jobs – all combining to give these big cars a sense of speed, even at rest. A masterly reworking in 1957 made cars that were effectively unchanged mechanically look completely different, with sharp fins and aluminium trim panels.

Classic mid 1950 Chevrolets are considered to be among the most attractive the company ever made, with the '55, '56 and '57 Bel Airs (commonly called TriFives) being those most eagerly sought by collectors – especially convertibles. In 1958, the Impala arrived to share senior status with the Bel Airs, which thereafter – though retaining great mid-range status and selling in large numbers – slowly started sliding down the totem, finishing up as no-frills fleet cars in the 1970s.

**COUNTRY OF ORIGIN:**
USA

**FIRST MANUFACTURED:**
1953 (until 1975)

**ENGINE:**
Numerous options, usually the 3.9 l (235 cid) Straight Six or 4.3 l (265 cid) V8

**PERFORMANCE:**
Varied by model and engine, but the '53 launch model was capable of 87 mph (140 km/h)

**YOU SHOULD KNOW:**
In 1955 the 50-millionth car built by Chevrolet finally rolled off the line . . . and by accident or design it turned out to be a Bel Air hardtop that was especially trimmed in gold to mark the momentous milestone.

# DAIMLER SP250 (DART)

**COUNTRY OF ORIGIN:**
UK

**FIRST MANUFACTURED:**
1959 (until 1964)

**ENGINE:**
2,548cc OHV V8

**PERFORMANCE:**
Top speed of 123mph
(198 km/h); 0–60 mph
(97 km/h) in 9.2 secs

**YOU SHOULD KNOW:**
Take a head-on look at
the SP250 (Dart) engine
grille, and you won't
be surprised that some
enthusiasts call it 'the
Catfish'.

**Launched in New York as the Dart, Daimler's first sports car was officially renamed the SP250 after Dodge claimed copyright. The car was a barefaced attempt to ride the wave of popularity for British sports cars in America, and it looked much more transatlantic than the Triumph or MG competitors on which its chassis was based. Daimler's boldness, and hurry to enter the market, resulted in confused styling. From the front, the fibreglass moulded lines curl sinuously down to the wide grille. From the rear three-quarter view, the futuristic horizontal and vertical lines forming the SP250's outrageous fins seem to belong to another car.**

Even so, the awkward design looks sexy – but it is the authoritative throaty rumble from the SP250's twin exhausts that confirms it. Powered by a 2.5 litre V8 engine, the SP250 is a joy to drive. Once initial problems of the chassis (the doors on the original 'A' spec version had a tendency to fly open on tight bends) had been ironed out, the car began to fulfil its destiny as a two-door, open-topped king of the road. It was, and is, fun. Its responsive acceleration appeals as strongly to enthusiasts as it once did to the British police, who fielded a number of automatic versions as high-speed pursuit vehicles.

The real surprise is that Daimler ever made the SP250 (Dart). For decades the company had been associated firmly with upmarket family saloons and limited production of luxury limousines (clientele included the British Royal Family). The SP250 is really a delightful aberration. Its oddity, as well as its success, marks it as a product of a very specific, late 1950s social climate.

# FIAT 500

The Fiat 500 is an adorable bubble of a car conceived by a philosophy so successful that in 2007 it was relaunched in its umpteenth incarnation. The philosophy was originally dictated by post-World War II economics. Fiat took its prewar 500 (the 'Topolino', of 1936) and created the first true 'city car', capable (just) of carrying four people in completely basic, no-frills, pitifully low-powered, rear-engined, bony discomfort. The 'Nuova 500', designed by Dante Giacosa, instantly became the definitive 'Cinquecento'. Never mind it was necessarily small, cheap and utilitarian. It was reliable, and almost as basic to maintain as the scooters it replaced. Most of all it was loved because it was insanely cute.

The Cinquecento did for Italy what the 2CV did for France. It was classless, meaning you got jounced about on Italy's cobbled streets and uneven tarmac just as much on a romantic date as you did packing the family to market; and its appeal has endured as much as the simple purity of its engineering and styling. Between 1957 and 1975, Fiat introduced at least six versions, losing the 'suicide doors', switching the engine from rear to front, experimenting with chrome add ons, and calling the 500 the 'Bambino'. But as any owner will confirm, it eventually proved more fun to keep your old, battered friend on the road than to buy new.

Only in 2004, with the 'Trepiuno', did Fiat rediscover its original 500 magic – the radically modern redesign looks much more like a descendant of the classic Cinquecento than anything in between; and the 500 Abarth, the Sports version based on the Trepiuno, caused a sensation in 2007 for marrying low cost to fabulous performance, comfort and sporty looks. If any car has a philosophical pedigree – of doing a simple thing with brilliance and flair, cheaply – suited to the economic climate, it's the Fiat 500.

**COUNTRY OF ORIGIN:**
Italy

**FIRST MANUFACTURED:**
1957 (until 1975)

**ENGINE:**
479 cc, 499 cc, 594 cc
Straight Two, air-cooled

**PERFORMANCE:**
Top speed of 59 mph
(95 km/h)

**YOU SHOULD KNOW:**
There's an all-electric Fiat 500 made by NICE Car Co and the Italian firm Micro-Vett. Powered by lithium ion batteries, it has a range of 55 m (89 km) and a top speed of 55 mph (89 km/h) – plenty for a typical day in the city.

# FORD THUNDERBIRD

Think the Pacific surf thundering in, and the Coast Highway glinting silver, snaking past the sunsplashed canyons. The Thunderbird – the 'T-Bird' of legend – was born to the infectious upbeat of Jan & Dean and the Beach Boys, synonymous with youth and fun and the fulfilled promise of a comfortable post-World War II America. In fact it was devised as the first 'personal luxury' car to be available at a mass-market price. It only looked like a sports car, its two-seater bodywork slung low, but with a longer, heavier body, just enough tailfin and features borrowed from bigger family cars to give it its characteristic, solid sleekness. No mere sports car of the era could match the T-Bird's standard fittings (power steering, brakes, windows, radio, heater, choice of transmission and five possible colours) at the price.

The original Thunderbird was thought to be a little soft and loose to drive; but it was the perfect ride for America's growing Interstate Highway system, and when its V8 was on song, its performance easily matched the beautiful styling, at speeds well over 100 mph (160 km/h). More than 50 years later, riding a T-Bird still feels just as thrilling: the interior is a microcosm of the 1950s USA, once described as 'like a contemporary juke box, stylized and brash'.

Since the day it was first shown (on which orders for 4000 were placed!) the Thunderbird legend has grown steadily. Its evolution has gone full circle from two-seater to four-seater, luxury and Continental luxury, two-door sport coupe and back to 'retro' two-seater, in just thirteen generations spanning every automotive development. But no technology can recreate the spirit in which the 1955 Thunderbird was conceived, received and driven. The gods still smile at the thought.

**COUNTRY OF ORIGIN:**
USA

**FIRST MANUFACTURED:**
1955 (until 2005)

**ENGINE:**
4.8 l (292 cid) Y-block (OHV) V8

**PERFORMANCE:**
Top speed of 110 mph (177 km/h); 0–60 mph (97 km/h) in 9.5 secs

**YOU SHOULD KNOW:**
Only an accident of good taste prevented the car from being named the 'Hep Cat' or the 'Beaver' – these were serious suggestions before the 'Thunderbird' saved the day.

# FORD ZEPHYR MARK II

**COUNTRY OF ORIGIN:**
UK

**FIRST MANUFACTURED:**
1956 (until 1962)

**ENGINE:**
2,553 cc OHV Straight Six

**PERFORMANCE:**
Top speed of 89 mph (143 km/h); 0–60 mph (97 km/h) in 17 secs

**YOU SHOULD KNOW:**
A factory-modified Mk II rallying version had a top speed over 101 mph (163 km/h) and achieved 0–60 mph (97 km/h) in less than 10 secs.

By the middle of the 1950s Ford of Britain was reaching its industrial zenith. Success at every market level was maintained by constant innovation and improvement. With its Consul/Zephyr/Zodiac range, Ford had already struck gold in both sales and motorsport. A Mk I Zephyr (originally known as the Zephyr Six) had won the Monte Carlo Rally in 1953 and the East African Safari in 1955, enhancing the car's reputation for good value. Problems of understeer and limited performance were overcome with easily made modifications that improved handling and added as much as 20 mph (32 km/h) to the top speed.

Success bred success. In 1956 the new Mk II Consul/Zephyr/Zodiac models were acclaimed as 'the three graces', thanks to their stunningly family-friendly new lines. The Mk II Zephyr benefited most. Longer, heavier, wider and more powerful, its popularity as the biggest mass-market family car was assured – considerably helped by a run of competition successes crowned by winning outright the 1959 RAC Rally.

It was the Mk II Zephyr which opened the door for Ford's later adventures with the Cortina and the Escort. Many are still competing in Classic and other events: and drivers' reports of powering a Mk II up a snowy mountain pass, or controlling the well-behaved heavyweight hurtling through mud-clogged forest lanes, continue to excite everyone who has ever dreamed of their family car transforming into a supercar. The Zephyr Mk II is the car that proves you don't have to be rich to be a winner.

# JAGUAR XK150

**COUNTRY OF ORIGIN:**
UK

**FIRST MANUFACTURED:**
1957 (until 1960)

**ENGINE:**
DOHC Straight Six
(available as 3.4/3.4S and
3.8/3.8S)

**PERFORMANCE:**
A 3.4 l XK150S FHC
achieved a top speed of
132 mph (212 km/h) and
0–60 mph (97 km/h) in
7.8 secs

**YOU SHOULD KNOW:**
What we now know as
Jaguar Cars was founded
in 1922 as the Swallow
Sidecar Company.
After World War II,
the company had to
change its name because
of 'associations' with
the initials forming its
previous logo – SS.

**Though Jaguar is now a subsidiary of Ford, the marque is still esteemed for its pre- and post-World War II reputation for luxury saloons and competitive sports cars. In 1948, Jaguar had thrilled the motoring world with its XK120, still sought after and enjoyed for its mean, lean, sporting lines. Nine years and the XK140 later, the company's wealth of racing and marketing experience was poured into the XK150, the last and most glamorous of its species. Obvious family resemblances were misleading: the XK150's subtly improved, but still old world styling incorporated extensive modernization that paved the way for both the stylistic Great Statement of the E-Type and the mechanical glories of the XK engine-powered sports saloons of the 1960s.**

In fact the first XK 150s were not as quick as their predecessors. Their beefed-up curves (with the new one-piece windscreen, wider bonnet and wing line raised almost to door level, the heavier car still looked as athletically poised and dangerous as the leaping mascot itself!) relied on the XK140's standard 3.4 engine. But from 1958, the 3.4 and (later) 3.8 litre versions could be tuned to 'S' form, restoring real performance to match the car's aura of stylish menace. You could have a Fixed Head Coupe (FHC), a two-to-three seater like the Drop Head Coupe (DHC), or the Roadster.

In the XK150's short production life (to October 1960), almost 10,000 owners succumbed in equal measure to the magic of the three versions. Subsequently, in his first film as actor/director, Clint Eastwood immortalized one of them in *Play Misty For Me*. In every way, the XK150 bears the hallmarks of discriminating taste: like so many Jaguars, it talks quietly, and walks the walk effortlessly, on demand.

# LAGONDA 3.0 LITRE

The Lagonda was a marque of automotive aristocracy more than equal to its luxury sports car competitors, Bentley, Invicta and Railton. When Rolls-Royce bought him out, W O Bentley in fact chose to move to Lagonda, which was acquired in 1947 by the industrialist David Brown at much the same time as Aston Martin, for whose salvation he depended on Bentley's legendary engineering. Brown put the available 2.6 litre Bentley engine first into his Aston Martin DB2, and only in 1948 into his first Lagonda, a wonderful but old-fashioned, somewhat stately magnificence.

It was 1953 before he announced the new 3 litre Lagonda, powered by a revised Bentley engine capable of topping the magic 100 mph (161 km/h), and featuring the advanced design of a cruciform-braced chassis and all-round independent suspension. Initially, though seating four, it came only as a two-door closed saloon or a convertible drophead coupe (styled by the Swiss coachbuilder, Graber). Though fast, the column-change gearbox detracted from its sporty appeal.

By 1954, the gear change was floor mounted, and drivers could feel they were truly participating in one of the era's great motoring experiences. The saloon appeared with four doors, and the drophead coupe just got better. You bathed in leather and walnut, with every available extra installed as standard in a vehicle of supremely discreet elegance, while the engine effortlessly dealt with the solid weight of genuine luxury. Five people could be comfortable in a 3 litre Lagonda; and even with the ample boot filled with luggage, the car fulfilled its fastest specs.

HRH the Duke of Edinburgh thought so, too, and had his 3 litre Lagonda Drophead Coupe finished in Edinburgh Green with Battleship Grey upholstery. He even persuaded his wife, HM The Queen, to use it in 1959 on the occasion of the official opening of Britain's first motorway, the M1.

**COUNTRY OF ORIGIN:**
UK

**FIRST MANUFACTURED:**
1953 (until 1958)

**ENGINE:**
2,922 cc DOHC Straight Six

**PERFORMANCE:**
Top speed of 104 mph (167 km/h); 0–60 mph (97 km/h) in 12.9 secs

**YOU SHOULD KNOW:**
This beautiful car was unfortunately more expensive than its obvious rivals, and only 270 were ever made including all its configurations. It was succeeded in 1961 by the Lagonda Rapide, another super luxury saloon – but after that Aston Martin had to go it alone.

# LOTUS ELITE

**COUNTRY OF ORIGIN:**
UK

**FIRST MANUFACTURED:**
1957 (prototype); 1958
(production) (until 1963)

**ENGINE:**
1,216 cc Straight Four

**PERFORMANCE:**
Top speed of 115 mph
(185 km/h); 0–60 mph
(97 km/h) in 12.2 secs

**YOU SHOULD KNOW:**
If you enjoy automotive
mathematics,
investigate the Lotus
Elite's incredible drag
coefficient. Those gentle,
delicate curves contain
nothing superfluous.
The Elite's beauty is
dedicated to achieving
its coefficient of 0.29,
brilliant today, and simply
unheard of in 1957.

Its streamlined elegance flabbergasted the motoring world when it was unveiled at the London Earls Court Motor Show of 1957. The Lotus Elite's fibreglass monocoque engineering was the very first combination of its kind. It was also the first 'regular', roadgoing, production sports car created by the maverick engineering genius, Colin Chapman and his team, even if the first line-produced car was not made until mid-1958 (and bought, incidentally, by the celebrated jazz musician, Chris Barber).

Though there was a steel subframe to support the engine, suspension and essentials like the door hinges, the Elite's featherweight and advanced aerodynamic construction, balanced on four-wheel independent suspension, made it a dream to handle. It was a wonderfully quick car. In fact to begin with, the 1.2 litre engine made it almost overpowered – but it provided the Elite with the authentic sports car performance that gained it, among many triumphs, six class victories in the Le Mans 24 hour. The interior had carefully matching, stylish practicality – including a metal dashboard shaped exactly like the Elite's exterior profile.

There were major problems. The drive was bolted directly to the monocoque without even rubber cushions. The noise was horrendous. Forget 'opening the windows': curved on two planes so they couldn't wind down into the doors, the only option was to remove them completely and stow them in special pockets behind the seats. Worse, the glass fibre bodywork was liable to crack.

Not even shifting body manufacture to the Bristol Aircraft Company resolved the Elite's shortcomings. Yet its performance belied its fragility – and when you see one today, zipping along with fluid elegance, it's impossible to forget that the Lotus Elite is a car whose subsequent influence entitles it to be universally lauded as a genuine ancestor.

# MG
# MGA

After 20 years of the highly traditional 'T' series sports car, MG appeared to break with its usual modus operandi'. The MGA came to its public as an unknown Adonis, the first MG with a full-width body and streamlined curves. In fact, though the styling was indeed radically new, it had (as always with MG) been evolved over four years from a prototype shell based on the 'TD' series, and progressively refined.

The engine was a BMC B series already chosen for the MG Magnette sports saloon. Its size meant the hood line could be lowered, reducing the drag coefficient. Mutterings about 'underpower' were stilled when the MGA (suitably handicapped) totally outperformed its predecessor and stablemate, an MG TF 1500. The MGA's stylish aerodynamics alone were shown to add just under 10 secs to its top speed.

The MGA faced the future squarely. Traditionalists were disappointed, but the company was firmly fixed on innovation and improvement. Almost immediately the engine was uprated (from 68 to 72 bhp). Then came a 'bubble-top' coupe version with the sports car luxury of wind-up windows, and the first of a procession of stylistic adjustments throughout the car's production. The Twin-Cam of 1958 looked normal, but revelled in a competitive ability to hit 114 mph (183.5 km/h) or more. In anything but expert hands, it was unreliable. In its place came the MGA 1600 Mark I & II, which did most of the same things, and stayed on their respective feet. Finally, every development was incorporated into a few, leftover, twin cam chassis and designated the MG MGA 1600 Mk II Deluxe. It was now a brilliant, beautiful, high-performance sports car (with a really snappy name!), but its time had passed. Luckily, the MGB was waiting in the wings.

**COUNTRY OF ORIGIN:**
UK

**FIRST MANUFACTURED:**
1955 (until 1962)

**ENGINE:**
1,489 cc OHV Straight Four

**PERFORMANCE:**
Top speed of 98 mph (157 km/h); 0–60 mph (97 km/h) in 15 secs

**YOU SHOULD KNOW:**
Besides starring in a 1970s Kellogs Corn Flakes commercial on Golden Gate bridge, the MGA has an excellent Hollywood pedigree. Among other films, it features in *Animal House* (1978) and *Guess Who's Coming to Dinner* (1968). Most conspicuously, Elvis Presley liked the red 1960 MGA 1600 Mk I roadster he uses throughout *Blue Hawaii* (1961) so much that he bought it. You can see it at Graceland.

# MERCEDES-BENZ 300 SL

**At least one major poll declared the Mercedes 300 SL 'Gullwing' to be 'Sports Car of the [20th] Century'. And it's true: more than 50 years after its introduction, its aerodynamic finesse has the undimmed, futuristic beauty of a timeless thoroughbred; and its original ergonomic brilliance still makes it one of the most pleasing cars you will ever drive.**

New York City saw the Gullwing first, at the 1954 Auto Show. The two-seater closed sports car was the road model of Daimler-Benz's hugely successful 300 SL racing car. It was the company's response to urgent prompting by their official US importer, who accurately foresaw an eager market for a top-quality Mercedes sports car. It was a sensation. The importer immediately ordered a thousand. The aerodynamic streamlining spoke of muscular sophistication, and the visual drama of the unfolding gullwing doors released the full potential of the car's inherent panache.

Performance depended not just on the light weight of its aluminium skin, but on the rigidity of the tubular frame, which necessarily reached much higher than usual up the side. Normal doors were impossible – and so was any proposal for an open-top version. Instead, customers could choose from five rear-axle ratios for their preferred balance between straight line speed and acceleration, all of which benefited from the Gullwing's revolutionary new direct fuel injection system, another first for a petrol-powered production car and not even installed in the Gullwing's race-only predecessor.

Climbing in was an adventure. Once there, the ergonomic lay-out, like everything else, was years ahead. The road-holding and hanling were precise but effortless. Steering was direct, power instantaneous. This dazzling automobile cloaked you in its own charisma, and it still does.

**COUNTRY OF ORIGIN:**
Germany

**FIRST MANUFACTURED:**
1955 (until 1957)

**ENGINE:**
2,996 cc Straight Six

**PERFORMANCE:**
Top speed of 146–61 mph (235–260 km/h) according to axle ratio; 0–60 mph (97 km/h) in 10 secs

**YOU SHOULD KNOW:**
To squeeze beneath the Gullwing's remarkably flat bonnet profile, the engine had to be tilted more than 45 degrees to the left.
Gullwing owners could make the most of their car's space by ordering a set of luggage made to measure.

# MINI COOPER

**COUNTRY OF ORIGIN:**
UK

**FIRST MANUFACTURED:**
1959

**ENGINE:**
997 cc Straight Four

**PERFORMANCE:**
Top speed of 85 mph
(137 km/h); 0–60 mph
(97 km/h) 17.5 secs

**YOU SHOULD KNOW:**
Customized Minis or
Mini Coopers were stars
in films like *The Italian
Job*, *A Shot In The Dark*,
and the Beatles' *Magical
Mystery Tour*. Owners
included Steve McQueen,
Enzo Ferrari, Marianne
Faithfull, all four Beatles,
and Peter Sellers (whose
Mini had wicker side-
panels designed by the
Rolls-Royce coachbuilder,
Hooper).

In 1959 the Austin/Morris Mini changed the face of motoring. Just 3 m (10 ft) long, it was the most efficient and effective use of road space ever seen. The apparent miracle of Sir Alec Issigonis's design was to create a front-wheel drive, two-door, four-seat economy saloon that sacrificed nothing to exact steering, superb handling, and super-agile response. At the time of its first launch, BMC (which included Austin and Morris, and marketed the Mini under both to keep the names before the public) lent a Mini to John Cooper, whose racing cars were then approaching the peak of their success (in several formulae, including two Formula 1 World Championships). He was immediately fascinated. By 1961 his 'idea' for a hot Mini had been researched, tested and produced – to a tidal wave of public and professional applause.

It was a social revolution as much as anything. The Mini Cooper, brilliant on the track and multi-winner of Monte Carlo Rallies, was the car of Britain's about-to-be 'swinging 60s' elite. In London the unofficial race track was Belgrave Square (there was much less traffic than today). The manic screeching of tyres at night is said to have only been tamed when a local policeman got his own Mini Cooper to give chase.

The Mini Cooper, and of course the even snappier Cooper 'S', have added to their legendary exploits with every incarnation. Like the Mini itself (and the MINI, as current owners BMW distinguish their versions), the Cooper has appeared in dozens of configurations, from economy to super-deluxe and back again. It has always guaranteed and delivered pure thrill; and that's why so many people continue to admire and drive one more than 50 years on.

# MORGAN 4/4

The company was famous for its three-wheelers when Morgan announced its first '4-4 – four wheels and four cylinders' cars in 1936. It returned from war production in 1950 with its Plus-4, a commercial success but a demographic step too far upmarket for the marque's core enthusiasts. So in 1955 Morgan introduced the Morgan 4/4 Series II (note the subtle change from 4-4 to 4/4) as a lower-powered, lightweight, nippy return to the company's original principles. Ever since, through succeeding generations of power plants and every kind of technical evolution, the car has existed in a category of its own.

Sturdy but light, built from aluminium on an ash frame, the Morgan 4/4 has survived many experiments in modern materials, and innumerable cycles of fashionability. In effect, the experience of providing fast, fun, recreational transport at the lowest practicable cost, to which the original Henry Morgan devoted himself in 1910, locked the company into a way of doing things which it has never been able to change without compromising the reasons for its success. Owners and drivers of the Morgan 4/4 of any era get particular pleasure from tinkering. Closed factory systems and computerized technology inhibit it, so Morgan avoids them where it can. The outward, still 1930s, styling is a hallmark of the 4/4's longstanding promise of keen handling and performance characteristics that can readily be modified to suit an individual's requirements (or expectations). The Series II, and every subsequent version, comes with all the technical mod cons of the day – but it always looks and drives like you've just roared in, rimed with dust where your goggles sheltered your eyes, from the Mille Miglia or the Indy 500, or even Box Hill. The Morgan 4/4 is, par excellence, the sports car of Everyman's imagination. That's why it's still going strong.

**COUNTRY OF ORIGIN:**
UK

**FIRST MANUFACTURED:**
1955 (Series II) (until 1959)

**ENGINE:**
1,172 cc flathead Straight Four Ford 100E

**PERFORMANCE:**
Top speed of 75 mph (121 km/h); 0–60 mph (97 km/h) in 26.9 secs

**YOU SHOULD KNOW:**
You get a very direct ride in a Morgan 4/4, but the car has never been built for raw power. Its success is the result of decades of cunning, balancing the least available power to the least available structural weight.

# NISSAN SKYLINE

**COUNTRY OF ORIGIN:**
Japan

**FIRST MANUFACTURED:**
1957 (until 1963)

**ENGINE:**
1,482 cc, 1,862 cc OHV
Straight Four

**PERFORMANCE:**
Top speed of 87 mph
(140 km/h)

**YOU SHOULD KNOW:**
Though you won't see
it badged on Nissan
cars, the Prince marque
still exists within the
Nissan company. After
the Tachikawa Aircraft
Company turned from
making World War II
fighter planes to making
electric cars in 1947, it
moved on to make petrol-
driven cars in 1954 –
simultaneously changing
its name to Prince Motors
to honour the Japanese
Crown Prince Hirohita. It
still does.

**For years, the Nissan Skyline GT-R series has starred in road and track races, and in some of the world's most successful video games, like Gran Turismo. Its latest incarnation, the Nissan GT-R (the 'Skyline' got dropped in 2007) R35 uses 'launch control' to achieve 0–60mph (97 km/h) in 3.2 secs, and blasts on to a top speed of over 192 mph (309 km/h). Appropriately for a Japanese car, it owes much to its ancestors, the Nissan Skyline ALSI-1 and ALSI-2 first introduced in 1957.**

Back then, what we know retrospectively as the Nissan was actually a Prince Skyline, made by the Japanese auto manufacturer that merged with Nissan-Datsun. It was a luxury four-door sedan or a five-door station wagon, updated within its first year with a more powerful engine and the first quad headlights arrangement ever seen on a Japanese car. It had all the virtues of contemporary cars designed for Middle America, on which it was based, but not many of their vices. In terms of automotive history, its success was not just its virtuous good looks or its well-mannered competence (it agreed politely when you wanted to accelerate, then took off, gracefully), but the mere fact of its existence.

The Nissan Skyline set a benchmark by establishing Japanese capability to match worldwide technical and aesthetic auto evolution. Since the ALSI-1, the Skyline's genealogy has included sports and super sports cars, pickup trucks, luxury sedans, and one of the finest families of GT cars ever made anywhere. You still see lots of Nissan Skyline GTs from each of the last three decades, barely resembling anything of their lineage except pure quality of design, and inspirational – sometimes titanic – technology under the hood.

# PANHARD DYNA Z /PANHARD PL17

**COUNTRY OF ORIGIN:**
France

**FIRST MANUFACTURED:**
1953 (until 1959 Dyna Z;
1965 PL17)

**ENGINE:**
848 cc–851 cc Flat-twin

**PERFORMANCE:**
Dyna Z – top speed of
81 mph (130 km/h)
Dyna Z 'Tigre'/PL17 –
top speed of 90 mph
(145 km/h)

**YOU SHOULD KNOW:**
While the column shift
made the Panhard
Dyna Z more spacious,
other controls were less
obvious. Since the brake
lights had a dual function
as reversing lights,
you could start the car
without a key – in reverse
with the brake on.

**Halfway through its development of the Dyna Z sedan, the Panhard Car Company was partially integrated with Citroën. By the time the car had evolved into the Panhard PL17, that merger was evident in the modified styling, and you can see the future of Citroën's most famous profiles emerging.**

Stylistically, the Panhard Dyna Z tells the story of French car design in the 1950s. When it was launched in 1953, it was a comfortable but economic six-seater mid-range saloon, still made of aluminium (which evaded the postwar proscription on steel for cars) on a front and rear steel tube subframe. With characteristic élan, Panhard created a smooth, rounded (even slightly bulbous), futuristically sleek profile. The Dyna Z looked good, and novel. By 1956, the bodies were made of steel, and the suspension improved to take the weight – but the car remained light enough to lift a back wheel on tight corners, or slide the passengers across the bench seats if it didn't.

Reliability was dealt with while Citroën used their influence on the design for the Dyna Z's successor. The Panhard PL17 of 1959 (the 'L' referred to Levassor, Panhard's original partner) looked like a new model, but was the Dyna Z in all important technical senses. The PL17 flattened the Dyna Z's curves into streamlined simplicity, but left the fairly extreme curvature of the front of the hood in what we now recognize as a prototype of later Citroëns. Even at the time, it was a radical aesthetic, but over half a century later, the Panhard PL17 still holds its own as a progressive profile. In the light of the revolutionary engineering being developed by Citroën, perhaps it shouldn't be surprising that the Dyna Z engine was never developed to match, and this was almost Panhard's last car.

# PLYMOUTH FURY

1956 was the year of 'The Forward Look', when Plymouth sought to amaze its competitors and the US public with tailfin 'developments' and a series of ingenious in-car devices. In addition to the V8 'Hy-Fire' engine from the previous year, the 1956 Plymouths could have push-button 'Powerflite' automatic transmission and 'Highway Hi-Fi', a record player designed to keep the stylus in the platter's groove while you avoided potholes in the road. Plymouth marketing was a cameo of the economic optimism of the era – but it couldn't prepare the company for the kind of enthusiasm that greeted the summer launch of its new hardtop coupe, a limited edition to crown its range: the first Plymouth Fury.

It only came in white, with a gold stripe worked down each side to emphasize the high fins looming over the twin exhausts that spoke of the 240 bhp inside. It was beautiful, fast and difficult to get your hands on. It raised the profile of every Plymouth model, and the company began its most successful era. The Fury's role as high-performance standard-bearer for Plymouth increased with its staggering tail size. Its proven reliability and performance even endeared it to US Police forces (who also, apparently, greatly admired its unexpectedly soft ride). By 1959, the Fury's name was attached to most Plymouth high-end models (pushing the Belvedere, Savoy etc. down the marketing pecking order); and a new 'Sport Fury' was created as a limited edition with numerous options for making it even more flashy (it already came with a trunk lid appliqué intended to look like an exterior spare tyre, but resembling a trash-can top). In the giddy euphoria of the day, the ruse worked, and went on working. The Plymouth Fury is a marketing milestone as well as one of America's hottest 1950s cars.

**COUNTRY OF ORIGIN:**
USA

**FIRST MANUFACTURED:**
1956 (until 1959)

**ENGINE:**
5.0 l (303 cid) V8

**PERFORMANCE:**
Top speed of 110 mph (177 km/h); 0–60 mph (97 km/h) in 10 secs

**YOU SHOULD KNOW:**
Since 1961, the name 'Fury' has been attached to several generations of Plymouth models and series. The villain of Stephen King's novel *Christine* is a demoniacally possessed 1958 Plymouth Fury which manipulates two odd people to fall in love, and slaughters anyone who gets in the way.

# RILEY 1.5

**COUNTRY OF ORIGIN:**
UK

**FIRST MANUFACTURED:**
1957 (until 1965)

**ENGINE:**
1,489 cc Straight Four

**PERFORMANCE:**
Top speed of 84 mph
(135 km/h); 0–60 mph
(97 km/h) in 24.8 secs

**YOU SHOULD KNOW:**
The Riley 1.5 had a high
final drive in the axle,
which meant it could
cruise comfortably at
speed. For a small car, it
also proved surprisingly
lively in contemporary
races and rallies. Its Riley
ancestors would have
approved.

**Throughout the 1930s and 1940s Riley was numbered among Britain's most successful manufacturers of sports cars, sporting saloon, and even luxury limousines. Their characteristic, slightly raffish and aristocratic styling did not survive the 1952 merger of the Nuffield group (including Riley) with Austin, which formed BMC. It took five years for the merger to bear fruit: twin replacements for the Morris Minor 1000, to be launched as the Wolseley 1500 and then later, the Riley 1.5.**

It was a radical change for the Riley. Fifty years of sporting elegance was replaced by a four-door, mid-size family saloon on which awkward curves vied uncomfortably with straight lines. The Riley 1.5 looked like it couldn't decide if it wanted to look American, or just a little like a Jaguar, if only by its suggestive grille shape. It was safe, solid, comfortable, and at least it was more powerful than the Wolseley, with which it shared so many Morris Minor components. Both were fitted with the BMC B-series engine, but the Riley's twin SU carburettors gave it substantially more clout. It also had some of the same attention to interior detail of its more magnificent Riley predecessors, like the walnut veneer and extensive dial arrangement of the fascia.

The Riley 1.5 was successful enough to warrant a Mark II version, an almost entirely cosmetic style-tweak that enabled it to be sold in a sporty duo-tone version; and in 1961, a Mark III, with lower suspension. In fact, BMC's Australian-built Riley 1.5s incorporated more changes than were ever made in Britain. In its place of origin, the Riley 1.5 is a monument to motoring decency. Impeccably behaved, and both comfortable and speedy, it belongs neither to the past nor the future. It's in the middle.

# VAUXHALL PA CRESTA

**Few cars are so evocative of Britain's late '50s obsession with American culture as the PA range. The introduction of the PA Cresta was the culmination of several years' gradual Americanization of the Vauxhall marque and the drift away from the small-car market with which it had been associated in the prewar years. General Motors (Vauxhall's parent company) had given the first subtle signs that the marque was evolving in a new direction with the introduction of the Wyvern family saloon in 1948, and by 1954 understated echoes of American styling had become apparent in Vauxhall's Velox and Cresta saloon range, indicating the start of a new era in design that paved the way for the 1957 launch of the PA Cresta, a deluxe version of the PA Velox.**

The PA's flashy tailfins, clustered rear lights, whitewall tyres and wrap-around windows were blatantly transatlantic, emulating the brash good looks of the Buicks and Cadillacs rolling off General Motors' Detroit assembly line. Its paintwork came in bright (optional two-tone) colours with plenty of gleaming chrome trim while the plush interior was fitted with leather upholstery and pile carpet, and included the luxury of a fitted heater as standard. Three people could easily sit together along the front benchseat, with the handbrake neatly stowed under the dashboard and the gearshift mounted on the steering column, leaving the floor completely clear for feet. A beautifully designed tri-sectioned rear screen gave panoramic visibility while the all-sync three-speed gearbox and independent front suspension ensured a smooth ride.

If the starchier members of the establishment considered the PA too outré for words, it was certainly the prestige statement car that every hip '50s glamour-seeker aspired to. More than 81,000 PA Crestas were built and today it is a highly sought-after classic.

**COUNTRY OF ORIGIN:**
UK

**FIRST MANUFACTURED:**
1957 (until 1962)

**ENGINE:**
2,262 cc Straight Six ('pushrod' OHV until 1960)

**PERFORMANCE:**
Top speed of 90 mph (144 km/h) with acceleration of 0–60 mph (97 km/h) in 16.8 secs

**YOU SHOULD KNOW:**
Ironically, despite (or maybe because of) the PA Cresta's rock 'n' roll image, the Queen of England had a rare estate version for her own personal use.

# VOLVO AMAZON 120 SERIES

**COUNTRY OF ORIGIN:**
Sweden

**FIRST MANUFACTURED:**
1956 (until 1970)

**ENGINE:**
1580 cc, 1778 cc, 1896 cc
OHV Straight Four
(Volvo B16, B18 or B20
engines)

**PERFORMANCE:**
Top speed of 108 mph
(174 km/h)

**YOU SHOULD KNOW:**
The 120 series was a
bestseller for Volvo for
more than a decade and
nearly half the Amazons
sold in Sweden are
still on the road today.
Their astoundingly
good condition attests
to Volvo's quality
production.

**Arguably the car with which Volvo established its reputation as a manufacturer of safe, solid and attractive mid-range cars, the Amazon is perhaps the most famous and easily recognisable car that Volvo has ever produced. Designer Jan Wilsgaard's take on the classic Chrysler tailfins and bull nose was influenced by Italian and British design as much as American; the Amazon has a restrained elegance about it that still impresses today.**

The Amazon was designed to be the sophisticated, up-to-the-minute successor to the rugged but staid postwar PV series, but almost as soon as it went on the market a problem arose: its name. Sole title had already been registered by a German motorbike manufacturer which meant that Volvo's use of it was restricted to the Baltic countries. Throughout the rest of Europe the car had to be marketed by model number alone. Despite this marketing gaffe, the car quickly gained a reputation for reliability and durability and Volvo soon also demonstrated concern for safety, offering fitted front-seat safety belts as standard on its 1959 sports version.

The basic model (known as the 121) was a three-speed manual with rear-wheel drive, fitted with a single Stromberg carb, 1.6 litre engine. In 1958 a four-speed, twin carb sports version (122S) was produced. Further models and more powerful (1.8 and 2 litre) engines continued to be introduced and by the time production ended you could have chosen from a selection of two- and four-door saloons as well as estate versions, with a number of engine options.

Volvo's numbering system for the 120 series is notoriously confusing, depending partly on which country the car was marketed in. In theory, four-door saloons are designated 120s, two-door saloons as 130s and estates as 220s; and an S on the end indicates a sports model. However, they are by no means always badged according to this system. To establish beyond doubt what a particular model is, it is best to consult the type number in the engine compartment.

# VOLKSWAGEN TYPE 2 (CAMPER)

**The Type 2 KombinationsKraftWagen, or 'Kombi', was originally intended as a utilitarian commercial transporter for the numerous new business enterprises that sprang up after World War II. It was built on a modified Type 1 (Beetle) platform and almost as soon as it was introduced it became clear there was a market for a passenger version with removable seats – the campervan was born. The split-windowed early models, known as 'splitties', had various styles of interior layout and degrees of luxury, of which the best-known are the thousand or so original 'westies' produced by Westfalia, VW's official coachbuilders.**

From its inception, the Type 2 was recognised as a uniquely versatile new type of vehicle. The novelty of its very un-American low-powered, air-cooled rear engine and space-saving boxy shape appealed enormously to the US market and in the 1960s it was adopted by the counter-culture as the ultimate fashion accessory for living out the hippie dream – the epitome of wanderlust chic. The VW Camper's great attraction lies in the fact that it is extraordinarily easy to drive with excellent visibility and easy steering and, although it has the acceleration of a snail and is neither particularly comfortable nor very economical, these are small prices to pay in return for the towering sensation of power you feel at the wheel – a veritable king of the road.

Over the years, the Type 2 has evolved through a multitude of styles to come almost full-circle: the latest model is a retro second generation 1970s 'breadloaf' version but with more power, a water-cooled engine and a vintage price tag. Too much to hope, though, for a remake of the original classic 'splittie' – it is destined to remain a rusty collector's piece for dreamers.

**COUNTRY OF ORIGIN:**
Germany (also produced in Brazil and Mexico)

**FIRST MANUFACTURED:**
1950 (Split-screen until 1967)

**ENGINE:**
Depending on model, ranges from 1,131 cc to 2,000 cc Flat Four (air-cooled until 1984)

**PERFORMANCE:**
Top speed of 60 mph (97 km/h); 0–60 mph (97km/h) in 75 secs

**YOU SHOULD KNOW:**
The VW Type 2 Camper has acquired almost as many nicknames as it has had incarnations. As well as 'kombi', 'westie', 'splittie' and 'hippie van/bus', you may hear it referred to as a 'microbus', 'bulli', 'loaf', 'bay' or 'vee-dub'.

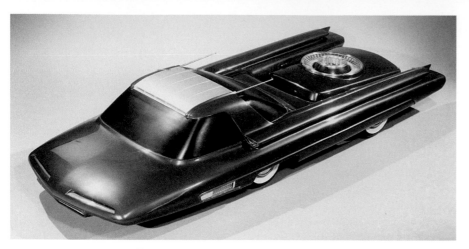

# FORD NUCLEON

## CONCEPT CAR

**COUNTRY OF ORIGIN:**
USA

**FIRST MANUFACTURED:**
1958

**ENGINE:**
N/A

**PERFORMANCE:**
Power capsule with radioactive core (different 'sizes' were 'designed' to be interchangeable according to varying demands of performance or distance to be travelled)

**YOU SHOULD KNOW:**
At least the Nucleon contributed to the design of the DeLorean-based time machine featured in the film *Back to the Future*.

**The Big Three of 1950s Detroit car makers all had elite design teams charged with transforming half-baked dreams into roadgoing realities. Ford's Nucleon seized the high ground of the Atomic Age by suggesting a brave new world in which the internal combustion engine was replaced by a small nuclear reactor! In 1958, nuclear power was pregnant with possibility. There was every reason to think the Nucleon might presage an automotive revolution; and every reason to fear that possibility.**

Ford's designers envisaged a genuine scientific pedigree for the Nucleon and its claim to travel 5,000 miles on a single charge, but unwittingly acknowledged their own economy with the truth by stressing how the Nucleon was designed to keep passengers as far from anything radioactive as possible. In fact they had no real notion of how nuclear energy could be harnessed in any way applicable to a car, and the Nucleon remained a scale model of a theory about an idea.

As the *New York Times* much later remarked, it was one of a number of concept cars that 'each deserves credit for charging full-throttle down an amusing blind alley'. The Nucleon never got any throttle at all. It was actually one of the great conceptual 'rollers' – so called because they had to be rolled onto the stage, lacking any means of self-propulsion. Half a century later, you still wonder 'what if?'

# OLDSMOBILE GOLDEN ROCKET

## CONCEPT CAR

General Motors was more circumspect with its concept cars than its 1950s competitors. It had evolved an annual show called the General Motors Motorama which travelled from city to city giving potential customers a close look at the company's latest models. Each year, the star of the show was a one-off machine that incorporated the most extreme thinking of the designers, stylists and engineers who created the production models that people actually bought and drove. The difference was that all GM's concept cars, up there on the platform amid the 'ooohs' and 'aaahs' and the glitzy lighting, were equally driveable. Behind the glamorous presentation and the 'shocking' extremity of design was a carefully graded marketing exercise which might, as the Corvette had already proved, take fire in the public imagination, and create a whole new production success.

The Oldsmobile Golden Rocket Concept car of 1956 typified General Motors' ability to dramatize stylistic and technical innovation. It looked like an aggressive shark flanked by the fuselages of two fighter planes, with their chrome propeller cones as bumpers (pretty but ineffective, since the 'shark' nose protruded by several inches in the middle). With its wraparound front and split rear windows tapering into a teardrop, and arrow-flight fins curling slightly outwards above the slimmed sweep of the cigar-tube rear profile, the all-golden car really did suggest a rocket. It embodied the future. Open a door, and a roof panel raised automatically, the seat rose three inches and swivelled outwards, and the steering wheel tilted for better access. The Golden Rocket was full of ergonomic and technical innovations which influenced whole generations of production vehicles. It was everything a concept car should be – sacrificing safety considerations (the car would never be made in this form) for a glimpse of attainable desire. A beautiful and clever car.

**COUNTRY OF ORIGIN:**
USA

**FIRST MANUFACTURED:**
1956

**ENGINE:**
5.3 l (324 cid) V8

**PERFORMANCE:**
N/A

**YOU SHOULD KNOW:**
The Golden Rocket Concept car starred in several Motorama travelling shows. Its 'wow!' factor tempted General Motors into naming a 1957 production series the Golden Rocket 88, but these cars, though a close relative, looked nothing like the concept original. The only surviving concept model changed hands for $3.24 million.

1960s

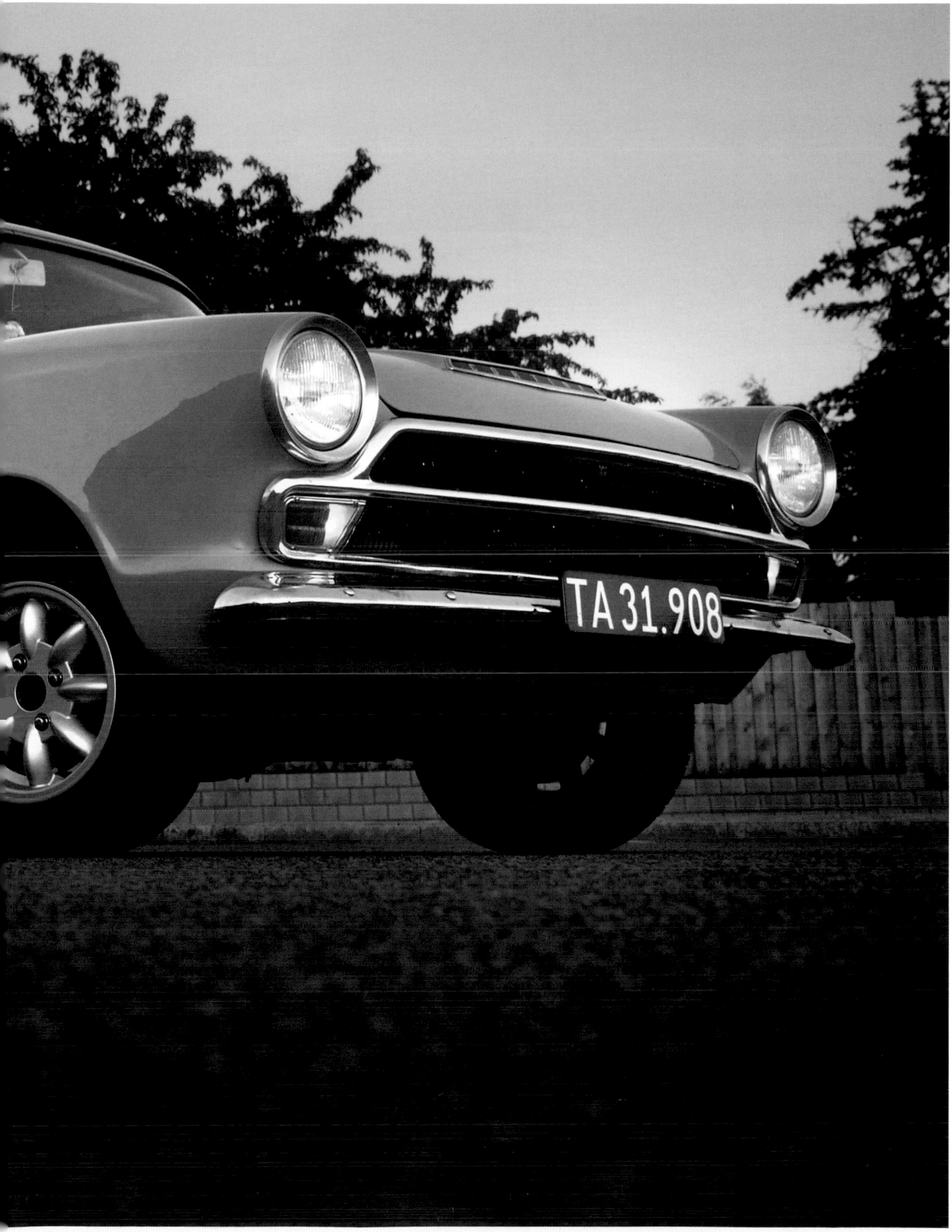
TA 31.908

# ALFA ROMEO T33 STRADALE

**COUNTRY OF ORIGIN:**
Italy

**FIRST MANUFACTURED:**
1968 (until 1971)

**ENGINE:**
1,995 cc V8

**PERFORMANCE:**
Top speed 162 mph (260 km/h); 0–60 mph (97 km/h) in 5.4 secs

**YOU SHOULD KNOW:**
You can see an Alfa T33 Stradale in the Alfa Romeo Museum in Arese near Milan, Italy.

For some years Alfa Romeo competed successfully on the race track by using modified production cars, but in 1967 the company adopted a new approach – the 2 litre Tipo 33 racer was built from scratch. This prototype was to become the basis of the legendary Stradale, a roadster born from racing car technology that not only vies for title of most beautiful car ever made but also performed in the same league as any supercar of the day.

Technically, the Stradale was virtually identical to the T33 racer but with a longer wheelbase and a lower-tuned engine, a custom-built, powerful but compact, lightweight alloy shortstroke V8 designed by Alfa's racing engineer, Carlo Chiti, and a Valerio Colotti six-speed transaxle gearbox. The cars were assembled individually entirely by hand at coachbuilder Carrozzeria Marazzi of Milan to a daring futuristic design of Franco Scaglione. The beautifully sculpted aluminium body had the first butterfly doors (opening upwards and outwards) to be found in a production car and side windows that arched seamlessly into the bubble roof. The finished product oozed sex appeal in a way that was far ahead of its time.

Anyone lucky enough to get behind the wheel of a Stradale is in for the experience of a lifetime. The car literally begs you to let go and give in to your lust for speed. But dream on! You've got about as much chance of driving one of these gorgeous million-dollar roadsters as you have of going to the moon. Only 18 were ever made and even they were outside the grasp of any but the very deepest pocket – the Stradale was one of the most expensive cars on the market, selling at $17,000, more than five times as much as the average car at that time.

# ALVIS TF21

**Alvis had a 'good' World War II, switching from the specialist car market to the manufacture of aero engines thus ensuring a healthy profit. But the war had shaken up society, creating a more egalitarian climate in which the minority privilege of elite sports cars and luxury tourers had no place. This top-end specialist market had been Alvis's customer base so it isn't surprising that the company folded; the only wonder is how it was able to give such a long-lasting swansong.**

Alvis's final cars were an imaginative line of 3 litre saloons and drophead coupes, starting with the TA21 in 1950 and ending with the TF21 in 1966 – the last-ever Alvis car. Alvis's short-stroke six-cylinder 3 litre engine supplied plenty of power whatever the revs (150 bhp in the TF21) but carriagework was a dying art and Alvis were only able to go into production by going abroad – to renowned Swiss coachbuilder Hermann Graber. Together with Mulliner Park Ward, by now a subsidiary of Rolls-Royce, Graber saved the day. He built some stupendous one-off models while Mulliner produced the rest in batches to his modified design.

The TF21 was the model with which the company closed its doors on the car industry for good, with not a whimper but, rather, a thundering great bang. Though it is generally agreed that the apotheosis of the 3 litre series was a remarkably beautiful Graber-inspired TD21, there is something incredibly special about the TF21. Only 106 were ever made and the experience of sitting behind the wheel of this luxurious motor easily beats driving a contemporaneous Jaguar or Bentley. Alvis faded from the car market with its reputation still at its height. Sadly the company was swallowed up by British Leyland in 1967 and reverted to general engineering.

**COUNTRY OF ORIGIN:**
UK

**FIRST MANUFACTURED:**
1966

**ENGINE:**
2,993 cc Straight Six

**PERFORMANCE:**
Top speed of 120 mph
(193 km/h)

**YOU SHOULD KNOW:**
Founded in Coventry by engineer T G John (1880–1946) originally a naval architect, Alvis made exclusive cars for 47 years (1920–1967) which are renowned for their character and the high quality of their workmanship. They have survived well and are still driven in competition racing. A TF21 drophead coupe in good condition can cost around $65,000.

# ASTON MARTIN DB5

**COUNTRY OF ORIGIN:**
UK

**FIRST MANUFACTURED:**
1963 (until 1965)

**ENGINE:**
3,995 cc Straight Six

**PERFORMANCE:**
Top speed of 140 mph
(225 km/h); 0–60 mph
(97 km/h) in 8.1 secs

**YOU SHOULD KNOW:**
The Aston Martin DB
series was named
after David Brown, its
managing director. He
bought the company in
1947 and sold it in 1972.

**Possibly the most successful ever example of car product placement, the DB5 achieved film star status in its own right in the hands of Sean Connery as James Bond's over-the-top set of wheels in the film *Goldfinger*. The must-haves for the car chase in the hills above Monte Carlo included twin pop-out 30 calibre Browning machine guns, a three-way revolving front number plate, smokescreen generator, spiked nail dispenser, oil-slick spray nozzle to dispatch tailgaters and a passenger-seat ejector for the instant removal of unwanted company. The car's starring role in the film led to sales of over a thousand DB5s – a record for the Aston Martin company. The DB5 was the epitome of style and if your sights were trained on Miss Moneypenny, the DB5 was the unchallenged transport of delight.**

The DB5 replaced the relatively long-lasting DB4, in two-door, four-seater coupe, convertible or estate versions. The DB4's 3.7 litre engine was revved up to 4 litres for the DB5. Earlier models maintained the DB4's four-speed manual transmission plus optional overdrive, or the three-speed automatic alternative but these systems were soon superseded by a standard five-speed manual gearbox. The three SU carburettors of the earlier DB5 model produced a top speed of about 140 mph (225 km/h). The Aston Martin Volante, introduced in late 1964, was slightly more powerful.

While its price/performance ratio couldn't match such contemporaries as the Jaguar E-Type (at about half the price tag), the DB5's classic design was infinitely more refined than the E-Type's blatantly vulgar appearance. With its leather upholstery and classy wood interior fittings (though without power steering), it was a machine for the financially inoculated to die for, or even use as their licence for thrills.

# BMW 2002

The 2002 is a seminal car. It not only saved BMW from insolvency but put the BMW marque on par with top German manufacturers like Volkswagen. The world (and especially the US) was already primed for high-powered but nimble small sports saloons and BMW filled the niche to perfection with the 2002. It was synonymous with modernity: a two-door economy car that fulfilled practical everyday requirements – space for four people to travel in comfort (independent suspension with MacPherson struts) with room for luggage too – but which drove like a racer – speedy, agile and quick off the mark, handling better than just about any other small car on the market.

The 2002 evolved out of BMW's New Class sedans, first introduced in 1961. These were powered by BMW's four-cylinder M10 engine designed by one of the company's founding fathers, Baron Alex von Falkenhausen. Although the M10 was a 1.5 litre engine, it was cunningly designed so that it could easily be expanded to 2 litres. Von Falkenhausen and BMW's Planning Director Helmut Werner Bonsch discovered by chance that they had both independently put a 2 litre M10 into their own personal two-door New Class 1600s and been thrilled by the result. They decided to make a joint formal proposal for its production. And thus the BMW 2002 was born.

Based on BMW's New Class 1600, the 2002 was a sound economic proposition. BMW also introduced a hatchbacked three-door model, the 2002Ti (Touring international) and finally its star model, the 2002Tii (Touring international injection) fitted with a Kugelfischer fuel injection pump. With the introduction of the 2002Tii, BMW firmly established itself as a reputable quality manufacturer and set the standard for the entire class of small, high-performance cars, paving the way for the models on the road today.

**COUNTRY OF ORIGIN:**
Germany

**FIRST MANUFACTURED:**
1968 (until 1976)

**ENGINE:**
1,990 cc Straight Four

**PERFORMANCE:**
Top speed for the 2002 of 112 mph (181 km/h); top speed for the 2002Tii of 115 mph (185 km/h)

**YOU SHOULD KNOW:**
The 2002 and 2002Tii are classic cars for tinkerers BMW are not unaware of the nostalgia value of their charismatic car and have made it extremely easy for legions of dedicated 2002 enthusiasts to obtain spare parts.

# BMW 3200 CS

**COUNTRY OF ORIGIN:**
Germany (and partly Italy)

**FIRST MANUFACTURED:**
1962 (until 1965)

**ENGINE:**
3,168 cc OHV V8

**PERFORMANCE:**
Advertised top speed
124 mph (199 km/h)

**YOU SHOULD KNOW:**
Bertone designed and built a one-off convertible version of the 3200CS for BMW boss Herbert Quandt, the wealthy German industrialist who saved BMW from being swallowed up by Daimler-Benz in 1959. This unique car still exists and was exhibited to the public at the classic car show, Techno Classica 2003.

Designed as the successor to the BMW 503, the exceedingly handsome 3200CS four-seat sports tourer was BMW's top-range model in 1962. The body was designed and built by Italian car stylist Gruppo Bertone then freighted to BMW in Germany for mounting on the 503 chassis. It was the first BMW to be fitted with front disc brakes, and it had twin Zenith carburettors, a tweaked V8 engine, four-speed transmission and rear-wheel drive.

The coupe body, a typically distinctive Bertone design, introduced a new style feature – the 'Hofmeister kink' (named after BMW's director of design). This is the sharp-angled forward bend (or 'kink') towards the base of the C-pillar (the roof-support strut that separates the rear side-window from the rear windscreen) which has become the signature design of the BMW marque. Look at any BMW model sideways-on and your eye is automatically drawn to the C-pillar. The design philosophy at BMW has always been 'form should follow function' and the purpose of the Hofmeister kink is not simply to look pretty but to subliminally indicate that the drive lies in the rear wheels. The Hofmeister kink has since been incorporated into many different makes of car but it is still primarily associated with BMW.

The launch of the 3200CS was overshadowed by the simultaneous appearance of the BMW New Class 1500 sedan, one of a series of saloons designed to fill a gap in the market between mass-produced cars and luxury designer models. In its two-door version, the 1500 was so successful that BMW was barely able to keep up with production so the company dropped the 3200CS in 1995 after only three years. Sadly, it was to be the last of the big V8 BMWs.

# BORGWARD P100

**Nothing illustrated the brilliance of Carl Borgward as an automobile engineer better that Der Grosser Borgward (Big Borgward) introduced in 1960. The P100 was an exciting model that replaced the big six-cylinder Hansa 2400 Pullman, which had not been a notable commercial success. Borgward's all-new large saloon car was presented at the Frankfurt Motor Show in 1959 and had an angular contemporary design with panoramic rear window and small tail fins, reminiscent of the look Pininfarina was developing at the same time for cars like the Fiat 1800 in Italy.**

The P100 (also known as the Big Six) had the same type of integral three-box monocoque chassis as the company's successful Isabella model, and was powered by an evolutionary version of Borgward's own six-cylinder engine. It had revolutionary self-levelling air suspension (which the company christened Airswing), some time before this feature was introduced by rival Mercedes-Benz – the Stuttgart leviathan that was firmly in Borgward's sights when the new saloon was introduced. The P100's marketing campaign made much of advanced engineering features like that pneumatic suspension, underlining the fact that Mercedes now had some serious competition at the luxury end of the market.

Unfortunately, the Big Six suffered from an old Borgward drawback – unexpected mechanical problems that only surfaced after a car had been launched, rather than being sorted beforehand. Even so, when Bremen-based Borgward was unjustly forced into liquidation by its own state government (conspiracy theorists suggest with some covert encouragement from other German car companies seeking to suppress a feisty rival) over 2,500 P100s had been produced, suggesting that this fine car was on course to penetrate the market for big six-cylinder cars that had been dominated by Mercedes-Benz throughout the 1950s. But sadly it was not to be.

**COUNTRY OF ORIGIN:**
Germany

**FIRST MANUFACTURED:**
1960 (until 1961)

**ENGINE:**
2,238 cc Straight Six

**PERFORMANCE:**
Top speed of 100 mph (161 km/h); 0–60 mph (97 km/h) around 16 secs

**YOU SHOULD KNOW:**
The hard done by Carl Borgward didn't live to see the resurrection of the P100 in Argentina, using the Borgward production line. Devastated by the loss of his company, he died a broken man in 1963.

# BUICK SPECIAL SKYLARK

You could base a social history on the Buick Special Skylark. It was conceived as a conventionally cynical exercise in the idiom of contemporary supermarket salesmanship. The Buick Special had performed reasonably well for the company, which wasn't quite ready to launch a whole new series of models. The Special Skylark was going to pep up the existing range, and prepare America for the next one. Using the same chassis as the Chevrolet Corvair, Pontiac Tempest and Oldsmobile F-85, Buick based the new car's styling on the 1960 Buick Special two-door coupe. The Buick Special Skylark was launched in mid 1961 with a vinyl roof, lower body side mouldings, new rear light cluster, and the crucial, unique Skylark badging. Inside it was luxurious and well-made: a four-star rather than five-star car, with all-leather bucket seats as optional.

Buick's real target was the wannabe 'Wild Ones', 'the younger generation' just beginning to make the connection between rock 'n' roll and the highway ethic of 'the endless grey ribbon'. All the other manufacturers were chasing them but it was the Special Skylark that hit the spot. Improvements to the V8 engine gave it substantially more muscle than other comparable cars – a higher compression ratio and a four-barrel carburettor boosted it from 155hp at 4600 rpm to 185 hp. With its other features, the Special Skylark was something new – a sporty compact with a big-car feel. It was a pioneer.

By 1962, the transition from Special was deemed successful, and the identical car became simply the Skylark. This was available as a two-door convertible coupe as well as a hardtop. In 1963, the frame was made bigger, the engine became even more muscular – and the pioneer was absorbed into the next cycle of automotive marketing.

**COUNTRY OF ORIGIN:**
USA

**FIRST MANUFACTURED:**
1961 (until 1963)

**ENGINE:**
3.5 litre (215 cid) V8

**PERFORMANCE:**
Top speed of 107 mph (172 km/h); 0–60 mph (97 km/h) in 10.2 secs

**YOU SHOULD KNOW:**
The Skylark name regularly appeared on Buick cars, always denoting a step up in power or comfort from whatever series preceded it. The name is attached to numerous special editions and to whole series of cars. It still is – but every Skylark model has fulfilled its initial promise, at least to begin with.

# CADILLAC ELDORADO

**COUNTRY OF ORIGIN:**
USA

**FIRST MANUFACTURED:**
(Fourth generation) 1967
(until 1970)

**ENGINE:**
7.0 l (429 cid), 7.7 l (472 cid) or 8.2 l (500 cid) V8

**PERFORMANCE:**
Top speed of 120 mph (193 km/h); 0–60 mph (97 km/h) in 8.9 secs

**YOU SHOULD KNOW:**
The personal luxury car was a creature of the 20th century – although the Eldorado lingered on into the 21st century (just!) competitors like the Oldsmobile Toronado, Ford Thunderbird, Lincoln Mark and Buick Riviera had perished in the 1990s, predeceased by the Chrysler Cordoba in 1983.

The Eldorado is an automotive institution, having been a stylish presence for the second half of the 20th century. The name appeared in 1953 and had covered a multitude of models before the last Eldorado rolled off the line in 2002. However, they all had one thing in common – they were Cadillac's pampered playboys in the personal luxury car segment of the market. That was a strange but lucrative niche reserved for image-conscious buyers who wanted a smack-you-in-the-eye luxury car with oodles of style, at the expense of trifling practical concerns like boot space and good leg room for back-seat passengers.

This egocentric market was booming in 1967, when the fourth generation Eldorado was radically reworked. It shared a GM E-body with the Olds Toronado and also had that model's front-wheel drive system and Powerplant Package. The launch saw a car with an endless bonnet covering a hefty 7 litre engine, a short cabin and stubby rear end. The headlights were hidden and the front end sported a jutting triangle in the centre, giving this crouching speedster an aggressive appearance. And speedy it was, capable of rocketing well past the 'ton' with blistering acceleration to match. As would be expected by those please-themselves owners, handling and roadholding were exceptional, too.

Next year, there were cosmetic styling tweaks – and an even larger V8 motor. The 1969 advances saw the hidden headlamps appear, along with flashy options like a (then sensational) vinyl roof and a power sunroof. For the last year before another major revamp, the Eldorado acquired the ultimate boy's toy – a massive 8.2 litre engine that remained exclusive until it was adopted by the other big Caddies in 1975. This was the biggest production V8 ever made, and its cachet ensured that Eldorado sales remained brisk.

# BUICK RIVIERA

The Riviera was Buick's answer to the Ford Thunderbird – a 'personal luxury' car that gave the Thunderbird its first real competition and became a long-running success story. The 'Riviera' tag had first been coined in 1949 to describe a two-door pillarless hardtop. Buick was the first marque to put the style into mass production with its 1956 Roadmaster version and it had proved so popular that it was offered as an alternative body style on other Buick lines over the next few years. But the Riviera of '63 was the first time that the tag became a model in its own right. It soon became Buick's flagship car. Sales in the first three years topped 112,000.

The 1963 Riviera is considered a benchmark in car styling: a two-door pillarless hardtop sports coupe with frameless door windows (a completely new concept). Its streamlined elegance broke the mould and started a new era in American styling that introduced elements of sophisticated European design to large cars so that they appeared more than mere brash behemoths. The Riviera sold 40,000 in its first year – a huge success

Buick used a modified version of its standard chassis – slightly shorter and narrower – and fitted a standard Buick V8 engine and brakes, power steering and twin turbine automatic transmission, thus investing the Riviera with the same power as the larger Buick models for impressive overall performance. The bucket-seated interior was equipped with every conceivable luxury and a range of optional extras, including power windows and seats, cruise control, air conditioning and a tilt steering wheel. In 1964 the 401 engine was dropped and the car acquired its distinctive stylized 'R' badge that was to last until the end of the run 36 years later, by which time well over a million of these beauties had been produced.

**COUNTRY OF ORIGIN:**
USA

**FIRST MANUFACTURED:**
1963 (until 1999)

**ENGINE:**
6.5 l (401 cid), 6.9 l (425 cid) V8

**PERFORMANCE:**
Top speed of 115 mph (184 km/h); 0–60 mph (97 km/h) in 8 secs

**YOU SHOULD KNOW:**
There were eight generations of this fabulously successful car, each very different both externally and mechanically from the one before. The most sought-after versions date from 1963 to the early 1970s.

# CHEVROLET CHEVELLE SS 396

**COUNTRY OF ORIGIN:**
USA

**FIRST MANUFACTURED:**
1965 (until 1968)

**ENGINE:**
6.5 l (396 cid) V8

**PERFORMANCE:**
Top speed of 120 mph
(193 km/h); 0–60 mph
(97 km/h) in 6.6 secs

**YOU SHOULD KNOW:**
From 1970 GM dropped
a rule banning engines
larger than 400 cid
from mid-sized cars,
and the SS package first
acquired a 6.6 litre (402
cid) option, then a truly
monstrous 7.4 litre (454
cid) power plant that
cemented the Chevelle's
reputation as an awesome
muscle car.

In 1964 Chevrolet launched a new midline model – the Chevelle –
which was destined to be a great success for parent General Motors.
It also provided an opportunity to gatecrash the burgeoning muscle-
car market, ignited by the concurrent appearance of the Pontiac GTO.
Chevy's attention-grabbing riposte – codenamed Z16 – was the
storming Chevelle Malibu SS 396 that appeared in early 1965. The
SS stood for Super Sport and the 396 for a new big-block engine that
would give this medium-sized car sensational performance. Just 201
were made (including one now-vanished custom convertible) and they
catapulted the Chevelle SS to the forefront of muscle car production.

In 1966, Chevrolet cashed in with the Chevelle SS 396 becoming a
distinct series in its own right. This sports coupe was equipped with
tuned engine options and special features like enhanced suspension,
transmission and brakes to handle that serious high-performance
capability. But the Chevelle SS 396's distinct identity would last for
just three years, though all the goodies that made up the SS package
were henceforth available as an option. This deal had already been
offered on the '66 and '67 El Camino, but the formal El Camino SS
396 was available for one year only, 1968.

That exclusive SS badge still guaranteed grunt after the Chevelle
SS 396 series was discontinued, but times they were a-changing. The
1970s saw the American auto industry start to ease back from over-
the-top performance cars, with many engines being detuned to run
on low-lead fuel.

In 1973, General Motors marques underwent an across-the-board
revamp so – though the name remained the same – that year's Chevelle
was effectively a new model. The SS custom option lingered on,
though it no longer indicated the raw power of previous incarnations,
and the Chevelle itself reached the end of the line in 1977.

# DAIMLER DS420

The venerable Daimler company had gone as an independent entity but the new owner – Jaguar– let the name live on. In 1968 the last 'real' Daimler – the stately DR450 limousine – was replaced by the Daimler DS420. An unmistakable Daimler fluted grille remained, but the front end was given Jaguar four-headlight treatment and the new limo was built on a stretched Jaguar 420G floorpan at the Vanden Plas works. It also had a 4.2 litre Straight Six Jaguar engine.

However, the DS420's aspirations were altogether more upmarket. For this was Jaguar's cheeky attempt to take on the Rolls-Royce Phantom VI – a contest that wasn't entirely one-sided. The two luxury limousines were the same size with automatic transmission, independent suspension and disc brakes all round ensuring that the Daimler's ride was smooth and safe. Better still, it was half the Roller's price.

Various trim levels were available – from luxurious to opulent – and the DS420 had a glass screen allowing back-seat passengers to ride in splendid isolation from the chauffeur – suggesting the target market consisted of up-and-coming company directors who liked to travel in style. It was also popular at senior Government level (home and abroad) and used by top hotels to pamper premium guests. Last but not least it was much used in the matched-and-dispatched trade, sweeping brides to church (in white) or transporting grieving relatives and (suitably modified) the dear departed to funerals (in black).

Over the years around 4,100 DS420s were built, suggesting that Jaguar's ambitious plan was not without commercial merit. Production transferred to the company's Coventry plant in 1979, but the only change came in the shape of larger bumpers and a new rear numberplate surround. The enduring quality of these hand-built beauties is such that most are still around to delight dedicated drivers of a distinguished modern classic.

**COUNTRY OF ORIGIN:**
UK

**FIRST MANUFACTURED:**
1968 (until 1992)

**ENGINE:**
4,235 cc V8

**PERFORMANCE:**
Top speed of 110 mph (177 km/h); 0–60 mph (97 km/h) in 10.5 secs

**YOU SHOULD KNOW:**
Jaguar supremo John Egan obviously had faith in his own products – it is said that in the mid-1980s his DS420 was a mobile boardroom fitted with a TV, computer with printer and the inevitable drinks cabinet.

# DODGE CHARGER

**COUNTRY OF ORIGIN:**
USA

**FIRST MANUFACTURED:**
First generation 1966
(until 1967)

**ENGINE:**
Ranged from 5.2–7.0 l
(318–426 cid) V8

**PERFORMANCE:**
NASCAR versions top
speed around 150 mph
(241 km/h); 6.3 l road car
– 0–60 mph (97 km/h) in
6.4 secs

**YOU SHOULD KNOW:**
The Charger wasn't just
a boy racer's dream –
despite the high-quality
interior finish this was
also a very practical
vehicle, with rear seats
that would fold flat to
create a long load space.

**Flex your biceps and leap into a 1966 Dodge Charger. It wasn't the first muscle car on the block, but rather a hasty mid-year introduction to compete in a market crowded with performance cars like the Pontiac GTO, Chevelle SS 396, Buick Gran Sport, Olds 442, Plymouth Barracuda and Ford Mustang. A concept car had been presented at auto shows in 1965, which Dodge claimed would only be built if interest was high. But that was a gimmick – production was already approved and, having been slow away, Dodge was soon up to top speed.**

The wide, low Charger with its sweeping fastback had a beautiful state-of-the-art interior with bucket seats front and back and a console that reached to the back seat, plus a choice of V8s going all the way up to the 7 litre Chrysler 426 Street Hemi plant developed for NASCAR racing. This connection was no accident – national stock car racing was (and is) the premier American motorsport.

The Charger was the first production car to boast a rear 'spoiler', added to make it competitive – race cars had to be based on production models which were so streamlined that they acted like an aircraft wing and lifted at speed. It worked – a Charger secured a NASCAR win in 1966. This made it a big seller – success on the track immediately translating into brisk sales that topped 37,000.

Few changes were made for 1967, but competition was always cut-throat in America and the plethora of existing muscle cars were soon joined by the Chevrolet Camaro. Novelty value exhausted, Charger sales started to slide and a major revamp was ordered for 1968. This produced the 'Coke bottle' Charger whose sinuous lines replicated the famous beverage container, and the Charger series would continue through numerous modifications until 1978.

# FERRARI DAYTONA

**COUNTRY OF ORIGIN:**
Italy

**FIRST MANUFACTURED:**
1968 (until 1973)

**ENGINE:**
4,390 cc DOHC V12

**PERFORMANCE:**
Top speed of 150 mph
(241 km/h); 0–60 mph
(97 km/h) in 5.4 secs

**YOU SHOULD KNOW:**
All hell broke loose when
Ferrari discovered that
TV cops Crockett and
Tubbs were driving a
replica Daytona (built on
a Corvette chassis) in the
*Miami Vice* TV series – but
the offending machine
was conveniently
destroyed in an action
sequence and thereafter
a gen-u-ine Ferrari
Testarossa scorched the
screen streets of Miami.

Everyone calls it a Ferrari Daytona, but of course they're wrong – it's really the 365 GTB/4. Daytona it is, then. This late 1960s stunner was just that, representing a radical departure from everything that went before. The Daytona was created by long-time Ferrari collaborator Pininfarina and introduced at the Paris Motor Show in 1968. But to the dismay of many it was not like the slinky Pininfarina curves adored by aficionados. Instead, it had sharp-edged looks that reminded doubters of – whisper it if you dare – a Lamborghini.

Unlike the latest Lambo, however, the Daytona retained one traditional Ferrari characteristic – an engine up front, this time a meaty 4.4 litre DOHC V12 with six twin carburettors. But even this was a disappointment as Ferrari's racers had already gone mid-engined. With all that not going for it, the Daytona turned out to be rather successful and even (eventually) quite well liked. Around 1,400 were built.

The majority were left-hand drive GTB/4 coupes, though around 150 right-hand drive versions were made. The factory also issued 122 GTS/4 Spyders converted from coupes by Daytona bodybuilder Scaglietti. A mere seven of these were RHDs. The open-topped cars are so desirable that a number of Berlinetta coupes have magically turned into Spyders over the years, but these ringers can be distinguished from the real thing because the windscreen is more steeply angled. A total of 15 special lightweight competition Daytonas was also constructed.

There were a couple of related evolutions that don't have genuine 'Daytona' cachet. The 365 GTC/4 used an identical chassis and had a 2+2 coupe body by Pininfarina. The 365 GT4 2+2 was another four-seater with an angular look that had vague resemblance to a true Daytona, reiterating an angular style that Ferrari would use for cars like the Mondial in the 1980s.

# FIAT DINO

There's no getting away from it – the word 'homologate' had to be mentioned sooner or later, inevitably in a context involving Ferrari. Maranello was besotted with racing, but formulae in which Ferrari wished to compete required homologation – approval by the governing body (FIA) that a particular car is eligible to race. As getting the nod invariably depended on a specific number of road cars being produced, Ferrari often struggled as the company tended to concentrate on expensive custom racing cars with just a few offered for sporting road use.

And so to the Fiat Dino Spider. This stylish sports car was the forerunner of GT cars that Ferrari would market under the Dino name from 1968, and the two are sometimes confused. The purpose of the Fiat Dino Spider was to homologate Ferrari's 2 litre (and later 2.4 litre) engine for Formula Two racing by producing the required 500 road cars. This was the V6 power plant initially proposed by Enzo Ferrari's son Dino before his untimely passing at the age of 24. It came to fruition a decade after his death and enjoyed a successful run in cars that bore Dino's name.

Fiat went along with Enzo's co-production request and the delectable 2 litre Fiat Dino Spider was introduced at the Turin Motor Show in 1966, with a crisp four-seater coupe following a year later at the Geneva Motor Show. The Spider was designed by Pininfarina and the coupe by Bertone. The engine was at the front and was mated to triple Weber carburettors. These stylish Dinos sported a five-speed manual gearbox and had a live axle suspended by leaf springs. In 1969 engine size was increased and coil-sprung independent rear suspension introduced. Over 7,500 Dinos were made (all variants), amply justifying homologation, with around three-quarters of these being coupes.

**COUNTRY OF ORIGIN:**
Italy

**FIRST MANUFACTURED:**
1966 (until 1973)

**ENGINE:**
1,987 cc or 2,418 cc V6

**PERFORMANCE:**
Top speed of 130 mph (210 km/h); 0-60 mph (97 km/h) in 8.7 secs

**YOU SHOULD KNOW:**
Ferraris they are not, but the association is there – allowing financially challenged fans of the Prancing Horse to drive something that looks quite like a Ferrari and has a Ferrari engine . . . and is almost affordable.

# FORD BRONCO

**This gallant 30-year veteran was finally pensioned off in 1996, but not before going through five evolutionary stages. The first generation half-ton Ford Bronco lived from 1966 to 1977, and – choose your acronym – this compact ORV (Off-Road Vehicle) or SUV (Sports Utility Vehicle) was launched as a competitor for the Jeep CJ and Harvester Scout.**

The four-wheel drive Bronco was an original design that – unlike most Fords – owed little to any other model, though axles and brakes came from the 4WD Ford pickup truck. Unlike later SUVs it was intended to be a genuine rural workhorse. The two-door Bronco had robust suspension (though a heavy-duty option was available for real backwoodsmen) and the choice of a Straight Six or V8 engine. Low range gearing for heavy work was standard.

Simple, boxy styling made for economical manufacturing and a budget ticket price, with the Bronco offered as a wagon, popular half cab or roofless roadster (the latter soon dropped). Despite the affordable price, a long list of extras encouraged buyers to trade up from the base model. Apart from genuine treats like bucket seats or CB radio, these add-ons tended to be the sort of helpful tools appreciated by rural folk – towbar, winch, post-hole digger, power take-off for assorted farm machinery, snow plough and the like.

The 'Early Bronco' was a steady rather than spectacular seller, with around 231,000 shifted in a dozen years. The first major revamp in 1978 saw the Bronco evolve into an altogether larger vehicle to compete with the Dodge Ramcharger, Chevy Blazer and Jeep Cherokee – SUVs setting the trend towards luxury transport for the city and suburbs that were happy to go off road during vacations. Thereafter, until the model line ended in 1996, these big boys were known as 'Full-size Broncos'.

**COUNTRY OF ORIGIN:**
USA

**FIRST MANUFACTURED:**
1966 (until 1996)

**ENGINE:**
2.8 l (170 cid) or 3.3 l (200 cid) Straight Six; 4.7 l (289 cid) or 4.9 l (302 cid) V8

**PERFORMANCE:**
Varied according to engine – typically top speed of 75 mph (121 km/h); 0–60 mph (97 km/h) in 21 secs

**YOU SHOULD KNOW:**
Yes, there was a racing version – the Baja Bronco was prepared by Bill Stroppe for cross-country road races south of the border, like the Baja 500 and Mexico 1000. It had a roll cage, wide tyres and tuned engine.

# FORD CORTINA MK I

**COUNTRY OF ORIGIN:**
UK

**FIRST MANUFACTURED:**
1962 (until 1966)

**ENGINE:**
1,198 cc or 1,498 cc
Straight Four

**PERFORMANCE:**
With 1.5 l engine –
top speed of 85 mph (138 km/h); 0–60 mph
(97 km/h) in 21 secs

**YOU SHOULD KNOW:**
The Cortina's name was derived from the glamorous Italian ski resort of Cortina d'Ampezzo in the Italian Dolomites (which was cheeky, as Triumph had first used the Dolomite name in 1934) – and a notorious Ford publicity stunt saw Cortinas driven down the resort's fearsome bobsled run.

**As the Swinging Sixties got into gear, Ford was smarting from the mauling it was receiving from the trendy car of the moment – BMC's iconic Mini. Ford couldn't afford to retool to produce a competitive small car, so the company went with what it knew best – a new family saloon. The Cortina Mk I duly appeared in 1962 to take on Vauxhall Victors and Morris Oxfords.**

Initially this angular car with tapering flutes along the sides and signature 'Y' rear light clusters was the Consul Cortina, but a cosmetic facelift in 1964 saw the Consul bit quietly buried. The Cortina had arrived, and would be around for some time. It came with two or four doors, there was a choice of engines (1.2 litre or 1.5 litre) and trim levels (standard and deluxe).

It wasn't long before the Cortina family started reproducing. The 1500 Super arrived in January 1963, identified by tapered chrome strips along the flutes. A GT model with twin carbs, front disc brakes and modified suspension followed a month later. An estate car in deluxe or super made its debut in March, with the latter sporting fake wood panelling on the sides and tailgate. Over a million Mk Is would be sold, laying the foundations for what followed.

The Cortina just went from strength to strength. A Mk II version appeared in 1967, followed by the Mk III in 1970. The Mk IV occupied the 1975–9 slot and the Cortina 80 was the last of the line, the very final one being a silver Crusader that rolled off the Dagenham line in the summer of 1982. It had been a more-than-modest success along the way, becoming the UK's bestseller from 1967 until 1981, with 4.35 million units sold during the extended production run.

# FORD LOTUS CORTINA

**Although it was technically a variation on the Ford Cortina Mk I theme, the brilliant Ford Lotus Cortina deserves an entry all its own. This was one of the most interesting British saloon cars of the 1960s, making its debut in 1963 as the result of a partnership between Ford and Lotus Cars.**

Lotus supremo Colin Chapman had developed a twin-cam version of the Ford Kent engine for racing purposes. Ford's competition department asked Chapman to fit this into a thousand Ford saloons, so they could rally and race in Group 2. The deal was swiftly done and the Type 28 was born. Ford called it the Cortina Lotus, but for once the little guy won out and the world remembers this splendid custom car as the Lotus Cortina – which undoubtedly had a better ring to the target market of boy racers. Lotus did the mechanical stuff while Ford handled distribution and marketing.

A reinforced two-door Cortina shell provided innocent-looking wrapping around a potent 1.6 litre twin-cam Lotus engine that belted out 105 bhp. Lowered and revised suspension plus servo-assisted disc brakes ensured that the Lotus Cortina handled well, with wide road wheels and tyres providing limpet-like grip. Nobody who tried to beat one of these stylish sprinters away from the traffic lights had any doubts about what they'd just run up against – but just in case someone thought this special sports saloon was any old Cortina, a white paint job and green side flash proclaimed the Lotus Cortina's exclusive parentage.

Ford wanted to continue with the cooperative venture when the Mk II Cortina appeared, but Lotus declined and the Lotus Cortina Mk II was produced entirely by Ford from 1966 until 1970, with the Lotus badge being replaced by a bland 'Twin Cam' announcement after a few months.

**COUNTRY OF ORIGIN:**
UK

**FIRST MANUFACTURED:**
1963 (until 1966)

**ENGINE:**
1,558 cc DOHC Straight Four

**PERFORMANCE:**
Top speed of 108 mph (174 km/h); 0–60 mph (97 km/h) in 10.1 secs

**YOU SHOULD KNOW:**
The aim of creating a great sports racer was successful, with the Lotus Cortina enjoying many race victories. Unfortunately, it was prone to mechanical problems when used as a road car, but was so exciting that owners easily forgave its faults.

# FORD MUSTANG

**COUNTRY OF ORIGIN:**
USA

**FIRST MANUFACTURED:**
1964 (until 1973) Series 1

**ENGINE:**
Ranged from 2.9 l (170 cid) Straight Six to 7.0 l (427 cid) V8

**PERFORMANCE:**
1965 Mustang 4.7 l V8 – top speed of 120 mph (193 km/h); 0–60 mph (97 km/h) in 8.3 secs

**YOU SHOULD KNOW:**
Although the Mustang's cinematic debut was in the James Bond film *Goldfinger*, its best-ever role was starring alongside Steve McQueen in *Bullitt* when a 1968 Ford Mustang Fastback (actually two identical cars) driven by Lieutenant Frank Bullitt chased two baddies in a Dodge Charger to a fiery grave through the streets of San Francisco.

**The first generation Mustang was a revelation. Despite an inspired promotional campaign, Ford's most successful launch since the Model A in the 1920s still gave the Dearborn behemoth a pleasant surprise as 'Mustang Mania' swept the nation. Year One-and-a-half projections (the launch came midway through the 1964 model year) anticipated sales of 100,000 units, but the runaway Mustang sold 1.5 million inside 18 months.**

Best of all, the Mustang was basically a humble Ford Falcon in fancy dress, and its soaring success created a new class of vehicle – the pony car. These were compact performance cars with long bonnets and short rear ends – and those mega-Mustang sales soon spawned imitators like Chevy's Camara and AMC's Javelin.

As with most Ford lines one model could be many, with different body styles, a wide choice of engines, extras and trim levels allowing almost endless permutations. The Mustang launched with a hardtop and convertible, with a semi-fastback 2+2 coupe arriving in September '64 for the official start of the 1965 model year. There was a major first generation revamp in 1967 that produced all sorts of mechanical upgrades (including a new big V8 engine option) and also one of the most desirable manifestations of the Mustang – the full fastback. The Mustang Fastback has acquired iconic status over time and made a major contribution to establishing the Mustang as America's best-loved sporty car.

First generation Mustangs are the true classics, for when the second generation arrived for 1974 it was both smaller and heavier than the original 1964 car, thanks to new regulations that included pollution control laws. The Mustang series continues to this day but only fond memories – and lots of cherished cars – remain to commemorate the 'Golden Decade' when this mould-breaking car was at its very best.

# FORD CAPRI MK 1

**COUNTRY OF ORIGIN:**
UK (also built in Belgium and Germany)

**FIRST MANUFACTURED:**
1969 (until 1974)

**ENGINE:**
1,298 cc or 1,598 cc Straight Four, 2,550 cc or 2,994 cc V6

**PERFORMANCE:**
3000 GT – top speed of 122 mph (196 km/h); 0-60 mph (97 km/h) in 8.4 secs

**YOU SHOULD KNOW:**
The original choice of name for the Capri was the Ford Colt – but Mitsubishi had cleverly trademarked that iconic American title so Capri it became, revisiting the not-altogether-different Consul Capri of the early 1960s and borrowing a model name used by various Ford-owned marques in America.

**The European idea of a perfect pony car (long front, short back) was the Ford Capri – or more accurately it was Ford Europe's idea. The recently created conglomerate launched this trendy car in 1969, hoping to emulate the Mustang's success in North America. The Capri was based on the Cortina platform and had common styling but different engine specs for Britain and the Continent.**

Ford wanted to produce a fashionable car that would appeal to the widest possible market (or to put it another way, every pocket). Thus a variety of engines was offered. The initial UK options were 1.3 litre or 1.6 litre versions of the Ford Kent Straight Four, with a 2 litre Cologne V6 topping the offering. Before long, Brits with lots of dosh could choose sports versions like the 3000 GT with the Ford Essex V6 engine. That's the one that always featured in memorable car chases in 1970s TV series like *The Professionals*, frequently ending in a slewing handbrake emergency stop followed by a bonnet roll and brisk gunplay.

Competition glory was never far from Ford's mind, and a souped-up Capri duly appeared in 1971, powered by a 2.6 litre version of the Cologne V6 assembled by Weslake and featuring alloy cylinder heads. This was the Capri RS2600, which would prove to be a star of the European Touring Car Championship in the early 1970s. Never slow to appreciate the powerful aphrodisiac properties of track success, a luxury road-going version with a detuned engine and double-barrel Solex carb was available.

Business was encouragingly brisk, but Ford still gave the Mk 1 a facelift in 1972, introducing better suspension, more comfortable seats, rectangular headlights and enlarged tail lights. A significant revamp saw the larger Capri Mk 2 arrive in February 1974, complete with hatchback rear door.

# GINETTA G4

Who says there was no room for the start-up automobile entrepreneur in postwar Britain? The four Walklett Brothers certainly managed to found a successful car manufacturing business in 1958 (in the wilds of Suffolk) and ran it until their retirement in 1989.

The Ginetta G4 was an early introduction, in 1961. It had a fibreglass convertible roadster body that sported tailfins and was fitted with a Ford 105E engine. Unlike its immediate predecessors, the G4 was not designed specifically for competition use, though it was successful in that sphere. It was a classic 'drive to the track and race' car, which was equally at home on a motor-racing circuit or strutting its stuff to admiring glances when used as a road car.

This lightweight car had a space-frame chassis with double wishbones, coil springs and dampers in the front. Rear suspension consisted of a Ford live axle and there were drum brakes. Over the years the G4 enjoyed considerable evolution and improvement. A selection of Ford engines was offered, including a 1.3 litre Classic, 1.6 litre X-flow and a 1.5 litre Cortina GT power plant.

With the introduction of Series II in 1963, the roadster was joined by a coupe, which was essentially the same car with an add on hardtop. At the same time a BMC rear axle replaced the Ford live axle. The tailfins were dropped and enhancements like disc brakes were introduced to improve all-round handling and performance. The G4 Series III took over in 1966, though the only obvious change was then-modish pop-up headlights that rested on the front bumper when not in use.

Around 500 of these zippy sports racers were built in the 1960s and they still compete regularly at classic meets, piloted by enthusiastic drivers who appreciate unmistakably British motoring heritage.

**COUNTRY OF ORIGIN:**
UK

**FIRST MANUFACTURED:**
1961 (until 1969)

**ENGINE:**
Various, but originally a 997 cc Straight Four

**PERFORMANCE:**
1 l engine – top speed of 105 mph (169 km/h)

**YOU SHOULD KNOW:**
This great British sports car rides again in the form of the contemporary DARE Ginetta G4 – a sleek sports racer with a 1.8 l Ford Zetec that delivers a top speed of 130 mph (209 km/h) and a 0–60 mph (97 km/h) time of 5.8 secs.

# HILLMAN IMP

**COUNTRY OF ORIGIN:**
UK

**FIRST MANUFACTURED:**
1963 (until 1976)

**ENGINE:**
874 cc Straight Four

**PERFORMANCE:**
Top speed of 80 mph
(129 km/h); 0–50 mph
(80 km/h) in 14.7 secs

**YOU SHOULD KNOW:**
Rootes produced some
special Imp derivatives
like the Imp Californian,
and nifty badge
engineering transformed
the Basic Imp into
desirable alternatives like
the Singer Chamois, the
Sunbeam Stiletto and
Sunbeam Sport with its
tuned twin-carb engine.

**BMC's Mini caused a sensation in 1959, and rival manufacturers were caught on the hop by the popularity of that innovative new small car. But they all wanted a piece of the action and the Rootes Group's belated response was the Hillman Imp, which appeared in 1963.**

It was a huge gamble. Rootes had little experience of small-car production and the Imp (codenamed 'Apex') required a new factory, as further development at the company's Ryton base was impossible. The chosen site (after government arm-twisting and provision of generous grants) was Linwood near Glasgow. This necessitated a long round-trip for Linwood parts finished at Ryton, and involved a militant Scottish workforce prone to striking first and talking later. An added difficulty was the fact that the Imp's aluminium engine was another leap into the unknown.

All that considered, the Imp turned out to be an interesting and popular car. There were teething troubles after the daring design was rushed into production, but despite that the distinctive Imp was well received, being cheap to buy and economical to run. A lightweight engine was mounted behind the rear wheels and this required sophisticated rear suspension to counteract an inevitable tendency to oversteer.

The original Imp was a two-door saloon with a rear hatch. A coupe version was added in 1965. That year also saw the introduction of a van and estate car (effectively a van with windows), though these were discontinued in 1970. The Imp got a major revamp in 1966 to iron out early mechanical problems and Rootes continued to improve this attractive little car throughout its life. Around 440,000 were built, and they're as much fun to drive today as they were then. But ultimately the Rootes gamble failed – the expensive Linwood venture eventually ruined the company.

# HONDA S800

Japanese car manufacture after World War II was initially shaped by regulations that favoured the smallest of cars. Motorcycle maker Honda was keen to move into car production and showed a tiny S360 two-seater concept car at the 1962 Tokyo Motor Show. Officials decided it was too sporty to merit coveted 'light car' status, so Honda recklessly put in a 531 cc engine and launched the S500 anyway. They were rewarded with good sales figures and pressed on to marginally bigger and better things, introducing the petite S600 in 1964, that contained a brute of a 601 cc motor.

But it didn't stop there. At the urging of New Zealand racing drivers Bruce McLaren and Denny Hulme, Honda upped the power again. The S800 was previewed at the 1965 Tokyo Motor Show and would succeed the very successful S600 in 1966. The dinky S800 sports car was available in roadster or coupe form, with standard or SM trim levels, and extended the Japanese company's growing reputation for technical innovation, wringing extraordinary performance and impressive economy from a 791 cc engine.

At first the S800 employed chain drive and independent suspension, but Honda soon switched to a more conventional live rear axle. The next upgrade involved front disc brakes, followed by a major reworking in 1968 aimed at opening up the American market. This involved creating the S800M in an attempt to meet US regulations. This had lean carburettion, dual-circuit brakes, safety glass, reconfigured tail lights, outside marker lights and flush door handles. Amazingly (considering all those massive V8s propelling home-bred American cars), the S800's tiny but high-revving engine failed to meet US emission control standards. With entry to the most important export market in the world thus barred, Honda quietly ended manufacture of the S800 in 1970, after some 11,500 vehicles had been built.

**COUNTRY OF ORIGIN:**
Japan

**FIRST MANUFACTURED:**
1966 (until 1970)

**ENGINE:**
791 cc Straight Four

**PERFORMANCE:**
Top speed of 97 mph (156 km/h); 0-50 mph (80 km/h) in 9.4 secs

**YOU SHOULD KNOW:**
The S800 did its job by establishing Honda's credentials as an innovative car maker. Following its discontinuation in 1970 – as the company concentrated on motorcycles and conventional passenger cars – there wouldn't be another Honda sports car for three decades, until the Millennium saw the launch of the S2000.

# JAGUAR E-TYPE

**COUNTRY OF ORIGIN:**
UK

**FIRST MANUFACTURED:**
1961 (until 1975)

**ENGINE:**
3,781 cc, 4,235 cc Straight Six; 5,344 cc V12

**PERFORMANCE:**
Series 1 with 3.8 l engine – top speed of 149 mph (238 km/h); 0–60 mph (97 km/h) in 7.1 secs

**YOU SHOULD KNOW:**
The rarest E-Types are either those from the first batch of 500, which have flat floors and external bonnet catches (after which the floors were swiftly modified to provide more leg room and bonnet catches were repositioned internally) or the few Series 3 cars built using the old 4.2 litre Straight Six engine. Take your pick!

**The golden era of Jaguar Cars got off to a great start with the XK120 and XK150, but the company really hit the jackpot with the E-Type (XK-E in America). This is regarded as the finest-looking sports car of all time ('The most beautiful car ever made' was Enzo Ferrari's verdict) and also the most influential – leading the way for many fabulous brethren that made the 1960s a seminal decade for super sports cars.**

Series 1 was launched in 1961, consisting of two-door convertibles and coupes with a 3.8 litre engine carried over from the XK150S. The cars featured torsion bar front ends with independent rear suspension and disc brakes all round. A 4.2 litre engine was introduced in 1964, along with styling changes. The 2+2 version with a stretched coupe body appeared in 1966 and further modifications followed to meet American requirements, sufficient to justify the Series 1.5 tag applied by some.

Series 2 followed in 1968, retaining the 4.2 litre engine and all three body styles. Modifications towards the end of Series 1 were extended to meet US regulations, which also required the triple-carb UK engine to be detuned. Headlights had lost glass covers, a wraparound rear bumper appeared and the cooling system was improved. New seats added comfort, whilst air conditioning and power steering were optional extras. Series 2 carried the E-Type forward into the 1970s.

Series 3 ran from 1971 to 1975, and saw the introduction of a 5.3 litre V12, discontinuation of the short-wheelbase coupe and switch of the convertible to the longer 2+2 floorpan. The cars acquired an aggressive slatted grille, flared wheel arches . . . and boastful V12 badge. With 15,000 Series 3s completing an overall production run of 70,000, it was a fitting climax to 15 years of breathtaking sporting motoring.

# JAGUAR XJ MK 1 SERIES 1

Jaguar's strenuous efforts to make the grade as an upmarket volume purveyor of quality saloon cars took a step forward in 1968 with the introduction of the all-new XJ Series 1. The launch of the XJ (from Xperimental Jaguar) Series consolidated the company's saloon car offering into a single range. New XJ models provided a superb replacement for existing Jaguars (S-Type Mk 2, 420 and 420G, plus their Daimler counterparts) and the line would continue to be produced into the 1990s.

First out of the box was the XJ6 Mk 1. These comfortable saloons came with a choice of two Straight Sixes – 2.8 litre and 4.2 litre versions of Jaguar's renowned twin-cam XK engine. The former was considered to be somewhat underpowered and the latter outsold it by three to one. Power steering was standard and there was a choice of manual or automatic transmission. With either engine the XJ6 was famous for silky-smooth performance and crisp handling.

The particularly graceful styling was classic 'four-headlamp' Jaguar and the interior was lavishly appointed with wood and leather upholstery in the marque's finest traditions. A long-wheelbase version of the 4.2 litre XJ6 appeared towards the end of the run, offering more rear legroom, as did the top-of-the-range XJ12 with its powerful 5.3 litre V12 engine.

Around 82,000 Series 1 XJs were produced, plus another 16,000 of the Daimler equivalents of each Jaguar type, so there are still plenty around for anyone who owns a petrol station to drive and enjoy. Series 2 appeared in 1973 and did not acquire the best of reputations, with allegations of shoddy build quality said to stem from Jaguar's absorption into the British Leyland Group. The cars themselves weren't so different from Series 1 examples, but were modified to meet US regulations.

**COUNTRY OF ORIGIN:**
UK

**FIRST MANUFACTURED:**
1968 (until 1973)

**ENGINE:**
2,790 cc or 4,235 cc
Straight Six; 5,343

**PERFORMANCE:**
With 2.6 l engine –
top speed of 118 mph
(190 km/h); 0–60 mph
(97 km/h) in 10.5 secs

**YOU SHOULD KNOW:**
During the initial launch campaign Jaguar boss Sir William Lyons described the XJ6 as 'the finest Jaguar ever' – but he would say that, wouldn't he? Series 1 cars are universally considered to have the best build quality and are definitely the most collectable XJs.

# JENSEN INTERCEPTOR AND JENSEN FF

**COUNTRY OF ORIGIN:**
UK

**FIRST MANUFACTURED:**
1966 (until 1976)

**ENGINE:**
6,286 cc or 7,212 cc V8

**PERFORMANCE:**
With 6.3 l engine –
top speed of 133 mph
(214 km/h); 0–60 mph
(97 km/h) in 7.3 secs

**YOU SHOULD KNOW:**
Despite frequent
strikes at the factory,
a penchant for rapidly
rusting and a relatively
high ticket price, nearly
6,500 Interceptors
were produced in 10
years, which compares
extremely favourably with
anything the competition
managed to achieve.

Jensen Motors was founded by brothers Richard and Alan, who made vehicle bodies before World War II and were soon producing their own cars. The first Interceptor appeared in 1949 – a coupe with an Austin Six engine and a pioneering fibreglass body. The Jensen 541 replaced it in 1953, despite the demands of a major contract to produce bodies for the Austin Healey sports cars. In 1961, production of bodies for Volvo's P1800 was added and the booming company introduced the Jensen CV-8.

But the CV-8 soon looked dated, and Jensen decided to compete with big boys like Aston Martin and those luscious Latins. Although the CV-8's updated chassis, Chrysler V8 engine and TorqueFlite automatic transmission were up to the job, Italian styling was called for. A design by Carrozzeria Touring was realized by Vignale, who created the first production bodies. This stunning new fastback bore the revived Interceptor name and its look was distinctive, with a squarish front and rounded rear topped by a huge curved rear window that was also a hinged hatchback. The interior with its wood and leather was, however, reassuringly British.

Despite intense competition in the luxury GT market, the Interceptor sold well throughout the '60s and into the mid-1970s, despite build-quality problems and serious commercial pressures created by the collapse of Jensen's core body-building business. The Mk II arrived in 1969 and the Mk III in 1971 with a bigger engine. A yummy convertible was introduced in 1974 and a coupe in 1975.

The stylish Interceptor is deserving of a more-than-honourable mention in the book of British automotive success stories, but in many respects its importance is outweighed by that of a commercially unsuccessful companion model. Jensen Motors had been working with Harry Ferguson (of Massey-Ferguson tractor fame) since the early 1960s, and the innovative Irish engineer was intent on producing an effective four-wheel-drive system for race and road cars.

In 1961 the Ferguson P99 Climax scored a notable first and last. In the hands of Stirling Moss it became the first four-wheel-drive car – and last front-engined car – to win a Formula 1 race. On the road front, the joint venture led to the Jensen CV-8 FF shown at the Earls Court Motor Show in 1965. This was the debut of the FF road-car system (FF stood for Ferguson Formula) and it anticipated the world's first four-wheel drive supercar.

This was the Jensen FF, which deployed Ferguson's four-wheel drive system to great effect, also offering Dunlop Maxaret anti-lock braking, traction control and power steering. It shared Chrysler TorqueFlite transmission and 6.3 litre V8 motor with the Interceptor. To all intents and purposes both models were identical, though in fact the FF had a slightly longer wheelbase and an extra cooling vent in the front bumper. But technically it was a world ahead and was better to drive than the Interceptor, adding leech-like roadholding to its sibling's many qualities.

Unfortunately, mechanical complexity made it difficult – and expensive – to produce. Jensen FFs were built to order only, and the steep price ensured that relatively few were sold – some 320 in six years. And when Jensen started struggling in the early 1970s, the innovative FF was reluctantly discontinued – a classic example of a great car that was ahead of its time.

An attempt to enter the sports car market with the Jensen Healey was made after Donald Healey joined the company in the early '70s, but none of these moves could revive Jensen's fortunes and the company was dissolved in 1976, leaving the splendid Interceptor as a lasting memorial.

# LAMBORGHINI ESPADA S1

**COUNTRY OF ORIGIN:**
Italy

**FIRST MANUFACTURED:**
1968 (until 1970)

**ENGINE:**
3,929 cc 2 x DOHC V12

**PERFORMANCE:**
Top speed of 150 mph
(241 km/h); 0–60 mph
(97 km/h) in 7.9 secs

**YOU SHOULD KNOW:**
Granted the length and
slim profile of the Espada,
the name seems entirely
appropriate – in Spanish
espada is the sword used
by a matador to dispatch
the bull at the climax of
a corrida de toros, ideally
with graceful efficiency
and dashing style.
Presumably Lambo's
Rampant Bull was the
one that got away.

Long, wide and low are three words that spring to mind when describing the Lambo Espada S1 sports coupe that lit up the latter part of the 1960s, before the S2 and S3 versions carried the Espada through most of the 1970s. This typically Latin Grand Tourer was based on Lamborghini's Marzal concept car, designed by Bertone and shown at the 1967 Geneva Motor Show. With some additional styling notes borrowed from Bertone's sensationally reworked Jaguar E-Type Piranha, the Espada filled a gap in the Lamborghini range. It was a true two-door 2+2 four-seater and there was obviously demand for such a car, for the Espada became Lamborghini's best-seller of the period.

The Espada had fully independent suspension and disc brakes all round. Five-speed manual transmission was standard but an unusual automatic option was available – the three ratios were drive, first and reverse. The car was front-engined and – despite its flamboyant styling – did not have the pop-up headlamps beloved by designers of GT cars at the time. The interior trim was first-class and the only complaint was that rear-seat passengers were somewhat cramped. The Santa'Agata factory was a hive of activity as Ferruccio Lamborghini challenged Ferrari on all fronts, and the head-turning Espada was definitely a major gauntlet.

The Espada S2 appeared in 1970, and was in turn succeeded in 1972 by the S3 that lasted until 1978. Power output from the V12 was increased from series to series and the interiors saw major revamping, but there was little external change of appearance – though the S3 did acquire the ugly rubber bumpers required by new US regulations. Over 1,200 Espadas were built over the model's 10-year life – a sales record that added up to lots of lovely lira.

# LINCOLN CONTINENTAL

**The first Lincoln Continental appeared before World War II, with postwar production resuming until this big and exclusive automobile was discontinued in 1948. Then the Continental reappeared in 1956 as a separate one-model Ford-owned marque, but it was not until 1961 that the Lincoln and Continental names were reunited in an iconic design by the great Elwood Engel – a design considered by many to be his great masterpiece. The car's understated elegance won design awards and was soon copied by envious rivals such as Buick and Cadillac.**

The Lincoln Continental was smaller than previous versions, but still very much at the luxury end of the Ford family spectrum. If there was one distinctive design feature, it was that the back doors were rear hinged and opened from the front – the so-called 'suicide doors' common on prewar cars but hardly seen after 1945. With a few minor internal and external changes, the rectilinear design would last until the next Continental generation was launched in 1970, though it was stretched slightly in 1964 to give more rear-seat legroom.

The initial Continental offering was restricted to a pair of four-door models – the sedan and convertible – though a two-door coupe appeared subsequently in 1966, at which point a larger engine was introduced. In 1968 the Lincoln Continental Mark III coupe appeared but this famous car (as a result of being used on film to smuggle heroin in *The French Connection*) was sufficiently altered to be considered a completely different model. It was discontinued in 1971.

Despite enjoying great success throughout the 1960s, the Lincoln Continental nearly didn't happen – Elwood Engel's splendid design was originally intended for a new Ford Thunderbird, until an inspired decision was made to tweak and enlarge the car to create a revived Lincoln Continental.

**COUNTRY OF ORIGIN:**
USA

**FIRST MANUFACTURED:**
1961 (until 1969)

**ENGINE:**
7.0 l (430 cid), 7.5 l (460 cid) or 7.6 l (462 cid) V8

**PERFORMANCE:**
Top speed of 110 mph (177 km/h); 0–60 mph (97 km/h) in 12.4 secs

**YOU SHOULD KNOW:**
The open-top parade limousine in which John F Kennedy was assassinated in 1963 was custom built from a Lincoln Continental convertible – codenamed SS-100-X, it was subsequently armour-plated and fitted with a bulletproof roof, after which it continued in White House service for many years.

# LOTUS ELAN

**COUNTRY OF ORIGIN:**
UK

**FIRST MANUFACTURED:**
1962 (until 1975)

**ENGINE:**
1,558 cc Straight Four

**PERFORMANCE:**
Top speed of 118 mph
(190 km/h); 0–60 mph
(97 km/h) in 7.6 secs

**YOU SHOULD KNOW:**
Nobody could ever accuse the Japanese of being copycats, but it is known that Mazda bought, disassembled and closely studied a couple of first generation Lotus Elans – though of course the close resemblance of the subsequent Mazda MX-5 is a complete coincidence.

**The Lotus Elan roadster was a welcome debutant in 1962 – welcome to the manufacturer because it replaced the expensive-to-build Elite and welcomed by sporting drivers who appreciated performance-packed possibilities. It was even embraced by those who weren't minted but could wield a mean spanner, as the Elan was initially offered in kit form like the successful Lotus Seven.**

The Elan was an uncompromising manifestation of Colin Chapman's lightweight design philosophy and delivered acceleration and top speed far ahead of its time for this class of sports car. The power came from a 1.6 litre evolution version of the sturdy Ford Kent engine that had been fitted with a Lotus-designed Cosworth twin-cam alloy head (the engine also used in the punchy Lotus-Cortina). The Elan boasted independent suspension and disc brakes all round long before these became widely used standard features. It had a steel chassis and fibreglass body that kept the weight right down.

With its streamlined shape and pop-up headlamps, this modern-looking roadster was an instant hit. The Elan's favourable reception was complemented by the swift appearance of a hardtop option in 1963 and a two-seater coupe in 1965. The Elan's commercial success was finally cemented by the arrival of the handsome long-wheelbase Elan Plus Two in 1967. This was a genuine 2+2 coupe with a roomy cabin, which retained all the speed and agility of its predecessors – in fact it was even a tad faster, thanks to a slippery aerodynamic shape. The Plus Two continued in production until 1975, two years after the roadster and coupe were discontinued.

The Lotus Elan would be born again in the late 1980s for a six-year production run – differentiated from its illustrious ancestry by an M100 tag and lauded as a technical masterpiece in the finest traditions of advanced Lotus engineering.

# MAZDA COSMO 110S

**The one manufacturer to make a real go of the rotary engine originally designed by Felix Wankel was Mazda, and the Japanese company's first rotary-engined car was the Cosmo 110S, a GT car intended to headline the company's drive into mass-market car production.**

The Cosmo 110S was first seen at the Tokyo Motor Show in 1964 and pre-production models were extensively tested before the Series I L/10A Cosmo 110S was released – thus avoiding the trap that NSU fell into by hastily launching its Wankel-engined Ro80, which acquired a destructive reputation for engine failure. Mazda even went to the length of running a couple of 110S cars in an 84-hour endurance race in Germany.

This rather angular coupe had a twin-chamber rotary engine with two spark plugs per chamber, each with a distributor. A four-speed manual gearbox was standard. Suspension was independent at the front with a live rear axle and leaf springs at the back. The braking system consisted of front discs and rear drums. Considering that this was effectively a cross between a test bed and a marketing device, Series I sales of around 350 in two years can't have been too disappointing.

Serious business began in 1968 when the Series II L/10B was introduced. This offered increased power output from an enhanced engine, servo-assisted brakes all round, larger wheels and a longer wheelbase. There were also cosmetic styling changes that differentiated between the two versions, including a new grille with two additional air vents. The later Cosmo 110Ss were seen as an altogether better buy and Mazda sold nearly 1,200 before production was ended in 1972. Driving one today is nearly impossible – with the exception of a few that went to America, hardly any escaped from Japan.

**COUNTRY OF ORIGIN:**
Japan

**FIRST MANUFACTURED:**
1967 (until 1972)

**ENGINE:**
982 cc Twin-chamber Rotary

**PERFORMANCE:**
Series II – top speed of 120 mph (193 km/h); 0–60 mph (97 km/h)

**YOU SHOULD KNOW:**
The Cosmo name reappeared time and time again for Mazda – the Cosmo AP (from 1975) was known as the RX-5 for export purposes, the HB Cosmo ran through the 1980s and the Eunos Cosmo, with the distinction of a triple-rotor engine, was Mazda's top-of-the-range 2+2 coupe from the early 1990s.

# MERCEDES-BENZ 230 SL

**The racing-derived Mercedes 300 SL coupe with gullwing doors was the must-have sports car of the mid-1950s. It was the first of the SL (Sport Leicht = Light Sports) class that has continued to the present day, though subsequent SLs haven't quite recaptured the glamour of the sensually rounded 300 SL – also offered as a roadster and voted one of the top sports cars of all time.**

But Mercedes certainly tried hard. The 300 SL's companion car was the smaller but similar-looking 190 SL. Together they comprised the W198 SL class, discontinued during 1963 after the W113 SL class appeared in the form of the 230 SL. This marked the debut of the famous 'pagoda roof' SL with its six-cylinder fuel-injected engine and aluminium body panels, which reduced weight and improved the performance of this solidly built car. The 230 SL was a Coupe-Roadster, with an in-built soft top stored in a well behind the two seats and a removable coupe hardtop that enabled either configuration to be used.

There was a 230 SL California Coupe. It came with the coupe top only, though this could still be removed for open-top motoring – presumably in the ever-reliable California sun. In the space normally occupied by the soft top was a drop-down bench seat, but this was virtually useless and the 2+2 wasn't a hit.

The heavier R107 SL class superseded the W113 SLs in 1972, but not before the 230 SL had evolved, though this was not apparent visually as the main difference was larger engines. The 250 SL was offered in 1967 and 1968, whilst the 280 SL ran from 1968 to 1971. The production run of the three models was around 49,000, ensuring that these classics are not rare, with about 20,000 original 230 SLs produced.

**COUNTRY OF ORIGIN:**
Germany

**FIRST MANUFACTURED:**
1963 (until 1967)

**ENGINE:**
2,308 cc Straight Six

**PERFORMANCE:**
Top speed of 124 mph (200 km/h); 0–60 mph (97 km/h) in 10.5 secs

**YOU SHOULD KNOW:**
The 230 SL is the least desirable of the three 1960s SLs, as the smaller engine offers less impressive performance than later brethren, but this means that (despite a marked tendency to rust underneath) there are plenty around for anyone who fancies stylish pagoda-top motoring.

# MERCURY COUGAR

**COUNTRY OF ORIGIN:**
USA

**FIRST MANUFACTURED:**
1967 (until 1973)

**ENGINE:**
Various, from 4.7 l (289 cid) to 7.0 l (429 cid) V8

**PERFORMANCE:**
With 5.8 l engine – top speed of 104 mph (167 km/h); 0.60 mph (97 km/h) in 7.6 secs

**YOU SHOULD KNOW:**
The Cougar works team competed with honour – and considerable success – in the 1967 Trans-Am road racing series for production sedans, though it failed to topple the all-conquering Mustang and was rather mysteriously withdrawn from the following year's Trans-Am.

Blessed was the carmaker who invented a niche market which proved incredibly profitable. In the early 1960s that left Ford smirking, for their Mustang had become the first ponycar. This had involved the creation of a stylish compact capturing the free 'n' easy spirit of the age at an affordable price. Of course in the cut-throat world of US auto manufacture a unique niche soon became a genre with virtually every Detroit player trying to run a winning 'pony'.

Ford was greedy, and decided it might be possible for its Mercury marque to clamber aboard the bandwagon, even though Mercury cars were big. The answer was obvious – a bigger ponycar that might find its own niche within a niche. The thinking was sound. When the Cougar finally appeared in 1967 after a long development process it was an instant hit, with the elegantly designed standard hardtop and punchy XR-7 with their well-appointed interiors and huge options package selling well from Day One.

The Cougar ponycar would go on to enjoy a six-year run that saw the introduction of various evolutionary models, including a convertible from 1969 when range styling was updated for a second generation. Along the way there would be a choice of many engines, although sales declined steadily and never replicated the stunning success of the launch year.

The Cougar lasted as a ponycar until 1973, but enjoyed a much better run than some of Mercury's efforts to chase specific market share – around 615,000 of the various versions were sold over the years, and the Cougar pony has become a much-appreciated cherished car that has developed a cult following. The third generation was relaunched as a personally luxury car and the feline name is still in use.

# MERCURY MARAUDER

The Marauder name appealed to the good folk at Mercury, for they chose it for the big Ford engines the company used in the 1960s. Suitably enthused, they also applied the name to some early 1960s fastback versions of the Monterey, Montclair and Park Lane models. And in 1969 they went all the way, launching the Mercury Marauder as a fully fledged model in its own right.

This large, two-door coupe was a hopeful entry into the personal luxury car market, where self-indulgent quality cars tended to offer long fronts, short tails with fastback styling, luxury cabins and high performance. There were two types – those with big engines in smallish cars or alternatively big engines in biggish cars. The latter category included speedsters like the Ford T-bird, Buick Riviera and Pontiac Grand Prix and they were the ones in Mercury's sights.

The roomy Marauder certainly conformed to the latter stereotype, with a choice of versions – the standard offering having a 6.4 litre engine and the X-100 a larger 7 litre alternative. Despite being based on the Mercury Marquis – the pair had the same thrusting front end and shared interior components – the Marauder had a distinctive back end with fake side air intakes. It could be made more individual by ordering options like rear fender skirts (standard on the X-100), vinyl roof, bucket seats and a floor console for the gearshift.

Sadly (and not for the first time when Mercury was trying to cash in on perceived market trends) the Marauder failed to hit the spot, because the market for full-sized sporty cars had already started to evaporate – fast. Just 15,000 Marauders were sold in 1969, with the figure slumping to 6,000 the following year. Two years were enough for embarrassed management, and the Marauder swiftly passed into history.

**COUNTRY OF ORIGIN:**
USA

**FIRST MANUFACTURED:**
1969 (until 1970)

**ENGINE:**
6.4 l (390 cid) or 7.0 l (429 cid) V8

**PERFORMANCE:**
With 7.0 l engine – top speed of 126 mph (km/h); 0–60 mph (97 km/h) in 7.5 secs

**YOU SHOULD KNOW:**
Ford resurrected the Marauder name from 2003 to 2004, when it became the badge worn by a high-performance version of the Mercury Grand Marquis line, which was marketed as a 'muscle sedan'.

# MGB

**COUNTRY OF ORIGIN:**
UK

**FIRST MANUFACTURED:**
1962 (until 1980)

**ENGINE:**
1,799 cc Straight Four

**PERFORMANCE:**
Top speed of 103 mph
(166 km/h); 0–60 mph
(97 km/h) in 12.2 secs

**YOU SHOULD KNOW:**
For MGB purists, the last
year that really counts
is 1973 – for that's the
last year the car was
produced with traditional
chrome bumpers, rather
than the large, black
rubber monstrosities
introduced the following
year to comply with
US regulations.

**The rather voluptuous lines of the MGA were starting to look dated as the Swinging Sixties dawned, but the British Motor Corporation was ready with one of its few great success stories – the MGB. This brilliant sports car with its clean lines would be around for nearly 20 years and well over half a million MGBs (and derivatives) would be manufactured, making it the best-selling British sports car of all time.**

The two-seater roadster was introduced in 1962, and this neat convertible was joined in 1973 by the hatchback MGB GT coupe – nominally a 2+2, though the rear seating would only have been adequate if Snow White were driving. This version would continue to be produced in virtually unchanged form until it was dropped in 1974, though a meaty V8 evolution was offered from 1973 to 1976.

The roadster had a comfortable interior with wind-up windows and a parcel shelf behind the seats. The car featured a four-cylinder 1.8 litre engine and – unlike the MGA it replaced and the Triumph TRs with which it competed – had monocoque rather than body-on-chassis construction, which reduced weight and costs allowing the MGB to be sold at an attractive price. It was an instant success with sporty drivers because the MGB was (and is) a joy to drive, with good acceleration, excellent roadholding and an ability to top the 'ton' when flat out.

The roadster was upgraded as the Mk II in 1967, with an all-synchromesh gearbox and the option of automatic transmission. Various other cosmetic changes took place until the Mk III was introduced in 1972. This had a better heater and new fascia, and would be the final evolution. The last MGB rolled off the line at Abingdon in 1980, to end the era of mass-produced Great British sports cars.

# MGC

Mechanically speaking, the MGC's biography is not really so very different from the heart-warming MGB story, for the two models appear to be virtually identical. But that superficial likeness conceals considerable differences. Produced for just three years (1967 to 1969), the MGC was more than a performance-enhanced MGB fitted with a 2.9 litre Straight Six. It was intended as a replacement for parent company BMC's Austin-Healey 3000, which was discontinued in 1967.

Considerable modification of the MGB platform was required to accommodate the 2.9 litre Morris C-series engine with its polished aluminium head and twin SU carburettors. This took the form of a revised floorpan and bonnet with a characteristic bulge to allow for a raised radiator, plus a neat teardrop for the carburettors. There was a special torsion-bar suspension system with telescopic dampers and the standard gearbox was a four-speed manual. Overdrive or three-speed automatic transmission were options. The wheels were bigger than those on MGBs.

Very much following the MGB formula, both an MGC roadster and MGC GT were offered, but these powerful sports cars never really fired the public imagination. Despite their extra grunt and performance that far exceeded that of the four-cylinder car, the heavy engine adversely affected the nimble handling that had made the MGB so popular. However, the factory did produce a few lightweight MGC GTS racing models, and these competed with some success. The GTS cars were very attractive with flared wings and an aggressive bonnet bulge.

With around 9,000 produced during the shortish production run, the MGC is far rarer than its 'common' relation and therefore much sought-after by MG enthusiasts and collectors of classic sports cars. Happily, modern tyres and a little suspension tweaking can iron out those original handling problems to the complete satisfaction of today's owner-drivers.

**COUNTRY OF ORIGIN:**
UK

**FIRST MANUFACTURED:**
1967 (until 1969)

**ENGINE:**
2,912 cc OHV Straight Six

**PERFORMANCE:**
Top speed of 120 mph (193 km/h); 0–60 mph (97 km/h) in 10 secs

**YOU SHOULD KNOW:**
Sadly, the MGC would be the last all-new model to be created and produced by this great maker at the company's famous Abingdon works before it was closed in 1980.

# NSU RO80

**COUNTRY OF ORIGIN:**
Germany

**FIRST MANUFACTURED:**
1967 (until 1977)

**ENGINE:**
995 cc Double-rotor Wankel

**PERFORMANCE:**
Top speed of 112 mph (180 km/h); 0-60 mph (97 km/h) in 14.2 secs

**YOU SHOULD KNOW:**
The aerodynamic Ro80 (designed in the mid-1960s) was indeed ahead of its time – as anyone who compares it with the 1983 Audi 100 will confirm. The two cars have a virtually identical body shape.

Having pioneered use of the revolutionary Wankel rotary engine in the Wankel Spider roadster, NSU hoped to make a killing by producing a passenger car that would take full advantage of this exclusive engine. The result was the Ro80. It was a beautifully designed four-door saloon with an aerodynamic body, advanced engineering, superb performance and excellent handling. As well as that super-smooth engine, the Ro80 featured front-wheel drive, independent suspension all round, power steering and disc brakes, making it a really advanced vehicle.

Sounds too good to be true? Sadly, it was. NSU did not have the resources to undertake a thorough test programme on the new, twin-chamber rotary engine developed from the single-chamber version in the Wankel Spider. This proved to be a terminal weakness, though the patient would linger on for a decade.

It was quickly apparent that engine components were not up to the stresses placed upon them. Some rotaries even imploded, but mostly they just started losing power. Amongst other faults, chamber walls could distort and rotor tips wore rapidly, causing oil leaks. A service would sometimes correct the problem, but engines often needed a rebuild or even replacement after two or three years. Added to that was the fact that Ro80s were heavy on fuel and dealers found difficulty understanding the new technology. It all added up to a ruinous reputation.

NSU tried valiantly to save the Ro80 (and the company) by instituting a generous warranty programme, and actually sorted most of the engine problems by 1970. But the damage was done. NSU was acquired by Volkswagen and merged with Audi. The Ro80 was allowed to fade away, with production ending in 1977 after some 37,000 had been made. But some are still going strong, offering a unique driving experience.

# NSU WANKEL SPIDER

The long-established NSU car company was sold to Fiat in the 1930s, but the name was revived in World War II for production of the SdKfz 2, better known as the Kettenkrad – a small half-tracked all-terrain vehicle with a motorcycle front end. After hostilities ended, NSU restarted as a motorcycle manufacturer. Its innovative machines were very successful and NSU became a world leader in motorcycle production by the mid-1950s. This encouraged the company to start building cars.

The first four-wheeled offering was the small Prinz saloon, launched in 1957, but NSU might have become a footnote in postwar automobile history had it not been for the extraordinary Wankel Spider. At first glance there was nothing very special about the plainly styled but attractive little convertible that appeared at the Frankfurt Motor Show in 1964, based on NSU's four-year-old Sport Prinz coupe.

The special secret lay beneath a shallow luggage locker at the back – an innovative Wankel rotary engine positioned over the rear axle. This was an incredibly efficient single-cylinder power plant developed by the gifted German engineer Felix Wankel. A rolling rotor turned within the single combustion chamber converting combustion pressure directly into rotary movement, eliminating energy loss experienced in a conventional piston engine when reciprocating movement is converted into rotational movement. The result was a very compact high-revving engine that generated enormous excitement and was initially hailed the next great advance in automotive technology. It wasn't, but that's another story.

The little Wankel Spider was something of a test bed for the new engine, and NSU was not overly concerned with sales. The company was more interested in pioneering the engine concept that was intended to make its fortune, and only some 2,400 units were produced before the little roadster was discontinued in 1966. And after that the fun really began.

**COUNTRY OF ORIGIN:**
Germany

**FIRST MANUFACTURED:**
1964 (until 1966)

**ENGINE:**
498 cc Single-rotor Wankel

**PERFORMANCE:**
Top speed of 92 mph (148 km/h); 0–60 mph (97 km /h) in 16.7 secs

**YOU SHOULD KNOW:**
Despite the many licences issued to produce the Wankel engine, the only manufacturer to have overcome the technical problems and use it consistently in production cars has been Mazda, in such niche performance cars as the RX-7 introduced in the late 1970s.

# OLDSMOBILE JETSTAR I

**COUNTRY OF ORIGIN:**
USA

**FIRST MANUFACTURED:**
1964 (until 1965)

**ENGINE:**
6.5 l (394 cid) or 7.0 l (425 cid) V8

**PERFORMANCE:**
Top speed of 105 mph (km/h); 0–60 mph (97 km/h) in 9.5 secs

**YOU SHOULD KNOW:**
Remember that Oldsmobile weakness for muddying the minds of consumers? Pay attention – the Jetstar I (1964–5) should not be confused with the Jetstar 88 (1964–6) which was the Olds entry-level line (complete with fins on the front) that had no relationship whatsoever to the more expensive Jetstar I.

**Nobody could accuse Oldsmobile of resting on its laurels, for the company was constantly messing with model names, revamping, uprating, relaunching and introducing new models to keep a constant sense of excitement and innovation swirling around the brand name. Of course this was not a unique approach, applying to most other American manufacturers, but Olds was a master proponent of the black art.**

The policy was not always an unqualified success and sometimes a downright disaster. It isn't easy to decide which of these epithets applies to the Jetstar I, but it's certainly one of them. The car appeared in 1964 as the marketing gurus chased a double benefit. The Jetstar was a full-size high-performance car that would compete directly with the Pontiac Grand Prix – and offer a cheaper alternative to the company's own Starfire which was laden with luxurious standard features and therefore expensive. To leave the Starfire with some exclusivity, the Jetstar did not offer a convertible version, though they shared an engine.

Year One was hardly a triumph – Pontiac's Grand Prix outsold the Jetstar by four to one, and a hole was gobbled in Starfire sales by canny buyers who chose options that pushed the cheaper Jetstar towards the superior Starfire spec. Undeterred by these minor setbacks, Oldsmobile substantially reworked the Jetstar I for 1965, along with the rest of its full-size range.

In came curvy 'Coke bottle' styling, a more rounded roofline and a new engine – the 6.5 litre Rocket being replaced by the powerful 7 litre Starfire V8. And out went elderly Roto Hydramatic transmission in favour of the vastly improved Turbo Hydramatic system. The 1965 Jetstar I was actually a gem of a high-performance car, but it was all in vain. The 'Poor Man's Starfire' still failed to hit the sweet spot and was promptly discontinued.

# OLDSMOBILE STARFIRE

**The Starfire was a futuristic 1953 Olds concept car that never made it into production, though the name was then used for the most expensive Oldsmobiles of the 1950s – Model 98 Starfire convertibles. It was not until 1961 that the name borrowed from a Lockheed jet fighter plane was used for a stand-alone line.**

In the confusing world where cars were created to serve all sorts of real or imagined market segments, the new Starfire was Oldsmobile's bold tilt at producing a personal luxury car. Unlike Ford's competing Thunderbird, it was part of the Olds full-size lineup, sharing a body and wheelbase with the Oldsmobile 88s. A convertible was the first to appear, with a whopping price tag to cover a wealth of standard equipment. This included Hydra-matic transmission with floor-mounted shift, brushed aluminium side panels, power steering, electrically adjustable driver's seat, electric windows, leather bucket seats and a centre console with tachometer. The engine was the most powerful available – the 6.5 litre Skyrocket.

In 1962 a two-door hardtop with a convertible roofline doubled the Starfire range and comfortably outsold the original soft top. There was a styling update in 1963 but the Starfire's appeal was weakened by the debut of the Buick Riviera, which had the added appeal of unique styling that compared favourably with the Starfire's one-of-many-similar-Oldsmobiles appearance.

The Starfire limped through 1964, further weakened commercially by sharing a bodyshell with the cheaper Jetstar I. A major revamp across the Oldsmobile range in 1965 offered hope, with Starfire buyers getting the option of a larger engine and four-speed manual transmission. But the convertible was discontinued and many former standard features became options, to give a lower headline ticket price. It was all in vain. After 1967 the Starfire's flagship status went to the Toronado.

**COUNTRY OF ORIGIN:**
USA

**FIRST MANUFACTURED:**
1961 (until 1966)

**ENGINE:**
6.5 l (394 cid) or 7.0 l (425 cid) V8

**PERFORMANCE:**
With 6.5 l engine – top speed of 105 mph (km/h); 0–60 mph (97 km/h) in 9.7 secs

**YOU SHOULD KNOW:**
To ensure some element of exclusivity, Starfire buyers could mix 'n' match 15 exterior colours with four interior colours (blue, fawn, grey and red) – with a further six colours to choose from when it came to convertible tops (black, blue, fawn, green, red and white). Welcome to Glitzville, USA!

# PONTIAC GRAND PRIX

**COUNTRY OF ORIGIN:**
USA

**FIRST MANUFACTURED:**
1962 (until 1968)

**ENGINE:**
6.4 l (389 cid) or 6.9 l
(421 cid) V8; 6.5 l (400
cid) or 7.0 l (428 cid) V8

**PERFORMANCE:**
Varied according to
engine – but typically top
speed of around 130 mph
(209 km/h); 0–100 mph
(161 km/h) in 12 secs

**YOU SHOULD KNOW:**
The Grand Prix's sporty
profile was down to John
DeLorean, Pontiac's head
of advanced engineering
– who would become
notorious as the founder
of DeLorean Motor
Company, which went
spectacularly bust in the
early 1980s.

Many American model lines involve confusing nomenclature –
especially when names continue for decades – and so it is with the
1960s Pontiac Grand Prix, which made its debut in 1962 and has been
around ever since. But first series cars belong squarely to the Swinging
Sixties, as the second series (from 1969) dropped the Grand Prix from
Pontiac's upmarket full-size range into the mid-range.

The initial offering was developed from the Pontiac Catalina
coupe, without its predecessor's excessive chromework and with
sporty interior trim that included a centre console and bucket seats.
This was designed to make the Grand Prix the personal luxury car
for those who preferred to be seen in (and drive) a quality high-
performance model, to which end numerous fancy extras were
offered. The stratagem worked well, for the Grand Prix sold well
until it was demoted.

First generation cars were fitted with a 6.4 litre V8 from the
companion Bonneville, though various tuned versions were available
and a larger 6.9 litre option was offered. The engine choice remained
the same until 1967, when two improved versions of the old power
plants appeared at 6.5 and 7 litres respectively. The Grand Prix's
appearance evolved over the decade, too. The initial convertible-style
roofline was squared off with a concave rear window, and a major
restyle in 1965 saw all Pontiac models acquire the more rounded
'Coke bottle' look that was then modish. However, the Grand Prix did
not change as drastically as most.

Further styling changes were implemented in 1967, along with
the introduction of a convertible Grand Prix. But the end was nigh,
and though 1968 saw a new beak-nosed grille and bumper, the
convertible was swiftly discontinued and this would be the Grand
Prix's last year as a member of the full-sized Pontiac club.

# PONTIAC GTO JUDGE

When John DeLorean, Pontiac's chief engineer in the 1960s, named the first Pontiac GTO after the Ferrari 250 GTO, it was considered almost sacrilegious. The letters stand for Gran Turismo Omologato, that is, homologated (accredited) for GT racing. General Motors had banned advertising that associated their marques with racing, a keystone of Pontiac's strategy. DeLorean sidestepped the ban by creating the GTO as a performance 'option' of Pontiac's LeMans and Tempest models, a wily subterfuge senior management could collude with. By 1969, the GTO was still competitive, but Pontiac wanted a low-cost version, stripped of its accretion of luxury and 'performance enhancement' gimmickry. The Judge was born.

Almost immediately, economy was forgotten. Pontiac's raging desire to create the ultimate in street performance and muscular image made the GTO Judge more expensive than any other version. For the money you got a true muscle car, which reached its apotheosis at the end of 1970 when the long-stroke 455 engine became an option. Its top speed wasn't as high as other GTO Judge versions, but it wasn't particularly temperamental at low speed either. The Ram Air hood scoop was more style statement than functionally useful, like the rear spoiler, and for a short time it even had VOE (Vacuum Operated Exhaust) – in case people hadn't noticed the car when you pulled up, the VOE knob trebled the exhaust volume. Self-advertisement wasn't an issue. With its wide wheels, beefy front end and speed-whipped lines, the Judge was power incarnate in its day – and (though you could choose any colour) the Judge-exclusive, standard factory Orbit-Orange with blue/pink stripes made sure everyone saw it and knew it. As Road Test magazine noted, it was 'not for people who are shy about being looked at'. The Judge was a young man's dream.

**COUNTRY OF ORIGIN:**
USA

**FIRST MANUFACTURED:**
1969 (until 1971)

**ENGINE:**
6.6 l (400 cid) or 7.5 l (455 cid)

**PERFORMANCE:**
Top speed around 130 mph (209 km/h) according to engine tuning; 0–60 mph (97 km/h) in 6.1 secs

**YOU SHOULD KNOW:**
The Pontiac GTO series was produced from 1964 to 1974 by which time emissions requirements had sent performance and hence sales into decline. To the surprise of GTO fans (or 'Goats' as they call themselves) the name was reintroduced in 2004. The GTO Judge was named in honour of *Rowan & Martin's Laugh-In* TV show catch-phrase 'Here comes the Judge.' Seventeen convertible Judges were made, which are the rarest of all the GTOs.

# PORSCHE 904 CARRERA GTS

**COUNTRY OF ORIGIN:**
Germany

**FIRST MANUFACTURED:**
1963 (until 1964)

**ENGINE:**
1,966 cc DOHC Flat Four

**PERFORMANCE:**
Top speed of 160 mph
(257 km/h); 0–60 mph
(97 km/h) in 5.3 secs

**YOU SHOULD KNOW:**
The 904 was the first in
a line of sports racers
that would culminate
in the 917, which gave
Porsche its first outright
wins in the Le Mans 24
(1970 and 1971) – this
awesome beast hit 60
mph (97 km/h) in less
than 2.5 seconds on the
way to a top speed of
255 mph (410 km/h).
Phewwhatascorcher!

After easing out of F1 Grand Prix racing in the early 1960s, Porsche refocused on sports car racing. The versatile mid-engined Porsche 718 had featured in various classes since its debut in 1958, and was briefly replaced by the flying silver Porsche 804, which secured the company's only F1 victory in the 1962 French Grand Prix. But ending F1 involvement freed up funds to improve Porsche's competitiveness in the GT class.

The current GT competitor was the 356 Carrera 2, a modified road car that was looking tired compared to shiny stars being introduced by the likes of Alfa Romeo and Abarth. A new car was required, with a road-going version to secure homologation. One hundred would have to be produced to meet the rules, and the Porsche design team started with a blank sheet of paper. Lead designer was Ferry 'Butzi' Porsche, the founder's grandson.

His innovative solution was the first 'plastic' Porsche, with a very attractive fibreglass coupe body bonded to a steel chassis, which perforce carried a tuned four-cylinder engine from the Carrera 2, as the intended Flat Six was not ready. After testing, the stunning Porsche 904 Carrera GTS was revealed to the waiting world in November 1963. Waiting it was – Porsche's canny plan to get a 'free' sports racer worked out perfectly, with the vast majority of 90 cars allocated for public sale ordered within weeks. This ensured that the homologation rules were fully satisfied by the following spring, leaving Porsche 30 cars with which to go racing.

This exclusive machine duly enjoyed considerable all-round track success – including outright Targa Florio victory, class wins at Le Mans and second place in the Monte Carlo Rally. Porsche's 904 Carrera GTS remains the company's only true dual-purpose road/race car and is rightly regarded as one of the finest cars they ever made.

# PORSCHE 911S

Think Beetle, then think bigger, finally decide to create the world's most profitable car company – that was the audacious Porsche family plan, and how well it worked. The patriarch was Austrian engineer Ferdinand Porsche, designer of the Volkswagen Beetle before World War II, who would subsequently be imprisoned for alleged war crimes. But his son Ferdinand 'Ferry' Porsche operated Porsche AG and his grandson Ferdinand 'Butzi' Porsche was intimately involved in the development of the Porsche 911 – the car directly descended from the VW Beetle that would establish the company as a world-famous purveyor of superlative sports cars.

The classic 911 coupe was first shown in late 1963 at the Frankfurt Motor Show and went into production the following year. Like its mass-market Beetle ancestor, the 911 was a distinctive rear-engined, air-cooled car that would retain its characteristic aerodynamic shape for decades. The boxer Flat Six motor was teamed with a four- or five-speed manual gearbox for electrifying performance, steering was precise – though roadholding was best described as sporty.

But this would be an evolutionary series, and the first advance came with the 911S (for Super) that was introduced in 1966. Nothing looked very different, apart from the signature five-spoke Fuchs 'flower-petal' alloy wheels, but the engine had been uprated and the Weber carburettors tuned. Chassis improvements – including ventilated disc brakes all round, Koni shocks and a second roll bar – ensured the extra power was harnessed.

The first Porsche 911S was the sensational model that really established the line's performance credentials, though initially there were faults like plug fouling. But improvement and refinement would characterize the 911S at every stage of its long life, with a second generation (filling the next slot between 1969 and 1971) boasting a larger engine. But that was just the beginning of the success story – don't go away!

**COUNTRY OF ORIGIN:**
Germany

**FIRST MANUFACTURED:**
1966 (until 1969)

**ENGINE:**
1,991 cc Flat Six

**PERFORMANCE:**
Top speed of 131 mph (211 km/h); 0-60 mph (97 km/h) in 8.3 secs

**YOU SHOULD KNOW:**
The Porsche 912 is the almost-forgotten companion model of the 911, manufactured from 1965 to 1969 – it was Porsche's entry-level model and looked very similar to its big brother, the main difference being that it had a four-cylinder engine.

# RAMBLER AMERICAN CONVERTIBLE

**COUNTRY OF ORIGIN:**
USA

**FIRST MANUFACTURED:**
1961 (until 1963)

**ENGINE:**
3.2 l (196 cid) Straight Six

**PERFORMANCE:**
Top speed of 90 mph
(145 km/h); 0–60 mph
(97 km/h) in 12.9 secs

**YOU SHOULD KNOW:**
The Rambler American
was the last series to
bear the Rambler brand
name in North American
markets – though the
marque lived on into
the 1980s in far-flung
countries like South
Africa, Iran, Mexico
and Argentina.

In the late 1950s American Motors revived a name from the recent past, recycling the Rambler name from the Nash and Hudson compacts of the mid-1950s. The resulting Rambler American would last for 10 years. This workaday line had three distinct lives. The first generation was rather old-fashioned and consisted of a two-door coupe, two-door station wagon and four-door sedan. The dated look was hardly surprising – AMC had reused tooling dating back to the early 1950s.

The second generation looked sharper. Although American didn't retool, there was major restyling of the old bodies. In 1961 the three existing models were joined by a four-door station wagon and a very pleasing convertible. An attractive pillarless hardtop coupe was added in 1963, along with a 440-H sports special with bucket seats and tuned engine.

Of the six body styles, there can be no doubt which one best captures and holds the modern eye. The second generation Rambler American Convertible is considered to be something of a minor design classic, in that a new skin brilliantly disguised elderly mechanics and the clean, simple lines entirely escaped from the rounded 'bath-tub' look of previous cars, also eschewing the flashy fins popular at the time. With around 17,500 built, the Rambler American Convertible has a loyal modern following of weekend owner-drivers.

From 1964 to 1969, third generation Rambler Americans were very different after being completely redesigned. The range was trimmed to five body styles as out went the two-door station wagon and in came a wide range of engine options. The third generation ultimately saw eight different power plants ranging from the old 3.2 litre Straight Six up to a meaty 6.8 litre V8. There was, of course, a new convertible – which is also quite well regarded as a collectable (and affordable) 1960s ragtop.

# RELIANT SCIMITAR GTE SE5

**COUNTRY OF ORIGIN:**
UK

**FIRST MANUFACTURED:**
1968 (until 1972)

**ENGINE:**
2,553 cc Straight Six or
2,994 cc V6

**PERFORMANCE:**
With the V6 engine –
top speed of 121 mph
(195 km/h); 0–60 mph
(97 km/h) in 8.9 secs

**YOU SHOULD KNOW:**
Many cars on both sides
of the Atlantic were
named after the sleek
fighter aircraft of World
War II, but it was surely
a coincidence that the
1960s Reliant Scimitar
shared a designation with
the SE5 – that fine British
biplane that duelled with
the Red Baron's Fokker
Triplane in World War I.

**It all began in 1935 when bicycle company Raleigh decided to discontinue its three-wheeler delivery van. The van's designer was T L Williams, who founded Reliant to take over production. This led to a series of three-wheelers culminating in Reliant Robin economy cars and the extraordinary Bond Bug. However, the company also became active at the opposite end of the performance spectrum. First up was the punchy Reliant Sabre, but this was soon followed by the company's innovative Scimitar.**

The Scimitar SE4 appeared in 1964 as a two-door booted coupe. With around a thousand sold, the SE4 was successful enough to encourage the Scimitar's next evolution, which saw the completely redesigned SE5 model introduced late in 1968. With its sturdy chassis and cute fibreglass body, the SE5 was a head turner.

This four-seater GT was based on a design by British consultancy Ogle, which came up with a racy estate car with ample fold-flat rear load space accessed through the hinged, sloping rear window. The only car that came close to a similar layout was the Volvo P1800 estate, but the Reliant True Brit was the preferred repository for the muddy green wellies of sporty country types (famously, the Scimitar would acquire at least one high-profile fan, with the young Princess Anne rarely seen driving anything else).

There was a choice of Straight Six or V6 engines, but the latter was more powerful and proved the popular choice, leading to the former being dropped. Performance was excellent. The Scimitar had a snappy four-speed manual gearbox that later acquired overdrive, and Borg-Warner automatic transmission was offered as an option. Fewer than 2,500 SE5s were hand-built at Tamworth, but the upgraded SE5A (1972–5) would be the best-seller in a long line of Scimitars stretching ahead to 1995.

# RENAULT 4

**Renault had already tried direct competition with Citroën's 2CV. The company believed it could go one-better in 1961 with the Renault 4, a notionally more up-market car with very real improvements in power, space and capacity. Renault's chairman declared its first front-engine, five-door, new runabout to be 'an everyman's car . . . a woman's car, a farmer's car, a city car . . . suitable for motorists round the world'. He got that right, then.**

Hindsight tells the story of global, enduring success. It was based on common sense practicality, logic and simplicity, but it took some getting used to. Though the rear door revealed plenty of boot space, seats tipped, folded or removed to create room for unfeasibly large loads, making the Renault 4 the first true hatchback. You could look directly at the bonnet lid through the mesh over the face-high fresh air 'vent' (a hole in the car's skin). Economy dictated rubber mats, press-down flaps fashioned from the cutouts in the door panels instead of handles, sliding windows (no winding machinery) and heating with four controls all positioned out of useful sight. The biggest economy of all was continuity. The Renault 4 was barely developed throughout its long production run. Its size and shape never changed at all. The engine was perked from 747 cc to 845 cc from 1963, and only replaced with a smaller version of Renault's 1978 new 1108 cc engine in 1986.

The Renault 4 was basic and proud of it. It was remarkably comfortable to ride in. Its dash-mounted gear lever (thanks to 2CV) made much more space available; and if it might roll on cornering, it certainly never wallowed. It was classless, and it still is, though descendants like the Dauphine and Clio might argue otherwise. No wonder it sold over eight million, the fifth biggest-selling car in the world.

**COUNTRY OF ORIGIN:**
France

**FIRST MANUFACTURED:**
1961 (until 1993)

**ENGINE:**
747 cc OHV Straight Four

**PERFORMANCE:**
Top speed of 75 mph (120 km/h); 0–60 mph (97 km/h) in 38 secs

**YOU SHOULD KNOW:**
The Renault 4 is also known as the 4L – pronounced Quatrelle, which in French sounds like 'Four Wings'. In France the car is also called 'the hen coop on wheels'. In Colombia, one of 16 countries where the Renault 4 has been produced, it is affectionately called Amigo Fiel ('Faithful Friend'). In Argentina and Chile it's the Renolata – a play on the Spanish camioneta ('truck') and a dig at the 2CV, known as the Citroneta in consequence.

# ROVER P5B

**COUNTRY OF ORIGIN:**
UK

**FIRST MANUFACTURED:**
1967 (until 1973)

**ENGINE:**
3,528 cc V8

**PERFORMANCE:**
Coupe – top speed of
113 mph (182 km/h)

**YOU SHOULD KNOW:**
The P5 may have remained as an aspirational purchase for the British middle classes, but was classy enough to be acceptable to Royalty and Prime Ministers – Queen Elizabeth II used one, as did PMs Harold Wilson, Edward Heath, James Callaghan and Margaret Thatcher.

**The Rover P5 appeared in 1958, replacing the much-loved but elderly P4 (then a tired 25-year-old). The P5 was a larger car that took the Rover line up market, appealing as it did to senior businessmen and civil servants. It was also a very good car, soon becoming established as one of Britain's best-selling luxury motors of the 1960s.**

The Mk I was powered by a 3 litre Straight Six. This solid four-door saloon had independent front suspension, whilst servo-assisted front discs soon became standard. Automatic transmission, overdrive on the manual box and power steering were options. A minor upgrade in 1961 saw front quarter lights introduced, but that was just a holding operation until the Mk II appeared in 1962. This featured better suspension and a tuned engine, also offering the choice of a coupe version with sporty lowered roofline. The Mk III of 1965 was little changed, though the styling was updated and the engine's power output further tweaked.

In 1967 the best P5 of all appeared – the P5B. The B stood for Buick, for Rover had taken the American company's unsuccessful lightweight aluminium V8 and improved it out of all recognition (indeed, evolutionary versions would remain around for decades). This engine gave the P5B lots more grunt, which was teamed with standard Borg-Warner automatic transmission and power steering. Not much changed externally, but a pair of fog lamps gave the front a magisterial four-light look and (lest anyone should doubt that this was the new model) chrome Rostyle wheels were complemented by prominent '3.5 Litre' badging.

The P5B has become a collectable modern classic, and still gives drivers a superior feeling as they glide effortlessly amongst lesser vehicles. The saloon was produced in the largest numbers, making the coupe rarer and therefore more desirable.

# TOYOTA LAND CRUISER FJ40

The famous World War II Willys Jeep continued after 1945 as the civilian CJ model, offering a no-frills, rugged four-wheel drive vehicle. Toyota certainly thought it was a good idea, after building Jeeps to a Willys spec for American troops to use in the nearby Korean War. In the mid-1950s these Toyota Jeep clones evolved into the Land Cruiser, which would become the company's enduring four-wheel-drive flagship offering. After various developments of the Jeep format, the 40 series appeared in 1960 and would last for a quarter of a century.

This Land Cruiser line would establish Toyota's off-roaders as the toughest and most reliable money could buy – especially appreciated by Aussies who lived in the daren't-break-down Outback. The compact two-door FJ40 was the new generation's firstborn, with fresh body styling and low-range gearing. Mind you, the designer must have loved his set square, as the body was remarkably box-like with lots of precise straight lines.

The FJ40 was the short-wheelbase option, with fold-flat windscreen. Larger mid-wheelbase (BJ43) and long-wheelbase (HJ45) versions were offered later. The FJ had a petrol engine whilst the larger pair were diesel-engined. The FJ40's transmission evolved over time from three-, to four- and finally a five-speed automatic. Petrol engines also changed, from the F 3.9 litre (until 1974) to the 2F 4.2 litre (from 1974 to 1984). Body types over time would be two-door soft and hardtops, two-door pickup and four-door wagon.

Early FJ40s can be hard to find, especially in America, as the customizers love to fit them with alternative engines (and pretty much everything else) in order to indulge in the gravity-defying automobile art of rock crawling. But originals are appreciated as Toyota's true classic off-roaders, before the SUV started its inexorable drive into refined suburban streets.

**COUNTRY OF ORIGIN:**
Japan

**FIRST MANUFACTURED:**
1960 (until 1984)

**ENGINE:**
3,878 cc, 3,955 cc or 4,230 cc Straight Six

**PERFORMANCE:**
Varied according to engine and transmission – top speed typically 85 mph (138 km/h); 0–60 mph (97 km/h) in 29 secs

**YOU SHOULD KNOW:**
Classification of the Land Cruiser series involved an engine series designation (eg F = original petrol engine) and body style (eg 40 = original two door short wheelbase) separated by a J for Jeep. The Land Cruiser Series 40 contained literally dozens of different variations.

# TRIUMPH TR6

**COUNTRY OF ORIGIN:**
UK

**FIRST MANUFACTURED:**
1969 (until 1976)

**ENGINE:**
2.498 cc Straight Six

**PERFORMANCE:**
Top speed of 118mph (191 km/h); 0–60 mph (97 km/h) in around 9.5 secs

**YOU SHOULD KNOW:**
The TR6's fuel-injected engine failed US emissions requirements so models for export to America were a somewhat strangulated twin-carburetted version.

'Rattly, draughty, unpredictable in the wet, prone to disintegration . . . ' That's how celebrity car buff James May described the TR6. And coming from him, the words were glowing praise; for it is the sheer, unadulterated blokishness of the TR6 that was the secret of its success – a hunky machine, modelled along the lines of a classic British roadster but with the promise of high-performance tearaway thrills. When it came onto the market it immediately hit the spot, and by the time production ended in 1976 the TR6 was Triumph's best-seller – more than 94,500 had been built.

The TR6 was the consummation of a series which had evolved steadily through each model. Mechanically more or less identical to the TR5 (which itself was simply a TR4 with a pushrod six-cylinder engine) the TR6 had a classy new body, styled by Karmann. Its flowing lines gave it a beautiful old-fashioned shape and the interior had touches of opulence: pile carpet, wooden dashboard and comfortable bucket seats with plenty of leg room. A steel hardtop was included as an optional extra for instant conversion to a sports coupe. Built in Triumph's Coventry factory using the traditional body-on-frame construction method rather than the mass-production unibody technology that by then had become the norm, the TR6 had four-speed manual transmission with optional overdrive, rack-and-pinion steering and a fuel-injected engine – which gave so much power that Triumph had to detune it from 150 bhp to 125 bhp to make it more manageable.

The TR6 is a brilliant hobbyist's car for weekend tinkerering. Spare parts are readily available and inexpensive, the electrics are straightforward and there is enough room around the engine to wield a spanner with ease. And on the road, it fulfils every criterion of those boy racer dreams – a superb heritage toy.

# VANDEN PLAS PRINCESS 4 LITRE

**COUNTRY OF ORIGIN:**
UK

**FIRST MANUFACTURED:**
1960 (until 1968)

**ENGINE:**
3,995 cc or 3,909 cc
Straight Six

**PERFORMANCE:**
Princess 4 l R – top speed
of 106 mph (171 km/h)

**YOU SHOULD KNOW:**
The only other model
Vanden Plas built in
its own name was the
Pininfarina-designed
car simply known as the
Vanden Plas Princess
– it was a luxury four-
door saloon built from
1960 to 1964 that had
a 2.9 l engine and was
based on the Austin A99
Westminster.

Vanden Plas was a coachbuilding company that originated in Belgium and was licensed in the United Kingdom from 1910. After various ups and downs the British company built Bentley bodies in the 1920s, then worked for various makers including Alvis, Daimler and Rolls-Royce in the 1930s. After World War II Vanden Plas was acquired by Austin, who gave Vanden Plas the job of fitting bodies to the upmarket A135 Princess. From 1960 Austin successor BMC decided that Vanden Plas should be a stand-alone marque, so the Austin Princess turned into the stately Vanden Plas Princess 4 Litre.

This hand-built luxury limousine went through two generations before the Vanden Plas marque was abolished, with the name subsequently being used for top-of-the-range models by various companies within the merged British Leyland Motor Corporation from 1968, including Jaguar. The Princess 4 Litre had a relatively short life before being replaced by the Daimler DS420, Leyland's sole limousine offering.

The first Vanden Plas Princess 4 Litre was the former Austin Princess IV, which had been restyled in 1956 to eliminate the car's dated look, though mechanics were not much changed. These ceremonial limos were never big sellers (just 200 in nine years), but the Vanden Plas Princess 4 Litre R was a different story, with nearly 7,000 made between its launch in 1964 and the demise of Vanden Plas as independent marque.

This was an interesting vehicle as the Princess 4 Litre R had a Rolls-Royce Straight Six under the bonnet (signified by the 'R'). It possessed more rounded styling than its predecessor and lost the tail fins. It had the distinction of being the only mass-produced passenger car ever to have a Rolls-Royce engine and was something of a favourite with politicians, senior government officials and up-and-coming businessmen.

# VOLVO P1800

Forever associated with the TV Saint, the Volvo P1800 was well publicized by its appearance as Simon Templar's wheels in The Saint, starring Roger Moore. In fact, Volvo supplied several P1800 coupes for the long-running production, each in turn wearing the numberplate ST 1, after Jaguar refused to offer an E-Type. This canny move certainly enhanced sales of the P1800, which first appeared in 1961 after Volvo decided to enter the sports car market again (the 1950s P1900 roadster had been a disaster).

After various problems locating a suitable supplier, Volvo contracted Jensen Motors who agreed to do the business, using bodies from Pressed Steel at Linwood to produce this classic 2+2 notchback coupe designed by Carrozzeria Pietro Frua in Italy (where the designer who worked on the new car happened to be Pelle Pettersson, son of Volvo engineering consultant Helmer Pettersson).

Nepotism duly justified by a brilliant result, the first P1800s appeared to great public excitement in 1961. The engine was a specially engineered version of Volvo's reliable B18 plant with dual SU carburettors that gave ton-topping performance with brisk acceleration via a manual four-speed gearbox (optional overdrive available).

After 6,000 of the contracted 10,000 P1800s had been built, Jensen ran into problems and production was transferred to Sweden in 1963, at which point the name was changed to 1800S (S = Swedish assembly) and the engine was improved. The next big shake-up came in 1970, when the P1800E was introduced. This had a bigger fuel-injected engine and disc brakes all round. The last version appeared in 1972 – a striking hatchback estate car version designated P1800ES. This would be the only model built in the last year of production, 1973. Around 47,000 P1800s were produced and they are usable classics well up to the rigours of modern motoring.

**COUNTRY OF ORIGIN:**
Sweden (initially built in the UK)

**FIRST MANUFACTURED:**
1961 (until 1973)

**ENGINE:**
1,778 cc or 1,986 cc Straight Four

**PERFORMANCE:**
1800E without overdrive – top speed of 118 mph (km/h); 0–60 mph (97 km/h) in 7.1 secs

**YOU SHOULD KNOW:**
For some reason the B18 Volvo engine has a reputation as being rather robust and well built, perhaps because one Volvo P1800 has done over 2.7 million miles (4 million kilometers) – and counting – on its original B18 engine. Okay, so it IS rather robust and well built.

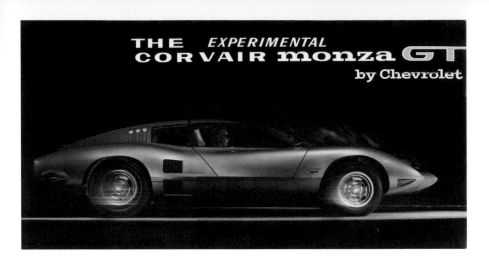

THE EXPERIMENTAL CORVAIR *monza* GT by Chevrolet

# CHEVROLET CORVAIR MONZA GT

## CONCEPT CAR

**COUNTRY OF ORIGIN:**
USA

**FIRST MANUFACTURED:**
1962

**ENGINE:**
2.4 l (145 cid) Flat Six
(with 'two carburettor
layout', a unique feature)

**PERFORMANCE:**
Top speed of 115 mph
(185 km/h); 0-60 mph
(97 km/h) in 10.8 secs

**YOU SHOULD KNOW:**
The Corvair Monza GT
appeared at many motor
shows during 1963 with
its fellow concept cars,
the convertibles Monza
SS (Sebring Spyder) of
1961, and Monza SS
(Super Spyder) of 1962.
Neither convertible
was anything like so
gorgeous or as technically
advanced as the Monza
GT, which rather lost out
by the association.

By 1962 General Motors had refined its notion of a concept car. Far from encouraging designs rooted in whimsy or science fiction, it restricted imaginative research to the realms of practical possibility. Cars could still be bizarre or weird or even fabulous, so long as every gizmo, attachment, style feature or technical surprise had a point.

Chevrolet's Corvair Monza GT was certainly extraordinary, and as dramatic as it was beautiful. It was also the most advanced Corvair ever made. By 1962, the Corvair was already a successful production model, a compact sports coupe of thrilling power but tricky handling, thanks to its rear-mounted engine. It provided GM with the perfect raw material with which to persuade Larry Shinoda, the designer revered for creating the Sting Ray Corvette, to demonstrate his lateral thinking and flair for styling.

Shinoda came up with a pocket-sized thunderclap. He shortened the standard Corvair wheelbase, and rotated the Monza GT's rear engine through 180 degrees to sit just forward of the rear axle. The weight redistribution transformed the handling problems of the standard Corvair – and that in turn enabled Shinoda to take full advantage of the Monza GT's aerodynamic potential. The headlights were hidden behind 'clam shell' lids in the sleek, low-slung, bumperless silver bullet; and the effortless billow of the streamlining that integrated the wheel arches and canopy into a single line was undisturbed by conventional interruptions like doors. For access, the entire canopy swept up and forward on front hinges, and the engine cover did the same from rear hinges.

The Corvair Monza GT was mean and lean enough to make its debut (at Elkhart Lake) in an actual race. It sprang into life fully formed, beautiful and successful. The mystery is that it remained just a wonderful concept.

# HOLDEN HURRICANE

## CONCEPT CAR

Typically forthright, the Australian Holden car company announced the Holden Hurricane of 1969 as 'Tomorrow's Holden'. It was the new Research and Development team's first creation, and it was conceived to show off and demonstrate the 'design trends, propulsion systems and other long range developments' of which Australia itself was capable. In 1969, the car was a catalogue of yesterday's wish-list made manifest so you could (just) imagine today what you might be driving tomorrow. Holden's timing was perfect, and the Holden Hurricane had a lot to say.

It was an aerodynamic wedge of pure speed, powered by the first fully Australian designed and built V8 engine. Directly as a result of this first appearance, the 4.1 litre Holden V8 went into production and sold a million cars in five years. The Hurricane had no doors: the entire, wraparound glass canopy lifted up and forwards, the steering wheel tilted, and the twin 'astronaut' seats rose up and pivoted for easy access, all at the touch of a single button. Once inside, the driver and passenger were lowered to a semi-reclining position, and the car wouldn't even start until the canopy was locked down and the seat-belts fastened. Safety innovations included foam padded interior trim and foam-lined fuel tank, integral headrests, pedals adjustable to the driver's height and a fire warning system. Other features were pure science fiction, like the automatic station-seeking radio, the 'Pathfinder' automatic steering indicator, the 'Comfortron' automatic temperature control and air conditioning, and wide-angle, rearward-looking camera connected to a dashboard console (instead of a rear mirror). The dashboard itself was crowded with electronic digital displays to monitor the gizmos – most people had never seen one before, let alone in a car.

The Holden Hurricane teased its awestruck admirers in 1969 – but it really was a glimpse of the future.

**COUNTRY OF ORIGIN:**
Australia

**FIRST MANUFACTURED:**
1969

**ENGINE:**
4,147 cc V8

**PERFORMANCE:**
N/A

**YOU SHOULD KNOW:**
Among professional designers, the Holden Hurricane's super-low slung, wedge shape was its most revolutionary feature – and you can see it echoed in the Bertone Stratos concept car of 1970, Ferrari's 1970 512S Berlinetta Speciale, and the 1972 Maserati Boomerang.

# AC 3000ME

**COUNTRY OF ORIGIN:**
UK

**FIRST MANUFACTURED:**
1979 (until 1984)

**ENGINE:**
2,994 cc OHV V6

**PERFORMANCE:**
Top speed of 120 mph
(193 km/h); 0–60 mph
(97 km/h) in 8.5 secs

**YOU SHOULD KNOW:**
The last AC 3000MEs were built north of the border after the AC name and car were licensed to the AC (Scotland) company formed for the purpose – but only 30 more cars were built at the factory in Hillington, Glasgow, before the new enterprise failed in 1985.

**Go looking for a crock of gold at the end of the nearest rainbow and you'll probably find it just before you manage to locate an AC 3000ME – just one hundred of these low-slung cars were built and they tended to rust. It all came about because AC boss Derek Hurlock was looking for a small custom-built luxury car with which to tackle the fuel-starved 1970s, and found the one-off Diablo prototype built by racing privateers Robin Stables and Peter Bohanna around an Austin Maxi engine. AC bought the rights and started developing it as the 3000ME.**

After somewhat prematurely showing an 3000ME mid-engined concept car containing the Ford Essex V6 engine at the 1973 Earls Court Motor Show in London, AC hit trouble when new regulations called for a crash test – which the AC 3000ME failed in 1976 at the very point when it was ready for sale. A major reworking of the chassis secured an A+ in the crash test, but AC's limited resources meant that the uprated car – now called the 3000ME – did not go to market until 1979. When it did, the wait must have seemed worthwhile for those lucky enough to secure one.

With its thrusting wedge-shaped front end, distinctive air intakes and advanced features, this was a handsome high-performance coupe with exceptional roadholding in best AC traditions. It had pop-up headlamps, five-speed gearbox, independent suspension and disc brakes all round. AC also included goodies like adjustable steering column, electric windows, sunshine roof, sun-dym laminated windscreen and windows, through-flow ventilation, electric aerial, alloy wheels and stainless steel exhaust. This was a terrific little car, but production delays meant the 3000ME arrived too late – the problem of competing with the formidable Lotus Esprit was insurmountable and production ceased at the Thames Ditton facility in 1984.

# ALFA ROMEO MONTREAL

**The first production Montreal was shown at the Geneva Motor Show in 1970 and attracted crowds of admirers – and no wonder. Alfa had come up with a very distinctive 2+2 coupe that seemed to tick all the boxes. For a start, it was a handsome, classically styled two-door sports coupe in the best Italian tradition, designed by Bertone. But the real appeal lay beneath the bonnet, where a fuel-injected 2.6 litre V8 lurked, capable of pumping out 200 bhp. With the help of a five-speed ZF gearbox and limited-slip differential this meant the Alfa Romeo Montreal was a mean performer, with rapid acceleration and an impressive top speed.**

The chassis and suspension of the Montreal came from the Giulia GTV coupe and the engine was a bored-out version of the 2 litre, four-cam V8 from the 33 Stradale, the road-going version of Alfa Romeo's Tipo 33 racing car. The Montreal's front end had four headlights mounted beneath unusual grilles that retracted when the lights were switched on. The fake air duct on the bonnet is in fact a necessary extension created as a power bulge. The prominent horizontal slats to the rear of the doors did work, but only as cabin vents.

Sadly, for all the initial excitement the Montreal failed to capture the hearts and wallets of many buyers. It undoubtedly suffered from entering a 'junior supercar' sector that was already looking crowded, not least by other sporty Alfas. Although it was not officially discontinued until 1977, Alfa had long ceased production and merely waited until the generous stick of unsold cars was finally shifted before announcing the Montreal's demise, with around 4,000 sold in eight years. It was a sad end for a rather impressive car that has happily received belated recognition from modern classic car collectors.

**COUNTRY OF ORIGIN:**
Italy

**FIRST MANUFACTURED:**
1970 (until 1977)

**ENGINE:**
2,594 cc V8

**PERFORMANCE:**
Top speed of 138 mph (222 km/h); 0–60 mph (97 km/h) in 7.5 secs

**YOU SHOULD KNOW:**
The concept car's first appearance was at Expo 67 in Montreal, Canada – the two prototypes had no name and were very different from the production model, but motoring press and public had christened this potentially exciting car 'The Montreal' and Alfa shrewdly went with the popular name.

# ALFA ROMEO JUNIOR ZAGATO

**COUNTRY OF ORIGIN:**
Italy

**FIRST MANUFACTURED:**
1970 (until 1976)

**ENGINE:**
1,290 cc or 1,570 cc
Straight Four

**PERFORMANCE:**
Top speed of 118 mph
(190 km/h); 0–60 mph
(97 km/h) in 11.2 secs

**YOU SHOULD KNOW:**
It won't be easy to find
a Junior Z to drive:
Zagato (despite stretching
production facilities to
the limit) only built 1,108
1300 JZs and a mere 402
1600 JZs – though the
effort did put Zagato on a
par with other carrozzeria
like Bertone and
Pininfarina in terms of its
commercial relationship
with Alfa.

The 1970s opened in style for lovers of sporty Alfa Romeos, who had been metaphorically licking their lips since the Junior Zagato was presented at the Turin Motor Show in November 1969. It was part of Alfa's 105 series and shared a floorpan – and lots of components – with the Giulia Spider, although the Junior Z was altogether more exclusive. Its public availability from the beginning of 1970 extended the 105 series GT Junior range, which had already sold well to those who wanted a stylish coupe that handled well and was fairly sporty – whilst also having a small motor to beat high Italian taxation on large engine capacities.

The GT 1300 Junior was made from 1965 until 1977, with a GT 1600 Junior added in 1972. But those with a nose for something special got really excited when the 1300 Junior Zagato hit the streets, for that added another dimension to their motoring pleasure. The Junior Z was a very different animal from the standard Junior 1300, with a classic short-tailed sporting coupe body aerodynamically crafted by Ercole Spada for Zagato of Milan, purveyor of fine automobile design to the likes of Aston Martin, Lancia and Maserati.

This was a fairly exclusive offering, with a strictly limited number built, and added excitement was generated amongst Alfa aficionados because it was very reminiscent of Giulietta Sprint Zagatos which had previously raced with great success, although the wedge-shaped 1300 Junior Z was not itself intended as a track star. Two years later this splendid little coupe was no more – but only because it was replaced in 1972 by the equally dashing 1600 Junior Zagato with its longer back end and improved performance. This would remain a low-production offering until 1976, when the new Alfetta range took over.

# AMC MATADOR COUPE

Would a car manufacturer ever tell a little white lie? AMC's marketing campaign certainly did in 1971, assuring the world that the Matador was an all-new car when it was a face-lifted 1970 Rebel. There was, however, a wide choice of engines and four body styles – two-door hardtop or coupe, four-door saloon and station wagon. Echoes of AMC's recent muscle-car adventures remained, with the Machine option package available on the two-door hardtop.

But wait! In 1974 AMC really did redesign the Matador, with second generation cars finally approaching that original 'all new' claim. The saloon and station wagon saw major changes, with a revamped front end that had a protruding section following the front bumper, earning the nickname 'coffin noses'. But the real surprise was the two-door's reincarnation as a completely different, radically styled coupe.

Although this streamlined car with its long bonnet and short rear deck won a 'Best Styled Car of 1974' award, the stretched fastback atop a short wheelbase with tunnel headlights was not to everyone's liking, though part of AMC's intention in producing this in-your-face machine was to create an aerodynamic something that could go NASCAR racing, and indeed it won five races. So in consequence the Matador Coupe was pretty speedy.

There was a choice of three engines over the production run, with a fourth big one added for 1974 only. Several trim levels were offered, along with a succession of 'designer' models – Oleg Cassini (1974–5), Barcelona 1 (1976) and Barcelona 2 (1977–8) – that had luxurious interiors. These (somewhat bizarre examples of 1970s kitsch) have become quite collectable, though it's fair to say that the Matador Coupe has never entirely captured the hearts of those of today's enthusiasts who look back to that generation of mighty 1970s American cars with affection.

COUNTRY OF ORIGIN:
USA

FIRST MANUFACTURED:
1974 (until 1978)

ENGINE:
4.2 l (258 cid) Straight Six; 5.0 l (304 cid), 5.9 l (360 cid) or 6.6 l (401 cid) V8

PERFORMANCE:
With 5.9 l engine – top speed of 116 mph (187 km/h); 0–60 mph (97 km/h) in 8.9 secs

YOU SHOULD KNOW:
A copper-coloured Oleg Cassini Matador coupe with its black interior appears in the James Bond film *The Man with the Golden Gun*, where it features rather dramatically as 'the flying car'.

# AMC
# PACER

**COUNTRY OF ORIGIN:**
USA

**FIRST MANUFACTURED:**
1975 (until 1980)

**ENGINE:**
3.8 l (232 cid) or 4.2 l
(258 cid) Straight Six;
5.0 l (304 cid) V8

**PERFORMANCE:**
With V8 engine – top
speed of 96 mph (154
km/h); 0–60 mph
(97 km/h) in 14.8 secs

**YOU SHOULD KNOW:**
The Pacer was originally
designed to have a
Wankel rotary engine but
when preferred supplier
General Motors canned
their Wankel development
programme AMC had to
hastily modify the Pacer
to take their own Straight
Six motor.

**The oil crisis of the early 1970s put the boys from Kenosha in their element. For AMC was all about producing affordable cars for the masses and swiftly came up with a compact to suit the mood of the moment. The futuristic Pacer had curvaceous lines, lots of glass and a handy hatchback, contrasting with the boxy offerings of most other makers. The little car quickly acquired the nickname 'Jellybean'.**

The term 'compact' was relative – the Pacer was wider than a Rolls-Royce Silver Shadow and the smallest of three engine options was a 3.8 litre Straight Six, paradoxically giving very poor fuel economy compared with imported compacts flooding in from Japan. An unusual feature was a passenger side door that was longer than the driver's to facilitate back-seat access. The car certainly fulfilled the design brief of being unique and the car-buying public responded well, shelling out for around 280,000 Pacers over time.

However, 145,000 of those sales were in the first year, and AMC was soon casting around for ways to bolster sales. Performance of the first edition was poor, with either Straight Six engine, so a more powerful version of the larger engine was offered in 1976, then a V8. Although rear seats folded flat to give load space, little remained with the seats up, so a station wagon version appeared in 1977.

AMC also started a hopeful drift from economy compact to luxury compact by offering various upgrade packages. The X was sporty, the D/L was a minor upgrade that became standard in 1978 and the Limited was a leather-upholstered offering loaded with extras that appeared in 1979. There were even specials like The Sundowner (for California) and a Levi's Package with blue denim interior trim and fender logos. It was all in vain, for this 1970s icon expired with the decade.

# AMC REBEL MACHINE

The Rebel name had been around since the late 1950s as a 'special' with a big engine and the American Motors Corporation's mid-sized Rambler bore the name from 1967 until 1970. And that was the one-and-only year the extraordinary AMC Rebel Machine was offered to the performance fraternity. The great champion of economy cars for the masses had finally caught muscle-car fever after dipping a toe in the water with the 1969 SC/Rambler developed with Hurst Performance.

The first examples of the racy Rebel Machine coupe had a garishly patriotic red-white-and-blue paint job, though this mercifully vanished from later examples and became a $75 option. The sporty interior was black with bucket seats separated by an armrest upholstered in (wait for it) red, white and blue vinyl, which never did vanish.

Colour scheme apart, AMC did a pretty good job – the Rebel Machine was an impressive performer thanks to a ram-air 6.4 litre V8 tuned to produce 340 bhp, assisted by a huge air scoop on the bonnet that fed the greedy engine via a vacuum-controlled butterfly valve. The engine was AMC's most powerful and came with modified heads, valve train, cam, intake and exhaust, plus a four-barrel carb. There was a four-speed manual gearbox with a floor shift from Hurst Performance, who had helped with the development programme.

The car had stiff suspension giving the Rebel Machine an elevated rear end and somewhat menacing raked look that more than hinted at its capabilities. It was street legal all right, though often used for drag racing. Around 2,300 were sold in 1970 and – whilst many were burnt out and bit the dust – there is still an enthusiastic band of supporters dedicated to restoring and preserving The Machine whilst revelling in its muscular All-American performance.

**COUNTRY OF ORIGIN:**
USA

**FIRST MANUFACTURED:**
1970

**ENGINE:**
6.5 l (390 cid) V8

**PERFORMANCE:**
Top speed of 125 mph (201 km/h); 0–60 mph (97 km/h) in 6.4 seconds

**YOU SHOULD KNOW:**
AMC really liked that colour scheme, and sold it hard just like this: 'What makes The Machine so unique? Let's start with the paint job. Red . . . white . . . and blue. Complete with stripes that glow in the dark, matching racing mirrors plus THE MACHINE decals inside, outside and on the back. Pretty wild.'

# BMW 6 SERIES

**COUNTRY OF ORIGIN:**
Germany

**FIRST MANUFACTURED:**
1976 (until 1989)

**ENGINE:**
Various, from 2,788 cc to
3,453 cc Straight Six

**PERFORMANCE:**
630CS – top speed of
131 mph (211 km/h);
0–50 mph (80 km/h)
in 5.9 secs

**YOU SHOULD KNOW:**
There can be slight
confusion about model
identification because
BMW released just one
6 series car at a time
in markets with tough
emission controls like
Japan and the USA, so
the 630CSi sent there
was actually a standard
630CS with a fuel-
injected 2,986 cc engine.

The first BMW 6 series appeared in the mid-1970s to replace the 2800 CS, 3.0 CS and 3.0 CSi coupes. The new E24 chassis was introduced in 1976 and that first 6 series would remain in business until the late 1980s. The clean, crisp styling by Paul Bracq was certainly up to the job, remaining virtually unchanged throughout and looking as pleasingly modern at the end of the production run as it had at the beginning.

The forward-leaning front end with familiar twin-kidney grille imparted a strong sense of purpose, supported by a wide bonnet, raked windscreen and rear window and neat boot. The side glass was divided by thin B-pillars that were unobtrusive. The cars had independent suspension and disc brakes all round, together with variable power steering for good road feel and the pioneering Check Control system that monitored engine systems, fluid levels and bulbs. The interior was luxurious, with twin bucket seats at the back separated by the extended front console, which joined the impressive angled 'Cockpit Design' dashboard.

There would inevitably be engine changes during the life of any such extended production run, but the 6 Series had more than most other long-lived European lines as the models evolved. The 630CS had a 3 litre carburetted Six, whilst the 633CSi was fitted with a 3.2 litre Six with Bosch fuel injection, adding serious power to style. The 1970s lineup was completed by the 2.8 litre 628CSi and 635CSi, each with fuel injection. The latter was fitted with an uprated 3.4 litre engine in 1982, and the final model was the awesome M635CSi introduced in 1983. These cars were so well built and satisfying that many are still in everyday use, driving as well today as when they came out of the box.

# CHRYSLER 300 HURST

**Despite the bold '300' in the title, this was no return of the fabled Chrysler 300 letter series of luxury cars that had been produced from 1958 to 1965 (or to put it another way, from A to L), though some consider the Chrysler 300 Hurst to be an honorary member of the elite 300 club. What is indisputable is that Chrysler press releases at the time did boldly refer to the 'Chrysler 300H'.**

If anything, the Hurst was even more exclusive than its sought-after predecessors, for this co-operative venture between Chrysler and famed customizer Hurst Performance appeared five years after the original series ended and was offered for just one year. Around 500 cars were produced, mostly hardtops with a couple of special convertibles thrown in for promotional purposes.

The two-door Hurst was a high-performance version of the large Chrysler 300, a car with a seemingly endless boot lid. The Hurst was identifiable by the fact that it was painted in Spinnaker White and Satin Tan (very close to gold). It also sported a scooped bonnet with fake power bulge and boot lid with moulded spoiler, both in fibreglass. There was no choice of engine – it was the 7.2 litre TNT V8 or nothing. This beast breathed through a dual-snorkel air cleaner and had booming twin exhausts, requiring beefed-up Torque-Flite transmission to put the power down and stiffened suspension to cope. All the Hursts had saddle-coloured leather interiors borrowed from the Chrysler Imperial, and featured bucket seats and a pull-down armrest.

Unfortunately, a communications failure between Chrysler and Hurst left each party thinking that the other would be handling promotion, so hardly anybody knew this muscular flyer was available. The 2,000-unit production target was not reached and the Chrysler 300 Hurst was not invited back for '71.

**COUNTRY OF ORIGIN:**
USA

**FIRST MANUFACTURED:**
1970

**ENGINE:**
7.2 l (440 cid) V8

**PERFORMANCE:**
Top speed of 120 mph (193 km/h); 0–60 mph (97 km/h) in 7.1 secs

**YOU SHOULD KNOW:**
It isn't easy to cut the mustard in a Chrysler 300 Hurst nowadays – of the original production run it is thought that around 250 of these huge muscle cars survive, the vast majority still in North America.

# CITROËN GS

**COUNTRY OF ORIGIN:**
France

**FIRST MANUFACTURED:**
1970 (until 1979)

**ENGINE:**
1,015 cc, 1,129 cc, 1,222 cc
or 1,299 cc Flat Four

**PERFORMANCE:**
With 1.0 l engine –
top speed of 92 mph
(148 km/h); 0–50 mph
(80 km/h) in 11.7 secs

**YOU SHOULD KNOW:**
Citroën persisted with
its Wankel dreams and
launched the two-rotor
GS Biorotor model in
1973 – but it proved to
be a nightmare with just
a few hundred sold . . .
and Citroën was forced to
buy those back in order
to avoid the expense of
producing spare parts.

**Better late than never – the arrival of the GS in 1970 plugged a gap that had cost Citroën dear over time. This four-door family car belatedly slotted between the Ami and 2CV economy cars and the luxurious DS – a vital market segment where rivals had been cheerfully cleaning up since Citroën discontinued the famous Traction Avant in 1957.**

At least Citroën's response met the standards of technical innovation and excellence for which the company was famous. When launched, the GS may well have been the world's most technologically advanced set of new wheels, with great aerodynamics and numerous safety features. It was an instant hit with the car-buying public, too, confirming in the nicest possible way what Citroën had been missing for all those years.

The in-house styling was typically French – which is to say unlike anything else on the market. It was a fastback saloon with an enormous amount of boot space, the spare wheel having been cunningly placed on top of the engine. There were two trim levels – GS Club and the superior GS Pallas. A van and estate car were quickly added to the range, though a hatchback did not appear until the uprated GSA series arrived in 1979. If the GS had a fault, it was that all four engines offered were rather feeble for the job.

Unfortunately, Citroën had let things slide too far, despite the success of the GS. A number of factors combined to bankrupt the company in 1974 – the expensively aborted development of a Wankel engine, the effort of launching the GS, the cost of a new factory to build the CX replacement for the ageing DS and the catastrophic impact of the 1973 oil crisis. However, a shotgun marriage to Peugeot presided over by the French government saved the day.

# DATSUN 240Z

**COUNTRY OF ORIGIN:**
Japan

**FIRST MANUFACTURED:**
1970 (until 1978)

**ENGINE:**
2,393 cc Straight Six

**PERFORMANCE:**
Top speed of 125 mph
(201 km/h); 0–60 mph
(97 km/h) in 8.3 secs

**YOU SHOULD KNOW:**
To help ensure continuing
American interest in
the 240Z, Nissan ran an
imaginative programme
in the late 1990s whereby
the company purchased
as many cars as possible,
had them professionally
restored and then sold
them through dealerships.

It had various different designations, ranging from Fairlady Z to the S30 Nissan/Datsun, but most people seem happy to agree on Datsun 240Z. This was the first of the company's Z-series sports cars, designed by Yoshihiko Matsuo. The rear-wheel drive, fixed-head coupe had clean and simple fastback lines with a sloping rear hatch. The six-cylinder engine was teamed with four- or five-speed manual transmission (or three-speed automatic box), whilst the 240Z had independent suspension, front disc brakes and rear drums. Internal trim was excellent, with reclining bucket seats, full instrument pack, radio and wall-to-wall carpeting. Air conditioning was available as an optional extra.

Performance was first class, with impressive top speed, crisp handling, tenacious roadholding, comfortable ride quality and notable reliability, adding up to a refined sports car that delivered unheard-of value in the price bracket. It made the Datsun 240Z a massive international success with Nissan unable to keep up with demand.

The main export market was the USA, where Nissan introduced the Datsun 240Z in 1970 – breaking out of the stereotype that Japanese imports were all boxy economy cars. Keen pricing undercut sporty imports like Jaguar and Porsche, ensuring that the 240Z was a huge hit with the American car-buying public, with the car's profile raised by considerable success on the racetrack. Regular upgrades were made over the years to conform to tightening American regulations.

A modified 240ZG was introduced in 1971 to homologate the 240Z for Group 4 racing. The two models were very similar, though 240ZG was sold only in Japan and had modified bodywork, notably an extended nose. There were various other evolutions of the standard Datsun 240Z – the high-performance Z432 and Z432R, the 260Z and 280Z. These well-made sports cars all combine stylish good looks with excellent performance, and they're fast becoming collectable classics.

# DE TOMASO PANTERA

If anyone were foolish enough to claim that the De Tomaso Pantera (a Panther in England) came from any country but Italy, they would instantly be branded as a liar – this stylish flyer is quite clearly a quintessentially Italian sports car. But appearances can be deceptive. Beneath that wedge-shaped fastback body lurked a powerful Ford Cleveland V8 engine, so the Pantera represented a unique cross between cutting-edge Italian styling and American muscle-car performance. Introduced in 1970, it would remain in limited production for more than two decades, initially aided and abetted by a formal tie-up with Ford of America that sold Panteras through the Lincoln-Mercury network.

The design was by Ghia (a company also controlled by Alejandro de Tomaso), with American Tom Tjaarda taking the lead. Unlike its predecessor, the Mangusta with its conventional chassis, the Pantera was of all-steel monocoque construction, with a mid-engine powertrain layout. There was independent suspension all round and the 5.8 litre V8 was teamed with five-speed manual transmission. The bodies were fabricated by Vignale in Turin and Panteras were assembled at De Tomaso's Modena factory.

It all started rather well, with a thousand cars shipped in Year One. Shortcomings soon surfaced – the cabin was cramped and tended to overheat rapidly, the driving position was rather strange and build quality left much to be desired  but these were offset by a combination of blistering performance, Italian supercar prestige and a low ticket price. But it ended badly. Despite shifting around 6,000 Panteras in the USA by 1974, De Tomaso had paid little heed to upcoming regulation changes. Reworking the car to meet them would have been prohibitively expensive, and the oil crisis was dampening demand for greedy cars. No Panteras were exported to America thereafter, though they continued to be made and sold into European markets.

**COUNTRY OF ORIGIN:**
Italy

**FIRST MANUFACTURED:**
1970 (until 1992)

**ENGINE:**
5,763 cc V8

**PERFORMANCE:**
Top speed of 159 mph (km/h); 0–60 mph (97 km/h) in 5.5 secs

**YOU SHOULD KNOW:**
Build quality of early Panteras wasn't great – a triumph of style over substance – and celebrity owner Elvis Presley once became so frustrated when his yellow Pantera wouldn't start that he blasted it with a gun.

# FORD ESCORT MEXICO

**COUNTRY OF ORIGIN:**
UK

**FIRST MANUFACTURED:**
1970 (until 1974)

**ENGINE:**
1,599 cc OHV Straight
Four

**PERFORMANCE:**
Top speed of 100 mph
(161 km/h); 0–50 mph
(80 km/h) in 7.9 secs

**YOU SHOULD KNOW:**
The Mk 2 Escort Mexico
was produced between
1975 and 1978 and
is much rarer than its
predecessor, having to
compete with the Escort
1600 Sport and the pokey
Escort RS2000 – just 2,500
examples were built at
Saarlouis in West Germany.

**One of the clever evolutions of the Ford Escort Mk 1 was the Mexico road car. The works team's Ford Escort RS1600s won the Daily Mirror World Cup Rally and also finished third, fifth and sixth. The winning car was driven by Hannu Mikkola and Gunnar Palm who conquered a gruelling 16,000 mi (25,750 km) course through Europe and South America, starting at London's Wembley Stadium in mid-April and finishing in Mexico City during late May.**

This extraordinary event attracted massive public interest, and Ford was a past master at turning motor-racing victories into hard cash by selling road cars that exploited the cachet of competition success. It was therefore no surprise to anyone when the distinctive Escort Mexico started appearing in showrooms up and down Britain. In fact, this custom version wasn't really so very different from any old Escort Mk 1, but that didn't stop it becoming a popular buy with dedicated motorsports enthusiasts.

The Escort Mexico did have the robust Ford Kent OHV engine, and shared the competition RS1600's strengthened two-door body shell, plus Rallye Sport suspension and brakes. Buyers obviously wanted to trumpet the fact that they had a special car, so the Mexico sported bucket seats and wide body stripes that contrasted with the rest of the paintwork. Extras like alloy wheels and four rather ostentatiously covered rally-style spotlamps on the front usually completed the impressive picture.

Escort Mexicos have become very desirable amongst those who like to own, maintain and drive collectable British cars from the 1970s. They are affordable, robust, easy to work on and still drive well. And with fewer than 10,000 produced during the four-year production run, the Mexico stands out from the large crowd of Escort Mk 1s that have dodged the scrapyard.

# FORD GRANADA MK I

**COUNTRY OF ORIGIN:**
Germany/UK

**FIRST MANUFACTURED:**
1972 (until 1977)

**ENGINE:**
Various, from 1,699 cc V4
to 4,942 cc V8

**PERFORMANCE:**
With 3 l engine – top
speed of 111 mph
(179 km/h); 0–50 mph

**YOU SHOULD KNOW:**
If the car's the star, the
Ford Granada's finest
hour was *The Sweeney*,
that tough 1970s TV cop
show that saw Inspector
Jack Regan and Sergeant
George Carter of Scotland
Yard's Flying Squad
pursuing assorted villains
all over London with the
help of a succession of
seriously abused but ever-
willing Granadas.

**The Ford Granada was launched in 1972 as a large executive saloon and/or capacious family car, replacing both the Zephyr and Zodiac in the UK and Taunus 20M and 26M in Europe. It was a truly European production number, being made both at Dagenham in the United Kingdom and Cologne in Germany.**

To add to the complexity of an apparently simple tale, entry-level Mk I models were badged as Ford Consuls until 1975, when they all became Granadas. In 1976 British production ended, leaving Germany to carry on alone. There was a choice of seven engines, some available in the UK only, some available in Europe only and some shared by both. There were four body styles – two- and four-door saloons, a two-door coupe and a five-door estate car. Some variations were not sold in the UK (like the fastback coupe with 'Coke bottle' styling), though a revised coupe was sold in the UK, but only as a Ghia option. Clear as mud!

Despite the Granada being yet another typically complex Ford model offering, the bottom line was simple enough – Ford had created another pleasingly designed, well-built car that went down a storm with the public and quickly became the sturdy mainstay of many a commercial fleet, hire car business, taxi operator, undertaker and police force.

The Granada Mk II appeared in 1977, with straight-line design and a square look. This lasted until 1985 when the Mk III appeared, though this was really a different car – called the Ford Scorpio everywhere but the UK and Ireland, where the Granada name was so potent that it was retained for the new model. There's no doubting the affection in which the Granada is held – there are well-supported owners' clubs and thousands of weekend drivers dedicated to keeping the Granada legend rolling.

# FORD TORINO GT CONVERTIBLE

One of the hardest tasks in American life during the 20th century must have been choosing a new car – especially a Ford. American manufacturers in general and Ford in particular delighted in being cavalier with the use of model names and loved offering endless permutations that must have left potential buyers with spinning heads. Nothing illustrates the point better than the Ford Torino.

In 1968 and 1969 the Torino was an upmarket sub series within the intermediate Ford Fairlane range. In 1970 the Torino became Ford's intermediate car with the Fairlane becoming the sub series. There were 13 models, five engine options, three transmission packages – and that's before even thinking about colour choice. Ah well, tens of thousands of happy campers managed to make a decision in the end, so perhaps Ford-buying wasn't that hard after all.

Certainly the top choice for someone looking to join the performance party was the 1970 Torino GT Convertible. This wide, low machine was sleekly styled with a distinctive egg-crate grille with hideaway headlights and full-width rear light panel. The comfortable cabin sported a raked windscreen, bucket front seats and simple dashboard. The really good bit was the great big lump under the bonnet – a 7 litre Cobra Jet engine. This put the GT Convertible right at the top of the muscle-car class at a time when these sporting bruisers were at the height of their popularity, before the impending oil crisis banished them to the world of happy memories.

With buyers spoiled for muscle-car choice, the Torino GT Convertible sold just under 4,000 units, making this speedy ragtop the rarest Ford intermediate. Today, scarcity value coupled with the fact that the GT was a terrific car in the first place has made this an ultra-collectable '70s icon.

**COUNTRY OF ORIGIN:**
USA

**FIRST MANUFACTURED:**
1970 (until 1971)

**ENGINE:**
Various, from 4.9 l (302 cid) to 7.0 l (429 cid) V8

**PERFORMANCE:**
With 7.0 l engine – top speed of 128 mph (206 km/h); 0–60 mph (97 km/h) in 6 secs

**YOU SHOULD KNOW:**
One of the more unusual options on the Ford Torino GT Convertible was a pair of broad reflective laser stripes that ran back along the front wings and across the doors before terminating, giving extraordinary colour effects as the light played on them.

# HONDA PRELUDE

**COUNTRY OF ORIGIN:**
Japan

**FIRST MANUFACTURED:**
1978 (until 1982) (First
generation)

**ENGINE:**
1,602 cc or 1,751 cc
Straight Four

**PERFORMANCE:**
With 1.6 l engine – top
speed 98 mph (158
km/h); 0-60 mph (97
km/h)

**YOU SHOULD KNOW:**
Early Preludes remain
great fun to drive and
are becoming quite
collectable, but it's
important to look for
a solid example that
is rust-free (a generic
problem) and has manual
transmission (automatic
transmission saps
performance).

Throughout the 1960s Honda's quirky little S800 sports car had provided a touch of performance frivolity against the solid backdrop of the well-built economy cars that were the Japanese company's stock in trade. The 1970s proved the value of that sober approach, establishing Honda as a major international exporter, but with that job safely done the Prelude was introduced in 1978 to compete with the successful Toyota Celica and broaden a Honda product range that then consisted of the sub-compact Civic and the mid-sized Accord.

The design of this neat two-door notchback coupe reflected that of the other two models, though the Prelude also had distinct echoes of the Mercedes-Benz SL. It was described by Honda as a sports compact and one unusual feature was the standard sunroof. Another was found on the dashboard, which featured a concentric speedometer/ tachometer combo, with the former encircling the latter.

First generation 2+2 Preludes had excellent build quality, good fuel consumption and were a pleasure to drive, though back-seat accommodation was cramped. They came with one of two overhead-cam four-cylinder engines (depending on which country they were sold in), the larger of which came out of the Honda Accord. Drive options were initially a five-speed manual gearbox or two-speed Hondamatic automatic transmission, though a more conventional four-speed automatic soon appeared. The Prelude had independent suspension all round and rack-and-pinion steering, giving excellent roadholding ability and nimble handling. It's fair to say that performance was brisk rather than outstanding, with early cars not quite capable of hitting the 'ton' and not therefore appealing to the sportiest of drivers.

The first generation was only produced until 1982, but set the scene for future progress. Thereafter four more generations would carry the Prelude triumphantly into the 21st century.

# LAMBORGHINI SILHOUETTE

**Rare as hen's teeth? Sure is! If you find one of these in a Palladian shed at the bottom of someone's country estate, it will increase the number of Lamborghini Silhouettes known to exist from 31 to 32 (out of an original production run of just 54 cars). These two-door, two-seater coupes had a removable targa lid for those who liked the wind in their hair, making this the first Lambo open-top. It was a refined development of the not-very-good Lamborghini Urraco 2+2 coupe designed by Bertone to compete with Ferrari's Dino and the Porsche 911, produced throughout the 1970s.**

Bertone also styled the Silhouette, which was an attempt to improve on the Urraco. The Silhouette had much softer lines than the angular Urraco and was altogether kinder on the eye. It also had revised suspension and a more powerful engine, making it lighter and faster. But the two models were so close in terms of what they offered the buying public that it hardly seems surprising that there was room for only one in the Lambo product range – if there is a surprise involved, it's that the Silhouette failed to displace the Urraco.

If the Silhouette failed, it was because the car had been created to target the US market, which required modifications like the fitting of a catalytic converter and various regulation requirements like plastic bumpers. This was a good car, but for good reasons (like poor build quality and the company's high-profile financial difficulties) American buyers regarded Lamborghini with suspicion and the project died. Still, all the effort that went into creating so few Silhouettes wasn't wasted – it contributed mightily to the altogether more successful Lamborghini Jalpa, launched in 1981 and destined for a seven-year run that would see over 400 units produced.

**COUNTRY OF ORIGIN:**
Italy

**FIRST MANUFACTURED:**
1976 (until 1979)

**ENGINE:**
2,996 cc V8

**PERFORMANCE:**
Top speed of 158 mph (255 km/h); 0–60 mph (97 km/h) in 7.6 secs

**YOU SHOULD KNOW:**
One concept car based on the Lamborghini Silhouette was built by Bertone and shown at the 1979 Geneva Motor Show – it was an elegant two-seater roadster that unfortunately never went into production.

# LANCIA STRATOS HF

**COUNTRY OF ORIGIN:**
Italy

**FIRST MANUFACTURED:**
1972 (until 1974)

**ENGINE:**
2,418 cc V6

**PERFORMANCE:**
Top speed of 143 mph
(230 km/h); 0–60 mph
(97 km/h) in 6 secs

**YOU SHOULD KNOW:**
One avid collector likes
the Lancia Stratos so
much that he has around
a dozen of the original
cars – and became
professionally involved
in the project to create a
revival NewStratos that
culminated in the debut
of a brilliant concept
car at the Geneva Motor
Show in 2005.

**The Lancia Stratos HF (HF = High Fidelity) was developed for the purpose of rallying, and very successful this extraordinary machine proved to be. Lancia had enjoyed great success on the rally circuit during the 1960s, but the Fulvia coupe was starting to struggle and a new contender was required.**

Happily, the recent takeover of Lancia by Fiat (who also bought a half share in Ferrari) provided the ideal opportunity to create something special. Bertone had presented a stunning Stratos Zero concept car based on the Fulvia at the 1970 Turin Motor Show, and this provided both a name and starting point for the new rally car that would be styled and built by Bertone. Out went Fulvia foundations and in came the midships drive train from Ferrari's Dino 246 GT. This was complemented with purpose-built independent suspension, crisp rack-and-pinion steering and disc brakes on all four wheels.

Around this potent mechanical package Bertone wrapped a short, wide coupe body with flared wheel arches, a louvered wedge of a bonnet and aircraft-style cockpit with wraparound glass – surely one of the most striking designs ever from the Grugliasco-based carrozzeria. No more than the 500-odd examples needed to homologate the Stratos HF for racing were built, and those that went for road use immediately acquired cult classic status. They made no concessions to private buyers, with strictly practical interiors and the edgy handling that made them fearsome rally cars.

The Stratos HF duly swept all before it, winning the World Rally Championship in 1974, 1975 and 1976, whilst also securing a notable consecutive three-timer in the prestigious Monte Carlo Rally from 1975. It would continue to win rallies in the hands of privateers into the 1980s, after Fiat pulled the factory plug in favour of its own-name Fiat 131 rally car.

# LOTUS ESPRIT

The long-running success story that was the Esprit started as a production spin-off from a concept car designed by Giorgetto Giugiaro. It was among the first of his renowned 'folded paper' cars, a clean-lined, sharp-angled wedge in the forefront of fashion. Colin Chapman, with the luxury supercar market in mind, immediately snapped up the design for Lotus. When the Esprit first appeared in 1976 it was somewhat disparagingly labelled a 'poor man's Ferrari' but it soon acquired snob appeal by appearing as James Bond's vehicle in *The Spy Who Loved Me* (1977) epitomizing British seventies glamour – powerful, exclusive, stylish, and (not least) a lot more reliable than a Ferrari. Altogether 10,675 Esprits were produced over the course of its 28-year run.

The Esprit S1 was a mid-engine, high-performance two-door coupe with a GRP (glass-reinforced plastic) body built on a steel backbone chassis, weighing in at less than 1000 kg (2200 lbs). Lotus used pre-existing parts to keep costs down and fitted a Lotus 907 lightweight alloy 2 litre engine with twin cams and 16 valves. From the start the car was praised for its superb handling, though there was the occasional gripe about insufficient power, especially in the USA where the engine was downrated to comply with emissions regulations.

Over the years, the Lotus Esprit went through several incarnations with a couple of major revamps. The body was restyled with rounder features in 1987 and was remodelled again in 1993, and throughout the 28 years of its production, continual mechanical improvements were made to enhance performance. All these tweakings have added to the original Giugiaro model's legendary status. The very last model was the 1999 Sport 350, which could do 0–60 mph (97 km/h) in less than 5 secs, but it is the 1976 Giugiaro S1 design that will be remembered as the iconic supercar of its era.

**COUNTRY OF ORIGIN:**
UK

**FIRST MANUFACTURED:**
1976 (until 2004)

**ENGINE:**
1,973 cc, 2,174 cc Slant Four (1976–96)

**PERFORMANCE:**
Top speed around 130 mph (209 km/h); 0–60 mph (97km/h) in 8 secs

**YOU SHOULD KNOW:**
Some models are extremely rare. To celebrate Lotus's success on the racetrack, an exclusive gold and black JPS (John Player Special) model was produced in a run of less than 150, and a mere 45 special red, blue and chrome 'Essex' versions of the 1980 turbocharged Esprit were made.

# PLYMOUTH DUSTER 340

**COUNTRY OF ORIGIN:**
USA

**FIRST MANUFACTURED:**
1970 (until 1976)

**ENGINE:**
5.6 l (340 cid) OHV V8

**PERFORMANCE:**
Top speed of 127 mph (205 km/h); 0–60 mph (97 km/h) in 6.2 secs

**YOU SHOULD KNOW:**
The name 'Duster' was intended (allegedly) to suggest the 'dust' you left in your speedy wake. Even more questionable monikers were given to subsequent versions, including the 'Twister' (it was: it looked exactly like a dolled-up 340, without the powerful 340 engine), the 'Space Duster' and the 'Feather Duster'.

The US motor corporations' 1960s philosophy of 'planned obsolescence' meant that every one of them felt compelled to challenge every model of every series produced by a rival. Intense competition combined with rapid technical evolution often led to 'junkyard styling' – creating a 'brand new' car out of existing, disparate components. The Plymouth Duster is proof that it could work, and brilliantly. With no money for a sporty, two-door compact to replace the Barracuda (the performance version of a Plymouth Valiant now elevated to a series of its own) Plymouth took the Valiant A-body platform, re-styled the rear as a semi-fastback, dropped in a hot, 340 cu in LA-series V8 – long proven for its power and reliability in Darts and early Barracudas – and hit their market bullseye.

The Plymouth Duster 340 made real muscle available to the masses. Lighter, more spacious and faster than much more expensive cars, the 340 was the performance leader of the Duster range, all of which shared its characteristics in proportion to their engine option. Plymouth's 'Rapid Transit System' allotted it the full armoury of performance enhancers at little extra cost – but apart from a pistol-grip for the four-speed manual option, dual exhausts and some discreet decals, there was nothing obvious to advertise the Duster 340's blazing capability.

You just had to drive one. The suspension was a little stiff, the ride punishing, and the economy trim devoid of excess comfort. On the other hand, it rode corners with contempt, and powered away with a throaty snarl. Even years later, when high speeds were curbed by the emissions rules, the 1970 Duster 340 still gave you more bang for your buck than its dozens of 'editions' or imitators from other companies. Quite probably, it was the most successful big 'something' ever to come from nothing at all.

# PONTIAC FIREBIRD TRANS AM

It was John Z DeLorean who had brought the Firebird to the American public in 1967. Super-sensitive to the steady clamour for muscle cars, his vision extended to fostering the Firebird's Trans Am performance version – but no sooner had its teething problems been solved for the launch of the Trans Am's second generation (known as the 1970-1/2 model), than the new Federal emissions regulations drew the fangs of every muscle monster on US highways. Pontiac's mega-punchy Super Duty 455 V8 engine, intended for the 1973 Trans Am, was a damp squib. Although it was constructed so that it could easily be converted for high-performance racing, its massive power was de-tuned to a street-legal whimper. Pontiac decided to kill it for 1975 – the year they re-drew the Trans Am's speedometer dial to show a maximum speed of just 100 mph (160 km/h) instead of its previous, 'Oh-my-lord!' 160 mph (258 km/h). The 1975 Firebird Trans Am arrived as a glorious, snarling, but apparently emasculated thug: the enormous firebird decal splashed across the hood was known as the 'Screamin' Chicken'.

Everyone wanted one. By 1975 it was the last muscle car around. Its engine options, the standard 400 V8 and the big block 455 V8 (re-introduced in the mid-year as the 'HO455', as carried by the sedate Pontiac Bonneville, but a big block just the same), were authentic, and so was every other potentially racing component. Pontiac contributed by improving visibility and handling. If they couldn't sell it as a rocket, they could and did make sure that within the legal limits the Trans Am was the last remaining tiger, poised, lethally quick at low speeds, and joyous to drive.

The Firebird Trans Am is most famous in the black and gold livery of the 1976 Limited Edition. It had gold Honeycomb wheels, grille, steering wheel spokes, body stripes and badging. A very few also had black chrome exhaust tips, and are relatively very valuable. Rising prices mean you now have to beware of clones for these and for all Firebird Trans Ams of the period.

**COUNTRY OF ORIGIN:**
USA

**FIRST MANUFACTURED:**
Second Generation 1970 (until 1981)

**ENGINE:**
7.5 l (455 cid) V8 (with catalytic converter)

**PERFORMANCE:**
Top speed around 120 mph (193 km/h) according to engine tuning; 0–60 mph (97 km/h) in 7.8 secs

**YOU SHOULD KNOW:**
The 1975 Trans Am has been called the 'Soul Survivor' of the 'Big Cube Birds'. Treasure it – it's the real deal.

For Release Monday September 16, 1974

# PORSCHE 911 TURBO

**COUNTRY OF ORIGIN:**
Germany

**FIRST MANUFACTURED:**
1975 (until 1989)

**ENGINE:**
2,993 cc Flat Six Turbo

**PERFORMANCE:**
Top speed of 153 mph
(246 km/h); 0–60 mph
(97 km/h) in 5.2 secs

**YOU SHOULD KNOW:**
Following the
unforeseen success of
the Porsche 911 Turbo,
every subsequent 911
generation has featured
a turbocharged version
distinguished by its
roadgoing modifications
of authentic race car
technology.

**The first production turbocharged Porsche 911 (known as the Porsche 930 in America) made its debut at the Paris Motor Show in 1974. It was Germany's fastest road-going sports car.**

Though turbochargers had long been used in motor sport, the 911 Turbo was the first production car to tame the beast. Its genesis was almost accidental. Porsche disbelieved its own ability to sell the 400 GT sports cars it was required to produce for GT racing accreditation. There weren't 400 racing drivers to buy them. Instead, the company installed creature comforts and safety measures well beyond the demands of street legality, and aimed at a production run of 1000. Even after a decade of the 911, the new Turbo made experienced Porsche enthusiasts gasp. Every aspect of the technical and design expertise the company had gleaned from its successes in motor sport had been put to good use.

The 911 Turbo body-shape was totally distinctive. The wheel arches were flared to fit the wider tyres; and the rear spoiler was so unfeasibly big it became known as the 'whale tail' (in the early models – when it was later shrunk, the nickname changed to 'tea-tray'). If you learned to manage the alarming turbo lag, and to control the quite stupendous transfer of power from the wheels to the road, the acceleration was moon-shot exhilarating. The car satisfied the new US regulations on emissions and impact bumpers, but seemed to defy them by opposing convention. Other cars got heavier and slower. The Porsche 911 Turbo used the new minimum weight for GT racers as a convenient guide, and produced power not just to compensate, but to take flight. For a 3 litre engine, its performance stretched credulity – and driving it is one of the greatest thrills you can have outside an aircraft.

# RANGE ROVER CLASSIC

If ever there was an accidental success story it's that of the Range Rover Classic. It was introduced in 1970 for the English county set, in the belief that a robust four-wheel drive vehicle that was more comfortable than the utilitarian Land Rover would go down well with those who rode horses, shot birds, hunted, attended agricultural shows and were always surrounded by wet dogs. As such, the first Range Rovers had vinyl seats and plastic dashboards that could be hosed down after green wellies tramped mud into the car.

Early two-door Range Rovers were built to deliver real cross-country ability. They had permanent four-wheel drive with low range for off-road work. Rover's V8 petrol engine was teamed with a four-speed manual gearbox. Advanced independent suspension offered coil springs all round with disc brakes front and back. To British Leyland's credit, they soon realized their new rural transport was appealing to a wider market, meeting the dual requirement of looking good and operating well both on and off the road.

This would mark the start of enhancement and uprating that would last for decades, resulting in the creation of the ultimate luxury SUV that European manufacturers like BMW, Volkswagen and Porsche eventually felt they had to challenge with their own awesome off-roaders primarily intended for imposing road use by wealthy drivers.

During the 1970s the Range Rover saw refinements like power steering introduced, but it was not until the early 1980s that significant change happened – including a four-door body and automatic transmission option. There were further style tweaks in the 1980s, plus innovations like the availability of diesel engines. A luxurious Vogue special edition was offered from 1983, and a stretched LSE model appeared in 1992. After 25 great years, second generation cars finally superseded the Range Rover Classic in 1996.

**COUNTRY OF ORIGIN:**
UK

**FIRST MANUFACTURED:**
1970 (until 1996)

**ENGINE:**
3,532 cc, 3,947 cc or 4,197 cc V8; 2,393 cc or 2,499 cc Straight Four Diesel; 2,495 cc Straight Four

**PERFORMANCE:**
With 3.5 l engine – top speed of 96 mph (154 km/h); 0–50 mph (80 km/h) in 11.1 secs

**YOU SHOULD KNOW:**
The series name was devised with the benefit of hindsight – Range Rover Classic was the tag used for first generation cars that briefly continued to be built alongside second generation cars in the 1990s, and Rover liked the name so much it retro-fitted the 'Classic' designation to all first generation Range Rovers.

# RELIANT BOND BUG

**COUNTRY OF ORIGIN:**
UK

**FIRST MANUFACTURED:**
1970 (until 1974)

**ENGINE:**
701 cc OHV Straight Four

**PERFORMANCE:**
Top speed of 75 mph
(121 km/h)

**YOU SHOULD KNOW:**
When a new 750 cc Reliant
Robin was launched in
1973, the Bond Bug 700s
were dropped in favour of
750 E and ES versions.
Apart from the larger
engine, these were more or
less identical to the earlier
models. It is estimated that
there are fewer than 900
Bond Bugs of any sort still
in existence.

The Reliant Robin, Regal and Rialto three-wheeler cars have a certain
air of eccentricity, a peculiarly British charm that is inextricably linked
with 'characters' like Mr Bean, or Del Boy in the TV series *Only Fools
and Horses*. Reliant was keen to dissociate three-wheelers from
this rather whimsical image and wanted to promote them instead
as sporty, fun cars for the young. With this in mind, the company
commissioned Tom Karen of Ogle Design to work on a prototype. When,
in 1969, Reliant took over its rival, the Bond Motor Co, it immediately
stopped production of Bond cars and used the Bond factory solely to
manufacture its own Ogle car. Although the Ogle was soon moved to
Reliant's own workshops, the company marketed its new model under
the Bond name.

The Bond Bug was a triangular fibreglass wedge built on a
modified Reliant Regal chassis with the same mechanics and 0.7
litre part alloy engine. Instead of doors, the top of the car (including
the side frames) was a hinged overhead canopy for people to climb
in and out like pilots. The Bug came in three versions: the 700 – a
very basic model without sidescreens; the 700E, which made slightly
more concessions to comfort; and the 700 ES, a de luxe version with
a higher compression engine, racing steering wheel, mud flaps and
wing mirrors, and the generous inclusion of a spare wheel. In terms
of power, the Bug matched a small four-wheeler but it was pricier
than the Mini, which meant it was bound to fail. Only 2,268 Bugs
were built (all painted a virulent shade of tangerine except for the six
white versions that were made as a special promotion for Rothman's
cigarettes). Unsurprisingly, this quirky little car now has a fanatical
following and is much sought after.

# RENAULT-ALPINE A310 V6

Renault's close association with Alpine was rooted in a shared racing philosophy. Until 1971 the collaboration was restricted to nimble, rear-engined coupes that broke easily and lacked both space and comfort. They were terrific for racing or rallying, but not a lot of fun for normal driving. The advent of the Alpine-Renault A310 in 1971 changed the perception of both companies, and the driving public. It was longer, wider, and roomier than its predecessors, though still conceived to the same Alpine-Renault formula of a rear-mounted engine set into a steel skeleton chassis and a separate fibreglass body. It was also faster, but unreliable. Only in 1976, when Renault had bought Alpine outright to redeem the company from financial catastrophe, did the A310 fulfil its destiny. With its new, 90-degree V6 engine, it became the only serious challenger to the Porsche 911 as the fastest rear-engine production car in the world.

It looked the part. A single aerodynamic line swept up and over from the front windscreen – but every curve was bitten off by a geometrically severe, angular ridge. The A310 V6 needed its new, little black rear spoiler to control its new capability; and with the wheel rims newly styled to look like the old, four-inch, reel-to-reel tape drums, it resembled a mobile, flattened bullet. Inside it retained Alpine's excellent driving position, but Renault now added a wholly unexpected level of comfort. It had grown up in every way, and it sold.

The A310 V6 soaked up punishment and it was reliable, but it was still a relatively lightweight, rear-engined sports car with every reason to fishtail when pedal hit metal. That, and Guy Frequelin's victory in the 1977 French Rallye, made it specially attractive to a younger and mostly male generation. The car's acceleration might snap your neck, but it was enormous fun.

**COUNTRY OF ORIGIN:**
France

**FIRST MANUFACTURED:**
1976 (until 1984)

**ENGINE:**
2,664 cc V6

**PERFORMANCE:**
Top speed of 137 mph (221 km/h); 0–60 mph (97 km/h) in 7.5 secs

**YOU SHOULD KNOW:**
The A310's V6 engine was a joint development between Peugeot, Renault and Volvo. Throughout the late 1970s and 1980s it powered dozens of different marques and models, including the DeLorean.

# ROLLS-ROYCE CORNICHE

**COUNTRY OF ORIGIN:**
UK

**FIRST MANUFACTURED:**
1971 (until 1982 coupe;
until 1987 convertible)

**ENGINE:**
6,750 cc V8

**PERFORMANCE:**
Top speed of 125 mph
(201 km/h); 0–60 mph
(97 km/h) in 10.2 secs

**YOU SHOULD KNOW:**
When Rolls-Royce first
experimented with
what would become the
Corniche, the celebrated
coachbuilder James Young
designed his own version
alongside that of MPW. It
never went into production,
and the few Rollers made
to Young's imaginative
genius are among the rarest
of the rare.

**The Corniche had a late baptism in 1971. The monocoque construction of the 1965 Silver Shadow range made it virtually impossible for traditional coachbuilders to practice their calling: there was no separate chassis on which to fit panel work.**

Rolls-Royce faced the problem by increasing their stake in Mulliner Park Ward (MPW), already their in-house specialist partner, in order to develop a two-door coupe (1966) and two-door convertible (1967) based on the Silver Shadow. By 1971, with Rolls-Royce in the throes of splitting the company into separate divisions to solve a financial crisis, the time was ripe for the publicity splash of a new model. Both coupe and convertible were revamped and powered up, and launched as the Rolls-Royce (and, of course, Bentley) Corniche.

MPW learned how to press panels and weld them to the Silver Shadow floor-pan. After technical assembly by Rolls-Royce in Crewe, which included the major modifications that justified the Corniche as an independent series, MPW completed the cars back in London. The hand-built quality showed, even if the 1971 'production' car didn't look very different. The sumptuous luxury extended to the finest detail, like the power-operated soft top which, alone, took as long as two weeks to make, fit and adjust. The bodyline still had the dip over the rear wheel arch that suggested the sporty monster sitting, poised on its athletic haunches.

You couldn't see many internal changes, but you could drive them. The Corniche wasn't about top speed, but about shifting its magnificent bulk with incomparably smooth ease, no matter what kind of road, throughout the low, mid and upper-mid ranges. Its stylish, measured glide became the benchmark of comfortable cruising. It was, literally as well as figuratively, designed for the Corniche. Monte Carlo and California absolutely adored it.

# ROVER SD1

**COUNTRY OF ORIGIN:**
UK

**FIRST MANUFACTURED:**
1976 (until 1986)

**ENGINE:**
3,528 cc V8

**PERFORMANCE:**
Top speed of 130 mph
(208 km/h); 0–60 mph
(97 km/h) in 7.7 secs

**YOU SHOULD KNOW:**
In its lifetime, the SD1
was never marketed
by that name. The
14 different versions
(including the Vanden
Plas and Vitesse of
the 1980s) were
identified by
their engines.

**The Rover SD1 of 1976 inspired either ecstasy or apoplexy. As a member of the new British Leyland group, Rover now had major in-house competitors like Triumph and Jaguar, with whom it expected to share parts and develop discrete elements of the company's extended range. It also had a brand-new factory of its own to produce the fruits of its Specialist Division – but that couldn't happen until the Division had learned the lessons of compromise from its early efforts.**

The SD1 went into production on a wave of infectious optimism shared by industry critics and the public. It was fast and safe – crash-tested, crumple-zoned, ergonomically brilliant and innovative. With the ever-versatile and seemingly endless tuneability of the 3.5 litre Buick V8 (though perhaps after more than a decade it could be called Rover's own), it made the most of its low weight. People spoke admiringly of its sporty handling, composed ride and modern design. It looked a little like a Ferrari Daytona (check the front end light assembly) with a hatchback designed by Pininfarina; and until Rover introduced a range of smaller engines some time later, it had a performance to match. The executive market for which it was intended glowed with reflected glory at its racing and rallying success. Mrs Thatcher's Cabinet Ministers all wanted one, and it was photographed underneath Concorde's needle nose as the 1976 Car of the Year.

Unfortunately, the new icon of postwar British car design was a manufacturing crock. Initial reaction had made favourable comparison with Jaguar and its ilk. Instead of upgrading the SD1, its price and build quality to match, Rover tried to give it a more 'economy' feel. Simultaneously, the first batch of cars began to rust, break down and fall apart. Conceived as a world contender, the SD1's future literally rotted away.

# SAAB 99 TURBO

The actual Saab 99 Turbo launch car was an almost iridescent pearl white. It stunned the 1977 Frankfurt Auto Show. The unique body colour dramatized Saab's revolutionary solution to every auto manufacturer's problem of maintaining performance in the teeth of increasingly strict emissions controls, in Europe and more importantly, the USA. The new model wasn't just turbocharged for high speed like a sports car. It was turbo tuned for low speed torque in a proper sedan intended for daily, including urban, driving. After a decade of upping the power of the Saab 99's Triumph Slant Four engine (always suitably doctored by Saab's own Zenith-Stromberg CD carburetor), and brief tests using the Triumph Stag's V8, Saab was the first manufacturer to dare this holy grail. Turbocharged cars (like the Porsche 911) were notoriously difficult to handle at low or variable speeds – but Saab devised the first 'closed loop' catalyst system, monitored by an oxygen sensor, to control the fuel injection on its existing 2 litre engine.

The Saab 99 Turbo's acceleration pattern had never been seen. There was no jerk when the Turbo cut in at just 1500 rpm, and though it went faster and faster as the boost increased, the really dramatic effects were on overtaking and mini-sprints from street or highway corner to corner. The 99 Turbo shrugged off the kudos of accelerating from a standing start and substituted stability and inspired handling at practical mid-speeds. It was a fundamental change of attitude, and brilliant engineering.

The Saab 99 Turbo wasn't pretty or even fashionable. It was striking in a 'jolie laide' kind of way, right down to its extraordinary 'Inca' alloy wheels. First-time drivers stepped out, puzzled by their own ease and comfort with such power at their disposal. They stayed struck, and delighted.

**COUNTRY OF ORIGIN:**
Sweden

**FIRST MANUFACTURED:**
1977 (until 1980)

**ENGINE:**
1,985 cc turbocharged Slant Four

**PERFORMANCE:**
Top speed of 123 mph (198 km/h); 0–60 mph (97 km/h) in 8.9 secs

**YOU SHOULD KNOW:**
The Saab 99 Turbo was designed as a three-door 'Combi coupe' – among the first family cars to be turbocharged since the 1963–4 Oldsmobile Turbo Jetfire – but in due course two (only) turbo limousine versions were produced (as part of a long wheelbase special edition), and called the Saab 99 Turbo Finlandia.

1980s

# BMW M3

**COUNTRY OF ORIGIN:**
Germany

**FIRST MANUFACTURED:**
1986 (until 1992)

**ENGINE:**
2,302 cc Straight Four

**PERFORMANCE:**
Top speed of 143 mph
(230 km/h); 0-60 mph
(97 km/h) in 7.6 secs

**YOU SHOULD KNOW:**
Homologation specials
continued to appear
regularly as the E30 M3
race car was improved.
The road car just
became more and more
impressive, too; and its
popularity means you
still see (and hear) them
frequently at anything
from events to shows
to the supermarket.
No other race car ever
proved so genuinely
versatile, and such fun.

The BMW M3 is the most successful example ever of racing homologation creating an internationally-acclaimed road car. Its genealogy is straightforward. The M3 is a high performance version of the BMW 3-series compact, based on the E30; but its racing engine has a broad pedigree in BMW motorsport. The engine's basic block layout derives from the M10 familiar from the earlier BMW 2002 and 320 series, overbored to resemble the specifications of the BMW M88 Straight Six. In fact the M3 uses a four-cylinder engine because it derived from their Formula One engine of the day. The roll-call of influences is an evolutionary history of motorsport – and no car has added to it more than the M3, which has won more road races than any other model in history, and dominated Group A Touring Car racing throughout its years of production.

The M3 doesn't look especially like the E30 whose soul it shares. Only the hood and roof panels are interchangeable, and the M3's obviously improved aerodynamics are emphasized rather stylishly by the famous 'box flared' fenders essential to accommodate the wider track and wheels. The stiffer body shell permits improvements to the suspension and power steering that, combined with the five-speed Getrag gearbox, add up to truly extraordinary road handling characteristics which more than compensate for a slight loss of top end speed. The trade press fairly worshipped it. Classic & Sports Car spoke lyrically of 'its beautifully balanced chassis, razor sharp steering, and sweet singin' twin-cam four'. Car and Driver described in awe how 'the M3 leaps through corners like a cat, its feisty engine spinning and spitting until you snatch another gear or the rev limiter grabs it by the tail'.

The M3, everyone without exception agrees, is the ultimate definition of 'a driver's car'.

# CHEVROLET CITATION

**History was firm but fair to the Chevrolet Citation. It was a great car, the biggest-selling car in America in its first year; but when it got found out, it had to pay the price of public failure.**

General Motors' new generation of modern, front-wheel drive cars was known as the 'X-family'. Pontiac, Oldsmobile, Buick and Chevrolet all created models that shared a basic mechanical layout – an efficient unibody with a transverse four- or six-cylinder engine – but Chevrolet offered more body styles of its come-hither Citation. Olds and Buick kept the four-door sedans for themselves, while the Citation had the three- and hugely popular five-door hatchback.

The Citation was a generational change, of car and market. For example, it was much shorter than the compact Nova it replaced, but had much more room inside; and to direct its appeal more specifically to a younger buyer, Chevrolet gave its coupe and three-door hatch added value as the X-11 models, with a considerably improved suspension package (so the said buyer could kid him or herself that he or she was being thoughtful) and 'bold exterior graphics' (beads and Manhattan come to mind). It wasn't so very different from other Citations, but then they were very good cars to begin with.

The point is that with targeted marketing proving so successful, the smug manufacturers became a bit careless. The Citation's transmission hose was liable to leak, and a number of engine fires prompted the recall of 225,000 cars. It was the first of many, until the Citation became one of the most recalled cars in history. Beefing up the X-11's engine stemmed the tide, but not for very long. Serious faults kept surfacing, reinforcing the sense of waste – and General Motors didn't really help themselves by sending specially engineered models for professional testing, deliberately concealing major problems that existed in the production vehicles.

In fact, the story of the Citation is worthy of Aesop.

**COUNTRY OF ORIGIN:**
USA

**FIRST MANUFACTURED:**
1980 (until 1985)

**ENGINE:**
2.8l (173 cid) V6

**PERFORMANCE:**
Top speed of 108 mph (174 km/h); 0–60mph (97 km/h) in 9.6 secs

**YOU SHOULD KNOW:**
It's a measure of how good the Citation looked when it was first introduced that *Motor Trend* magazine declared it to be 1980 'Car of the Year'.

# CHRYSLER LASER XT

**COUNTRY OF ORIGIN:**
USA

**FIRST MANUFACTURED:**
1985 (until 1986)

**ENGINE:**
2.2l (135 cid)
Turbocharged Straight
Four

**PERFORMANCE:**
Top speed of 115 mph
(185 km/h); 0–60 mph
(97 km/h) in 8.05 secs

**YOU SHOULD KNOW:**
The noiseless
disappearance of the
Chrysler Laser XT makes
a kind of sense since sales
of the Dodge Daytona
Turbo Z option, so similar
to the XT of 1986 (except
for the 'Swiss-cheese'
wheels), justified its
promotion as a model in
its own right. But logic
defies the resurrection
of the Laser name for
the 1990 Plymouth
Laser, Chrysler's tedious
collaborative variant of
Mitsubishi's Eclipse.

They were near-identical twins. Built on Chrysler's G platform (a shorter version of their old warhorse K platform), the new Dodge Daytona and Chrysler Laser launched simultaneously in 1984 to replace the Chrysler Conquest. Their restrained but eager styling made them two of the best-looking sports coupes ever made in America, an appreciation they have never relinquished. The Daytona already knew its target market of street performance-mad boy racers. The Laser was conceived as an upmarket version with the feel of European luxury comparable to increasingly popular imports. Initial performance matched aesthetics – but 1985 brought important mechanical changes that included the creation of the Laser XT version. Chrysler's own publicity never even mentioned the XT until 1986. By then, word of mouth had confirmed the XT's credentials as a supremely well-appointed powerhouse, an unlikely blend of menace and elegance that was beautiful.

It looked fast, standing still. The sharp rake of the nose was repeated in the windscreen, and balanced by the wraparound rear glass hatch with its attached spoiler. Louvres on the hood discreetly advertised the XT's turbo (an option on the basic Laser), but not the XT's improved power. Inside, a pleasuredrome of soft leather faced ranks of electronic dials and gauges (preferred over the digital instrument cluster of the XE, the XT's nearest relative); and hours of fun were guaranteed by disobeying the voice-activated warning system or the electronic 'navigator'. In fact just about the only extra you could add to the XT was a jeweller's hallmark.

The mystery is why Chrysler didn't make more of its masterpiece. It was fast, handled very well, and matched or outperformed anything else remotely near its price range. But it vanished, as it appeared, in silence. Finding one is like boarding a luxury Marie Celeste.

# DELOREAN DMC-12

**The story behind the DMC-12 is a scandalous tale of over-reaching ambition and ultimate ruination. Its production was surrounded by a murky aura of shady deals and sleaze, which involved Lotus Cars and the British government and ended in the arrest and trial of ex-Pontiac engineer John Z DeLorean on charges of cocaine smuggling.**

In the 1970s, DeLorean fell out with General Motors and trawled for high-profile backers to finance the setting up of his own company. His stated aim was to make an 'ethical' car. He commissioned Giugiaro, no less, to design a gullwinged-door body and sought technical inspiration from former GM engineer Bill Collins, who had a radical vision of using new materials technology to create a simple, super-safe high-performance car. But DeLorean abruptly sidelined Collins and talked Colin Chapman of Lotus into getting involved. The entire direction of the car changed. The DMC-12 ended up being built on the Esprit platform with a hotch-potch of proprietary parts and complicated electrics. Even though the car was targeted at the US market, De Lorean persuaded the British government into bank-rolling a purpose-built factory in Northern Ireland and after endless delays the DMC-12 finally started to roll off the production line.

The unpainted stainless steel body and gullwing doors looked slick enough but the rear-mounted 2.8 litre PRV (Peugeot-Renault-Volvo) V6 engine could only produce 130 bhp, the drivetrain was nothing to write home about and the retail price of $28,000 was more than twice as much as had been anticipated. The DMC-12 was underpowered and overpriced. Sales never matched expectations, and there were serious quality problems. DeLorean's reputation finally hit rock bottom when he was arrested by the FBI for cocaine smuggling. He was eventually found not guilty but by then his company was bankrupt and his name mud.

**COUNTRY OF ORIGIN:**
UK (Northern Ireland)

**FIRST MANUFACTURED:**
1981 (until 1982)

**ENGINE:**
2,849 cc V6

**PERFORMANCE:**
Top speed of 110 mph (177 km/h); 0–60 mph (97 km/h) in 10.5 secs

**YOU SHOULD KNOW:**
Two customized gold-plated versions of the DMC-12 were produced and a DMC-12 features as the time machine in the *Back to the Future* series of films. Around 9,000 DMC-12s were built, some of which were sent out of the factory in 1983, after DeLorean had gone bust, in a hopeless attempt to recoup British taxpayers' losses.

# FERRARI TESTAROSSA

**COUNTRY OF ORIGIN:**
Italy

**FIRST MANUFACTURED:**
1984 (until 1991)

**ENGINE:**
4,943 cc Flat Twelve

**PERFORMANCE:**
Top speed of 181 mph
(291 km/h); 0–60 mph
(97 km/h) in 5.2 secs

**YOU SHOULD KNOW:**
A unique, official, Testarossa Spider (convertible) was created as a present for Gianni Agnelli, then the head of Fiat. It was silver, with a white magnolia leather interior featuring a dark blue stripe above the black sills, and a silver Ferrari logo. Despite thousands of pleading requests, Ferrari refused to make any more.

With a pedigree as exalted and refined as any Arab stallion, the Ferrari Testarossa is one of the most beautiful and memorable cars ever made. Its name honoured the spirit of Ferrari's fabulous 1957 sports racer, the Testa Rossa ('Red Head'), and it replaced the 4.9 litre 512 BB (Berlinetta Boxer) of 1973, with the engine of which the Testarossa shared the capacity and a passing resemblance, but very few actual parts. But the Testarossa wasn't motivated just by evolution: it was built to cock a snook at Lamborghini, whose visually amazing Countach had surprised Ferrari, and at Porsche, whose creations threatened what Ferrari had always felt to be its pole position as supercar supremo.

The Testarossa shows Pininfarina at his most inspired and lateral-thinking. He kept the rear mid-engine, rear-wheel drive layout, lengthened the wheelbase, and increased the width to a mighty 78 in (1,976 mm). Then he added the Testarossa's signature feature, the side-strakes that changed car design for ever, and simultaneously solved three major technical problems. Instead of a single radiator in the front, there were twin radiators at the back, cooled much more efficiently via the strakes. The arrangement also solved the Boxer's problem of cabin overheating at a stroke. Thirdly, the strakes made the car wider at the back than at the front, improving its handling and stability. With its balletic balance, aerodynamics that gave negative lift (obviating the need for external spoilers), and despite its size, the Testarossa was fingertip light and agile to drive.

In an age of decadence, the Testarossa became synonymous with a social revolution, too. Everyone drooled – but Yuppies made it their ultimate status symbol as an icon of style, speed and plain wealth. Long after they got their come-uppance, the Testarossa remains immortal, a landmark among the best sports cars of all time.

# FIAT STRADA ABARTH 130TC

It was born in Italy as the Ritmo, but in Britain and North America it was called the Strada. For several years from 1978, this small family car appeared in equally dull versions whose only real claim to fame was that, thanks to Fiat's pioneering investment in automated assembly, it could be advertised as 'handbuilt by robots'. There was one exception, the 105TC sports model of 1981, intriguing enough to bring tuning and sports specialists Abarth into a collaboration with Fiat that produced the 2 litre Ritmo Abarth 125TC. It was good, but Abarth quickly saw it could be better. By 1982 they created the 130TC, a seriously hot hatchback with performance figures to see off contemporaries like the VW Golf GTi and Ford Escort XR3i.

The Fiat Ritmo/Strada Abarth 130TC was not an easy option. It had to follow where the standard Fiat Ritmo led, since so much of it (and all of the shell) was shared. Apart from the discreet spoiler on the hatchback, the wheels and interior trim, you couldn't tell that a veritable tiger was lurking under the bonnet. The Ritmo (Series 2) body was both blessing and curse. It was lightweight – the Ritmo's appeal had always been based on keeping it cheaper to produce than other comparable cars – so little of its power was dissipated just carrying, and its speed and acceleration were amazing. But the same manufacturing economies made it difficult to handle. Improved suspension and other tweaks couldn't compensate for the lack of rigidity or cornering balance needed to easily control the available surge of energy.

Britain in particular loved it. The Strada Abarth 130TC came with Recaro seats as standard, and that, together with the minor 1985 facelift, was good enough for the boy racers who made its tyre-shredding screech their calling card.

**COUNTRY OF ORIGIN:**
Italy

**FIRST MANUFACTURED:**
1982 (as Ritmo) 1984 (as Strada) (until 1988)

**ENGINE:**
1,995 cc DOHC Straight Four

**PERFORMANCE:**
Top speed of 121 mph (195 km/h); 0–60 mph (97 km/h) in 7.8 secs

**YOU SHOULD KNOW:**
The Fiat Strada Abarth 130TC was the only 1980s hot hatch that never used or switched to fuel injection. Instead, it came with twin carburettors, either twin Solex ADDHE or Weber DCOE40, and electronically controlled ignition timing.

# PEUGEOT
# 205 GTI

**COUNTRY OF ORIGIN:**
France

**FIRST MANUFACTURED:**
1984 (until 1994)

**ENGINE:**
1,580 cc or 1,905 cc
Straight Four

**PERFORMANCE:**
Top speed of 121 mph
(195 km/h); 0-60 mph
(97 km/h) in 8.9 secs

**YOU SHOULD KNOW:**
The most bizarre special
edition was the Peugeot
205 GTi 1 FM series of just
25 cars, made in 1992 for
the 25th birthday of BBC
Radio 1, UK. Each had
every extra available –
such as dark grey wheels,
black leather interior and
a special acoustic rear
shelf designed by Clarion
– and were individually
numbered with a brass
plaque. Radio 1 ran an on-
air competition to win one.

**The launch of the Peugeot 205 supermini in 1983 changed perception of the company and saved its fortunes; but it was the Peugeot 205 GTi version of 1984 that captured international hearts as the most popular hot hatch of its day. Small, perky but unassuming, four-square, with a wheel at each corner (squeezing extra space inside), the 205 GTi came in 1.6 litre and 1.9 litre versions. The combination of light weight, taut chassis, raw power and tight steering made it a byword for nimble flitting – with the proviso that with no electronic driver aids, you had to learn to contain its tendency to oversteer on high-speed cornering. Mastery of the 205 GTi's 'personality' became a point of honour among its many devotees (eventually, the car became difficult to insure because it was targeted by joy riders out to win their spurs).**

The 205 GTi's lightweight character came at the expense of safety features. It was a crumple zone. As safety issues became laws, the car's weight increased, and its top dog status was ended completely by the catalytic converter. Even so, its enormous success during its production led to many special editions and specialist versions like the stripped-down GTi Rallye; and many survive to demonstrate how exhilarating it is to be truly in control of a well-made mini-rocket.

There are, obviously, much more powerful hot hatches now, but few have ever matched the sensation of becoming one with the vehicle, that has been the defining judgement on the 205 GTi. It's why so many owners report having fallen in love with their car; and why there is still a strong market for them. The Peugeot 205 GTi is the definitive hot hatch of the pre-computer age – the best of the real thing.

# SUZUKI SAMURAI (SJ SERIES)

The Suzuki Samurai had more aliases than Mr Nice. The early star of the SJ series began in 1982 as the Suzuki Jimny (SJ-30), a 'kei car' of restricted dimensions and power that exempted a domestic vehicle from various swingeing Japanese road taxes. For export, the Jimny became longer, wider and more powerful, but less easily identifiable as versions of the same car under a plethora of names including Sierra, Potohar, Caribbean, Santana, Sidekick, Holden Drover (Australia) and Maruti Gypsy (India). There were two principal models: the 1 litre SJ410 (short and long wheelbase), and the 1.3 litre SJ413, introduced in 1984 as a five-speed manual with a wider axle, power brakes, a revamped body and new interior with redesigned dashboard and seats. With unofficial imports rising to the USA, Suzuki incorporated every feature they could think of, and in 1985 unveiled the Suzuki Samurai as their 1986 offering to the US.

The Samurai felt like the ultimate off-road 4WD, and in the 1980s, it was. Whatever combination of engine, body style or equipment you wanted was readily available, cheap and easy to modify. In 1988 it was even re-tuned for better on-road performance, as urban fans sought to improve its all-round practicality for school and mall runs. It could look macho (take the doors off for the 'riding shotgun in attack helicopter' pose) or feminine or surfer cool; jounce across the dunes; pick its way up a ravine; or just flit quickly through the back streets to work. Among pro-active off-roaders it was a byword for manoeuvrability, traction (especially towing), acceleration, handling, fuel economy and above all reliability.

In 2007, a heavily modified Suzuki Samurai (SJ413) with a supercharged engine set a new World Record for the highest altitude attained by a four-wheeled vehicle, of 6,688 metres (21,942 ft). That's off-roading.

**COUNTRY OF ORIGIN:**
Japan

**FIRST MANUFACTURED:**
1986 (until 1995 in the USA)

**ENGINE:**
1,324 cc Straight Four

**PERFORMANCE:**
Top speed of 81 mph (130 km/h)

**YOU SHOULD KNOW:**
A damaging report by the Consumers' Union in 1988 appeared to imply that the Suzuki Samurai was liable to 'unacceptable' amounts of rollover (a charge also levelled at the AMC Jeep CV-5 and the CJ-7). Suzuki sued for 'fraudulent testing', but by the time the CU had agreed that their choice of wording was unfortunate and actually meant something different (the case was eventually settled out of court in 2004) US sales of the Samurai had plummeted.

# TVR TASMIN 280I

**COUNTRY OF ORIGIN:**
UK

**FIRST MANUFACTURED:**
1981 (until 1988)

**ENGINE:**
2,792 cc OHV V6

**PERFORMANCE:**
Top speed of 130 mph
(209 km/h); 0–60 mph
(97 km/h) in 8.0 secs

**YOU SHOULD KNOW:**
Should you be privileged
to drive a TVR Tasmin
280i series II (produced
in the late mid-80s), be
warned that this model
is widely feared as one
of the 'scariest cars ever
in the wet'. Of course,
you might feel that only
makes the experience
more thrilling . . .

Every TVR sports car has been greater than the sum of its parts, and the Tasmin was no exception. Introduced as a replacement for TVR's M series Taimar, the Tasmin pillaged parts from a variety of other cars (mainly Fords) and reconfigured them with typical TVR chutzpah into a pocket rocket of real, if quirky, distinction. The Tasmin was almost a wedge car. For the first time ever, TVR appeared to be influenced by fashion: the Tasmin's profile and contours shared the 'origami' (paper-folding) characteristics made popular by design specialist Giugiaro. It was almost pretty – a departure for TVR that brought its own problems.

The Tasmin's wheelbase was short, but longer than the Taimar; and the chassis still came as the same space-frame built of small diameter, round and square-sectioned tubes. The hood was long for the 'front mid-engine' siting, and tapered into a droopy 'anteater' nose which contrasted oddly with the cut-off rear. The effect would have been sleek, but for the stumpy, fat B-pillar of the coupe's roof. The convertible got round that effect with a folding, Targa-style hoop which became standard for all TVR's convertibles thereafter. At least the convertible didn't pretend to be more than a two-seater – the rear seats of the 2+2 coupe were an optimistic joke.

But the car wasn't.

# ASTON MARTIN BULLDOG

## CONCEPT CAR

**COUNTRY OF ORIGIN:**
UK

**FIRST MANUFACTURED:**
1980

**ENGINE:**
5,341 cc Twin-Turbo
DOHC V8

**PERFORMANCE:**
Top speed of 191 mph
(307 km/h); 0–60mph
(97 km/h) in 5.2 secs

**YOU SHOULD KNOW:**
Within the Aston Martin
factory, the Bulldog
was known by the code
name K-9, after Dr Who's
robotic dog.

**When the Bulldog was unveiled in early 1980, it was intended as the first of a limited-edition run of 25, but it turned out to be so far-fetched that it never made it into production. Styled by William Towns, of Lagonda fame, the Bulldog takes the concept of wedge-shaped design onto a whole new plane.**

The Bulldog was designed to symbolize Aston Martin's intentions for the future, technically as well as aesthetically. On its test drive, it reached 191 mph (307 km/h), a remarkable feat at the time. Even more remarkably, it was theoretically capable of 237 mph (381 km/h), its twin-turbo V8 engine delivering around 650 bhp. The split-rim alloy wheels had blades around the edges which, though they may have looked as if they were intended for fending off bad guys in James Bond-style car chases, in fact fulfilled the function of directing cool air to the brakes in order to ensure reliability even at stratospheric speeds. The Bulldog also included the same innovative LED technology used in the Lagonda, and a rear view delivered via a TV monitor. It remains Aston Martin's only mid-engine car to date.

At the time, it was rumoured that the Bulldog project had been underwritten by a middle-eastern sheikh who then backed out of buying it. The car ended up in auction and was sold to a wealthy business tycoon from the Emirates. Eventually, it turned up in the USA but now resides back in the UK. The Bulldog is unlikely ever to be surpassed as Aston Martin's most bizarre creation. With its stunted height of just 110 cm (43 in), disproportionate width, massive power-operated gullwing doors and strange submerged headlights, it stands in the annals of automotive history as a madcap masterpiece from another dimension.

1990s

# AUDI TT

When Audi unveiled the TT coupe as a concept car in 1995, public reaction was so ecstatic that a production run was ordered, though in the event this was delayed by tooling problems. By the time the neatly rounded Audi TT 2+2 fastback coupe appeared in late 1998 – soon joined by an equally pleasing two-seater roadster – there was a long waiting list of eager buyers.

The cars were named after the famous Tourist Trophy motorcycle races on the Isle of Man, where Audi predecessor NSU had excelled over the years. When they finally arrived, the TT cars were based on the Volkswagen A4 platform used by the New Beetle, Golf and Skoda Octavia (amongst others). There was a choice of two transversely mounted, turbocharged 1.8 litre engines with different power output (a 3.2 litre Volkswagen VR6 was added in 2003). The less powerful 1.8 came with Audi's famous quattro all-wheel drive system or standard front-wheel drive, with the meatier engine having the quattro option only. The gearbox was five- or six-speed manual, with automatic and fast DSG (Direct-Shift Gearbox) as later options.

The delight of early buyers who finally got their Audi TTs to play with turned to dismay when they discovered the car could become dangerously skittish at high speed – a fault requiring the company to issue a recall so the cars could be modified with a rear spoiler and ESP (Electronic Stability Programme) to improved handling.

The second generation TTs were introduced in 2007, with a rear spoiler that deploys automatically at speed and a choice of fuel-injection engines, plus options like Audi Magnetic Ride active suspension. Launched at the Geneva Motor Show in 2014, the third generation TTs have a choice of TFSI or TDI engines, and all-wheel or front-wheel drive configurations. For the money, the Audi TT has always been a machine that offers a great driving experience, with crisp handling and impressive performance.

**COUNTRY OF ORIGIN:**
Germany (built in Hungary)

**FIRST MANUFACTURED:**
1998 (until 2006)

**ENGINE:**
1,781 cc Straight Four Turbo; 3,189 cc Staggered Six

**PERFORMANCE:**
Varied according to engine – minimum top speed of 137 mph (220 km/h); 0–60 mph (97 km/h) in 8.1 secs

**YOU SHOULD KNOW:**
A limited-edition performance model was released by Audi in 2005 – the TT Quattro Sport (in the UK, Club Sport in Europe) had a super-tuned version of the 1.8 engine, uprated suspension and brakes plus a special two-tone paint job. These are both scarce and desirable.

# BENTLEY CONTINENTAL R

**COUNTRY OF ORIGIN:**
UK

**FIRST MANUFACTURED:**
1991 (until 2003)

**ENGINE:**
6,750 cc V8 Turbo

**PERFORMANCE:**
Top speed of 145 mph
(233 km/h); 0–60 mph
(97 km/h) in 6.9 secs

**YOU SHOULD KNOW:**
The high-performance
Continental
R Mulliner model was
introduced in 1999 and
ran until 2003 – boasting
a top speed of 170 mph
(274 km/h). A limited
number of Continental
R Le Mans cars were
produced in 2001.

**Finally, in 1991, Rolls-Royce Motors got around to creating a Bentley that owed nothing to a Rolls-Royce sibling, apart from the engine. The Continental R cashed in on popularity the resurgent Bentley marque had been enjoying since the early 1980s, and also plugged the gap left in the corporate range by the demise of the Rolls-Royce Camargue back in 1986.**

This sleek two-door car with its raked windscreen was styled with more than a passing nod to aerodynamic efficiency, but was also a very handsome beast – spontaneous applause broke out when it was dramatically unveiled at the Geneva Motor Show. The interior finish and seating plan were similar to that of the well-proven Bentley Turbo R, though there were minor changes to the instruments and control panels, with a centre console that extended into the rear compartment.

The electric gear-selector was mounted on the console – the first time it had featured anywhere but on the steering column for an automatic Bentley – and controlled a new four-speed automatic transmission that delivered effortless cruising and improved fuel consumption (though that old cliché 'if you have to ask how many miles it does to the gallon you can't afford to run it' definitely applies). Another new feature of the Continental R was ETBC (Electronic Transient Boost Control). This could override the turbo when extra grunt was needed – for example during a hairy overtaking manoeuvre – by providing a further temporary boost when the turbo was already operating at maximum power.

In 2004 the new Continental GT superseded previous Continental models but the Continental R remains a grand tourer par excellence – and the beauty of these quality cars is that they retain their class and style long after they have sunk into the almost-affordable price bracket.

# BUGATTI EB110

Entrepreneur Romano Artioli acquired Bugatti rights in 1987 and set about resurrecting the iconic French marque by building expensive supercars that paid homage to the most famous of motoring names. An architect-designed factory arose near Modena, in an area already populated by the likes of Ferrari, Maserati and De Tomaso, and the great adventure was soon up and running.

Those talented designers Stanzani and Gandini (creators of the Lamborghini Miura and Countach) were hired, and in 1989 they presented plans for (according to Bugatti boasts) the world's most technically advanced sports car. With suitably symbolic drama, the Bugatti EB110 was introduced in Paris and Versailles on 15 September 1991, 110 years to the day after Ettore Bugatti's birth.

This mid-engined coupe had a 60-valve V12 with four turbos, coupled with a six-speed gearbox and four-wheel-drive to deliver sensational performance. The lightweight body was fabricated in carbon fibre and suspension was double-wishbone. The EB110 was long and low, having an aircraft-style cockpit with rounded glass front accessed by a pair of Gandini's famous upward-opening doors. A nice touch was provided by a glass engine-cover that provided a view of the impressive power plant. Another neat idea was the electronic rear wing that could be raised and retracted at will.

The following year the Bugatti EB110 SS appeared. This was even lighter and faster than the base model, with the ability to go from sitting on the tarmac quietly growling to a howling 60 mph (97 km/h) in a tad over three neck-snapping seconds. But Romano Artioli was about to learn the harsh lesson that producing the ultimate supercar is like trying to fill a bottomless money-pit. The new Bugatti company went bust in 1995 after producing around 140 EB110s (including SS models).

**COUNTRY OF ORIGIN:**
Italy

**FIRST MANUFACTURED:**
1991 (until 1995)

**ENGINE:**
3,499 cc V12 Quad-turbo

**PERFORMANCE:**
Top speed of 213 mph (343 km/h); 0–60 mph (97 km/h) in 4.5 secs

**YOU SHOULD KNOW:**
Always blame the tools! When in 1995 the world's greatest-ever racing driver crashed his banana-yellow Bugatti EB110 SS into a truck, Michael Schumacher was quick to point an imperious finger at . . . the Bugatti's inadequate brakes.

# CAMPAGNA T-REX

**Is it a boat? Is it a plane? Is it a starfighter? No, it's a motorbike. Or a three-wheeled sports car. Whatever, the futuristic Campagna T-Rex is definitely unlike any other form of wheeled thrillster devised by man. Actually, it's officially a motorcycle, though it does indeed have three wheels (two front, one back). The T-Rex is made in Quebec, Canada and had been around to delight those who've been aware of its exhilarating secrets since the mid-1990s, though the first street-legal examples were not imported into the USA until 2001.**

The T-Rex was (and remains) an affordable alternative to supercars costing many times the price, with sensational performance, great roadholding and the sheer sense of speed that comes from scorching along close to the road with the wind in your face. The original concept was developed by Formula Ford racing driver and F1 mechanic Daniel Campagna, with space-age styling by Paul Deutschman.

With a lightweight reinforced fibreglass body on a multi-tubular steel chassis and frame, the T-Rex has two adjustable seats, side by side, with carbon-fibre headrests. The T-Rex has three-point seat belts and a foot-pedal box. The wind deflector is also fabricated in carbon fibre. The wheels are aluminium and there is a six-speed gearbox (with reverse). Engines have evolved over time. The first power plant was a 1.1 litre Straight Four, followed by a slightly smaller engine, then a 1.7 litre cc V-Twin, succeeded by two more Straight Fours at 1.2 litres and 1.4 litres respectively. The top of line model is the 16SP, with an in-line six-cylinder engine from BMW. A special edition, of only 10 units worldwide, is also available. In 2018 the company announced the launch of a 100 per cent electric model.

The T-Rex was a long time in development, but well worth waiting for. Acceleration is electric and top speed is quite frightening. The vehicle may be a mere supertrike, but it drives like a sensational miniature sports car.

**COUNTRY OF ORIGIN:**
Canada

**FIRST MANUFACTURED:**
1996 (until the present)

**ENGINE:**
1,074 cc, 1,052 cc, 1,164 cc or 1,352 cc Straight Four; 1,735 cc V-Twin

**PERFORMANCE:**
With 4.0 l engine – top speed of 108 mph (175 km/h); 0–60 mph (97 km/h) in 9.9 secs

**YOU SHOULD KNOW:**
One mightily impressed motoring writer enjoyed an eye-watering test drive in this unique cross between a racing car and a superbike and promptly announced: 'Like its Jurassic namesake the T-Rex is a carnivore – one that eats cars for lunch.'

# CADILLAC ESCALADE

**COUNTRY OF ORIGIN:**
USA

**FIRST MANUFACTURED:**
1999 (until the present)

**ENGINE:**
5.7 l (348 cid), 5.3 l
(323 cid), 6.0 l (366 cid)
or 6.2 l (378 cid) V8

**PERFORMANCE:**
With 6.0 l engine –
speed-limited top speed
of 108 mph (174 km/h);
0–60 mph (97 km/h) in
8.7 secs

**YOU SHOULD KNOW:**
The Escalade is big
enough to need handling
with care, especially
around the parking lot; to
help out when reversing,
the fourth-generation cars
have a surround view
camera and Automatic
Parking Assist.

**American car makers can get hustled into precipitate action, and so it was with the Cadillac Escalade. This appeared in 1999 as a hastily conceived and poorly implemented response to numerous luxury SUVs from marques like BMW, Toyota and Mercedes that were appearing like a rash on roads everywhere. In particular, the boys at General Motors felt the need to tackle the Lincoln Navigator from arch rival Ford.**

Unfortunately, Cadillac was caught on the hop, and the first generation Escalade was little more than a badge-engineered version of the lesser GMC Yukon Denali. The five-seater was smaller than the rival Navigator and underpowered, with a stodgy 5.7 litre Vortec 5700 V8 engine that impressed nobody. It was, in short, a dog – but people seemed to like it nonetheless and Cadillac pluckily kept the Escalade going unchanged through 2000.

This allowed the company to play catch-up, improving the 2002 Escalade to create a genuine contender and launching this handsome bruiser in January 2001. It came with rear-wheel drive as standard, along with an improved 5.3 litre Vortec V8 engine. Four-wheel drive was optional, as was a 6 litre V8. The new model was an eight-seater and was available as a four-door SUV or upmarket four-door EXT (extended cab) pickup truck. An ESC wagon followed in 2003, completing the second generation line-up. These powerful cars were laden with standard features and built to thrill, offering an exciting driving experience for anyone wealthy enough to buy one (and keep filling the tank).

After a shaky start, Cadillac had a hit on their hands, with sophisticated yet rugged Escalades accounting for 40 percent of Caddy's annual sales. The line was rewarded with a full third generation redesign in 2007 to reinforce the Escalade's unexpected youth appeal, which had seen an ugly duckling turn into a lucrative swan.

Continuing the success, the fourth-generation Escalades were launched in 2015 with six-speed transmissions, updated in 2018 to a new ten-speed. The redesign was met with generally positive critical reception, however in 2016 the Escalade was named the worst large-sized luxury SUV in *Consumer Reports* magazine.

# FIAT CINQUECENTO

**Ital Design's Fiat Cinquecento was the replacement for the Fiat 126 and the name was a patent con – despite suggesting the engine was a modest 500 ccs, the truth of the matter was that the smallest engine offered in the new Cinquecento scoped out at an impressive 704 ccs. Naughty!**

This little city car had one body style – an angular three-door hatchback with a deep wraparound front bumper. Despite its square looks, the Cinquecentro was aerodynamically efficient and had some advanced features for a budget car. These included independent suspension all round, front disc brakes, side impact bars and crumple zones. It even had better rustproofing than Fiats of earlier generations, offering hope that the driver's foot wouldn't go through the floorpan after a few years of wet running. There were optional extras available, such as electric windows, central locking and a sunroof (the Soleil version actually came with a retractable canvas roof).

There were alternative engines, too. The basic 704 cc motor was reserved for the Cinquecento's home market (it was manufactured at the FSM plant in Poland), whilst everyone else got the long-established Fiat 903 cc engine (reduced to 899 cc in 1993 for fiscal reasons). The interesting point here was that the smaller power plant was mounted longitudinally, but the larger one was arranged transversely. Both configurations were produced simultaneously, which was a most unusual arrangement. The Cinquecento, unlike its predecessor, was a front-wheel drive car.

The Cinquecento Sporting was introduced in 1994, boasting the 1.1 litre FIRE engine from the contemporary Fiat Punto. This model boasted a close-ratio gearbox, lower ride height, roll bars and colour-coded bumpers and side mirrors. Inside there were sports seats, leather steering wheel and gear knob and a tachometer to underline Sporting credentials. This is definitely the one to zip around in!

**COUNTRY OF ORIGIN:**
Italy (built in Poland)

**FIRST MANUFACTURED:**
1991 (until 1998)

**ENGINE:**
704 cc, 903/899 cc or 1,108 cc Straight Four

**PERFORMANCE:**
Sporting – top speed of 93 mph (150 km/h); 0–60 mph (97 km/h) in 13.5 secs

**YOU SHOULD KNOW:**
Giorgetto Giugiaro was the Cinquecento's original designer, and he subsequently came up with a completely new version of the car. Waste not, want not – when Fiat decided not to pick up his concept he sold it to Daewoo of South Korea as the basis for their 1998 Matiz minicar.

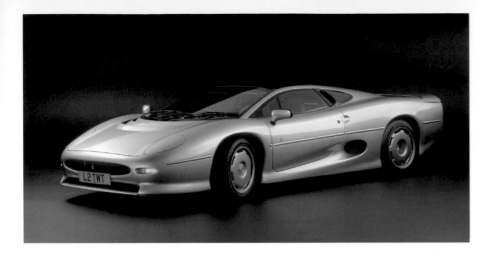

# JAGUAR XJ220

**COUNTRY OF ORIGIN:**
UK

**FIRST MANUFACTURED:**
1992 (until 1994)

**ENGINE:**
3,498 V6 Twin Turbo

**PERFORMANCE:**
Top speed of 220 mph
(354 km/h); 0-60 mph
(97 km/h) in 4 secs

**YOU SHOULD KNOW:**
If you ever come across
a parked XJ220, take
a peek through the
curved rear window and
admire the V6 engine
with its twin Garrett
turbochargers that can be
seen lurking within.

**In the late 1980s supercar fever was reaching is height, with established classics appreciating rapidly as speculators drove up prices and various manufacturers scrambled to take advantage by custom building awesome performance cars that were billed as the classics of the future (with a price tag to match the hype).**

Jaguar leapt aboard the gravy train in some style – coming up with the world's fastest production car, which ruled supreme in the speed stakes until the McLaren F1 shot past. But that's not to say that the XJ220 was an unqualified success story. It was initially conceived by Jaguar employees who came up with the idea of creating the ultimate road car and the mid-engined prototype certainly looked the part when it appeared in 1988.

The reaction was so positive that Jaguar announced that the XJ220 would go into production, as a strictly limited edition, with would-be buyers required to put down a substantial deposit to go on the waiting list. Dotted lines were signed upon and Jaguar set about turning their concept car into reality with the help of constructor Tom Walkinshaw Racing. The design by Keith Helfet was stunning, with flowing lines, a low cockpit and businesslike air scoops behind scissor-style doors. Sadly, by the time it was ready in 1992 the price had increased substantially, the supercar bubble had burst and many customers tried to wriggle out of their contracts. This controversy spoiled the debut of an excellent if expensive machine.

Despite the fact that Jaguar did not finally sell the last of 281 XJ220s until 1997, after drastically cutting the price, the XJ220 has become a sought-after collectors' car. But this stylish supercar did not prove to be a great investment, changing hands today at roughly a quarter of the original cost.

# JEEP TJ WRANGLER

The modern successor of that famous Willys wartime Jeep swaggered onto the scene in the form of the first generation YJ Wrangler, a robust off-roader introduced by Chrysler with a Jeep badge in 1987. Wranglers were initially built in Canada where – ironically – the Wrangler name couldn't be used because Chevrolet had already bagged it for a pickup. So Wranglers became the Jeep YJ in home territory. Production switched to the USA in 1992, but when the revamped second generation Wrangler arrived in 1996 the same restriction applied, with Canadian exports bearing the Jeep TJ name. To cut a confusing story short, the rest of the world now refers to the YJ Wrangler and the TJ Wrangler to differentiate between the two models.

The TJ Wrangler was much improved. It featured coil-spring suspension borrowed from the larger Jeep Grand Cherokee. The entry level TJ had a 2.5 litre four-cylinder motor (2.4 litre from 2003), but most opted for the big 4 litre Straight Six shared with the Cherokee and Grand Cherokee. There was a choice of transmissions over the production run, with three- and four-speed automatics or five- and six-speed manuals on offer. Stylistically, the TJ had more rounded contours than its predecessor, but this sturdy SUV remained a no-frills two-door soft top.

**COUNTRY OF ORIGIN:**
USA

**FIRST MANUFACTURED:**
1996 (until 2006)

**ENGINE:**
2.4 l (148 cid) or 2.5 l (150 cid) Straight Four; 4.0 l (241 cid) Straight Six

**PERFORMANCE:**
Top speed of 70 mph (120 km/h); 0–60 mph (97 km/h) in 29.7 secs (Hurricane 16)

**YOU SHOULD KNOW:**
A right-hand drive version of the TJ Wrangler was produced for export to left-side drive countries, and was also sold to the US Post Office so rural mail carriers could reach out to mailboxes without leaving the vehicle.

# LAMBORGHINI DIABLO

**COUNTRY OF ORIGIN:**
Italy

**FIRST MANUFACTURED:**
1990 (until 2001)

**ENGINE:**
5,707 cc or 5,992 cc V12

**PERFORMANCE:**
With 5.7 l engine –
top speed of 203 mph
(326 km/h); 0-60 mph
(97 km/h) in 3.9 secs

**YOU SHOULD KNOW:**
Diablos were very much driver's cars, not noted for an excessively luxurious interior finish, but those who always liked to keep track of time as they sped along the highway were able to order an optional dashboard clock by prestigious Swiss maker Breguet – that'll be another $10,500 please.

**Despite being a devil in disguise (well, in Spanish then) it wasn't necessary to sell one's soul to get a Lambo Diablo – just greeting the model launch in 1990 with a briefcase containing around $250,000 would do the trick. This wide, low-slung wedge with its characteristic grooved skirt and rounded air scoops in front of the back wheels was Lamborghini's long-awaited replacement for the Countach.**

The mid-engined Diablo had been under development since 1995, and was worth waiting for. This was no poseur's car, but an out-and-out performance model with a 48-valve 5.7 litre Lamborghini V12 with dual overhead cams and computer-controlled fuel injection. The brutish 492 bhp thus generated fed the rear wheels.

There was initially no choice of body style, as all Diablos were two-door coupes.

But interesting advances were afoot. After three years of tweaking the basic model a VT (for Viscous Traction) Diablo coupe appeared in 1993, followed by an open targa-topped version in 1995. Power was fed through a manual gearbox and four-wheel drive system to massive road wheels and fat tyres at each corner, making for adhesive roadholding, rapid acceleration and breathtaking top speed. The VT was uprated to a Version 2 in 1997, but when new owner Audi took over in 1998 the Diablo was given a 6 litre engine and major facelift even as a successor, the Murciélago, was developed.

There were various special editions in the Diablo's lifetime. The Diablo SE (1994-95 Special Edition) celebrated the company's 30th birthday. This hard-edged speedster could be further upgraded with the Jota package. The Diablo SV (Sport Veloce) lacked all-wheel drive. The Diablo SVR was a racing version created for a single-car pro-am series known as the Diablo Supertrophy. A few of these cars were subsequently modified for road use, reminding everyone of the Diablo's performance pedigree.

# NISSAN FIGARO

This curiosity was never meant to stray beyond the shores of Japan. The small, two-door Figaro convertible with its retro styling was a one-year wonder, being built only in 1991. It was styled by Shoji Takahashi and first shown at the 1989 Tokyo Motor Show, after which Nissan's special projects Pike Factory group brought it to market. The brief was to produce something looking like a 1960s classic but with all the performance and comfort of a modern car. The quirky Figaro definitely delivered.

Indeed, would-be Japanese buyers liked the concept so much that the original production run of 8,000 cars had to be more than doubled and still there weren't enough to go around, so a ballot was held. The Figaro was based on the Nissan Micra platform and had a 1 litre engine boosted by a turbocharger that provided plenty of zip, though in truth the Figaro was a triumph of style over performance. The engine was loud, the three-speed automatic gearbox laborious, steering skittish and wind noise intrusive. But who cared about any of that?

The Figaro came in four colours – topaz mist, emerald green, pale aqua and lapis grey – each representing a season of the year. The foldaway soft top in off-white was easy to erect and collapse, whilst there was a retractable glass rear screen.

Capacious front seats were trimmed in white leather and the CD radio that took pride of place on the dashboard had a satisfying Bakelite look to it, complemented by various chrome switches and knobs. Air-con, electric windows and power steering came as standard.

This was one of the most unusual cars to appear in the 1990s, and those attention-seekers who drive a Figaro today just love watching heads turning everywhere as this special little car buzzes by.

**COUNTRY OF ORIGIN:**
Japan

**FIRST MANUFACTURED:**
1991

**ENGINE:**
987 cc Straight Four Turbo

**PERFORMANCE:**
Top speed of 100 mph (161 km/h); 0–60 mph (97 km/h) in 13.5 secs

**YOU SHOULD KNOW:**
The fact that both the Japanese and Brits drive on the left encouraged a brisk trade in grey imports from Japan to the UK, and the Figaro became a popular choice with British buyers (especially celebrities) who wanted to be seen driving something rather eccentric.

# MERCEDES-BENZ SLK R170

**COUNTRY OF ORIGIN:**
Germany (also built in
South Africa and Mexico)

**FIRST MANUFACTURED:**
1997 (until 2004)

**ENGINE:**
1,998 cc or 2,295 cc
Straight Four; 3,199 cc V6

**PERFORMANCE:**
With 3.2 l engine –
top speed of 152 mph
(245 km/h); 0–60 mph
(97 km/h) in 6.5 secs

**YOU SHOULD KNOW:**
Hand-built engines
for the 32 AMG were
supplied by performance
specialist AMG – the
independent company
founded in 1967 with
a history of upping the
power output of Mercedes
engines that was taken
over by DaimlerChrysler
shortly before the 32
AMG was launched.

**Mercedes wasn't prepared to let the snazzy BMW Z3 and Porsche Boxster have the sporting arena all to themselves, and launched the SLK R170 compact roadster in 1997 to grab a slice of the action. This plainly styled but pleasing sports car followed the lead of Mitsubishi's 3000GT Spyder, featuring a retractable hardtop that changed a coupe into a convertible – a template that other manufacturers would copy.**

The SLK designation comes from the Mercedes mission statement for these cars – Sportlich, Leicht, Kurz (sporty, light and short). The R170 platform was new for 1997, and lasted until the R171 arrived in 2005. During the relatively short life of the R170 there were a number of models, differentiated by engine size and power output. Three different transmissions were offered during the run – five-speed automatic and five- and six-speed manual.

The basic 2 litre 200 version was produced throughout. The 2 litre 200K was also offered from 1997 to 2004, with an engine change in 2001. The 230K appeared in 1998 with a 2.3 litre engine, upgraded in 2001 – the 'K' stood for Kompressor (supercharger). The 320 with its 3.2 litre V6 engine did not hit the road until 2001, which year also saw the introduction of the high-powered 32 AMG model. Chassis production for all models was by Karmann in Germany, though some 320s were built in other countries as Mercedes vehicle production went global.

The most potent SLK R170 was the 32 AMG. This rare tyre-smoker scorched from rest to 60 mph (97 km/h) in 4.5 secs, with a top speed of 193 mph (311 km/h). Around 4,300 were built. A thousand stayed in Germany, two thousand went to the States and a few hundred to the United Kingdom. It's worth trying to catch one if you can for the ultimate SLK R170 driving experience.

# RENAULT SPORT SPIDER

After the demise of the Alpine A610 – a sadly underrated sports coupe – Renault's Alpine factory in Dieppe turned to building the Renault Sport Spider, a dashing open-top roadster that made its debut in 1996. The Alpine A610 had been an attempt to consolidate Renault's reviving fortunes with a halo performance car – and the Spider was intended to fulfill the same objective.

The concept was to produce a small racing car to be used in a single-model competition series, where driving skill alone would be the deciding factor. The commercial advantages would be to put Renault's name back up in sporting lights, with consequent marketing benefits for the whole range and the ability to sell a road-going version of the racer.

A concept car was presented at the Geneva Motor Show in 1995. This memorably lacked a windscreen and had butterfly doors, though these had vanished and a windscreen had been added by the time the production version went on sale. The mid-engined rear-wheel drive car was a handsome open-top roadster complete with roll bar to underline its racing pedigree. Indeed, the first cars built at Alpine's Dieppe factory were special Spider Trophy racing versions with a top speed of 156 mph (251 km/h).

This ensured that the road-going Sport Spider would satisfy the most demanding of sporting drivers. The lightweight aluminium chassis was fitted with GRP bodywork. In a technical masterstroke, engine and gearbox were a single transversely fixed unit using an oscillating hinge that effectively eradicated engine shake at speed. That engine was a 2 litre F7R borrowed from the limited-edition Renault Clio Williams hot hatch created by Renault Sport in 1992 for homologation purposes.

The Sport Spider's production was short, and these stylish but rare roadsters have become desirable amongst collectors betting on future classic status.

**COUNTRY OF ORIGIN:**
France

**FIRST MANUFACTURED:**
1996 (until 1999)

**ENGINE:**
1,998 cc Straight Four

**PERFORMANCE:**
Top speed of 131 mph (211 km/h); 0–60 mph (97 km/h) in 5.8 secs

**YOU SHOULD KNOW:**
The Spider racing series organized by Renault took place in the UK between 1995 and 1999, supporting the British Touring Car Championship. Far from creating a level playing field, the Spider Trophy's final season saw Andy Priaulx win all 13 races from 13 pole positions.

# SKODA OCTAVIA

**COUNTRY OF ORIGIN:**
Czech Republic

**FIRST MANUFACTURED:**
1996 (until the present)

**ENGINE:**
Various, from 1,298 cc to
1,984 cc Straight Four;
1,896 cc or 1,968 Straight
Four Diesel

**PERFORMANCE:**
With 2.0 l engine –
top speed of 139 mph
(224 km/h); 0–60 mph
(97 km/h) in 8.6 secs

**YOU SHOULD KNOW:**
The Octavia arrived in
the UK during 1998 and
was soon a staple of the
taxi and hire car business,
with its excellent build
quality, roomy interior
and competitive price.

**Those universal Skoda jokes were just starting to fade from the collective consciousness of petrolheads when the Octavia appeared in 1996, as it became apparent how quickly the Czech company had adopted Volkswagen quality control standards. To ram home the point these 'Volkswagens by another name' were sold at extremely tempting prices for the high specification and level of finish offered, with the intention of swiftly re-establishing the Skoda marque as a born-again player on the international scene.**

The first generation Octavia came as a five-door estate and also a strange hybrid saloon/hatchback combo that had a saloon-like back end and lifting tailgate. The styling was pleasant but unremarkable. The Octavia shared a platform with the Golf, Audi A3 and Seat Leon Cupra. The most distinctive Skoda option was four-wheel drive capability, available on both models, and these cars had a slightly higher ride height and a larger fuel tank. There was also a high-performance Octavia vRS. As with any model line having a German connection, there was a wide assortment of engines, all shared by other cars within the Volkswagen Group. There were five diesel variants, all at 1.9 litres, and twice that number of petrol engines, ranging in size from 1.4 litres to 2 litres.

The first generation was given a facelift in 2000, giving independent rear suspension and enhanced interior trim, and this remained on sale in some markets (as the Octavia Tour) after the second generation appeared in 2004. Again, many engine variants were offered (nine petrol and six diesel). There were changes to increase internal space and the new Octavia had a higher ride height to eliminate previous difficulties with tall curbs and ramps. The third generation, launched in 2013 was bigger still: 9 cm (3.54 in) longer and 4.5 cm (1.77 in) wider. For those wanting to be environmentally friendly, the GreenLine model, with a 1.6 litre diesel engine, produces only 85 grams of $CO_2$ per km. Further design updates came in 2017, with split front headlights.

# SUBARU IMPREZA TURBO

The compact Subaru Impreza was introduced in 1993 and has been motoring ever since. It challenged the likes of the Honda Civic and Toyota Corolla, but one of the Impreza's unique selling points was that it offered all-wheel drive. This worked well with the traditional Subaru flat boxer engine, minimizing body roll and providing first-class handling and roadholding.

There were three models in the new range – a two-door coupe, four-door saloon and five-door estate. Trim levels were LX, GL and Sport, though widespread distribution saw different names used in different markets. Likewise there was considerable variety in the engines used for the Impreza over time. The most powerful, though not the largest, was the 2.0 litre turbocharged and intercooled motor – marketed variously as the Impreza 2.0 WRX, Turbo 2000, 2.0 Turbo, 2.0 GT or 2.0 GT Turbo. The Turbo had wider tyres, bigger brakes and firmer suspension than the base model.

This was the innocent-looking four-wheel drive saloon or station wagon that inspired a generation of petrolheads after taking the world by storm in the mid 1990s. Despite the fairly basic interior finish of dull grey plastic and uninspiring seating trims, the Impreza Turbo's performance caused all that to be forgotten in the few seconds it took to blast past 60 mph (97 km/h). Endless variants (about 15) were produced before the chassis was uprated in 2001, since when another 25 have been offered, depending on the market. But inability to comply with emissions regulations, in Europe at least, have seen the end of the line. Just 150 of the aptly named WRX STI Final Edition were produced.

There couldn't be a better budget performance car for the aspiring boy racer to go looking for. It has become a cult car for good reason, being reliable, tough as old boots and fast as the wind. An Impreza isn't cheap to run, but the earlier models offer more boom for the buck than anything else in the same price bracket.

**COUNTRY OF ORIGIN:**
Japan

**FIRST MANUFACTURED:**
1993 (until 2018)

**ENGINE:**
1,994 cc Flat Four Turbo

**PERFORMANCE:**
Depended on variant – typically a top speed of 137 mph (220 km/h); 0–60 mph (97 km/h) in 5.8 secs

**YOU SHOULD KNOW:**
There have been numerous special editions of the Impreza Turbo, many attracting a good premium for their rarity value and superior internal finish. UK examples to look for include the RB5, Series McRae, Terzo, Catalunya and Prodrive WR Sport.

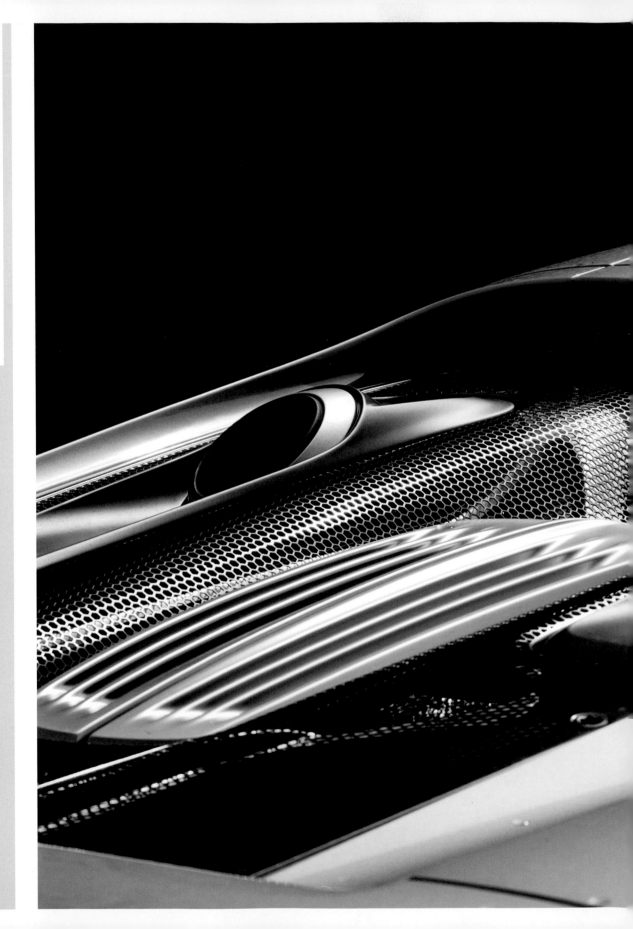

2000s

# ALFA ROMEO 8C COMPETIZIONE

**The Frankfurt Motor Show in 2003 saw the first appearance of an ab-fab Alfa Romeo two-seater coupe. Although its rounded body and streamlined profile were thoroughly modern, the prototype 8C Competizione had styling cues that harked back to great Alfas of the 1930s and 1940s and the name was a direct reference to the 6C Competizione that ran so well in Mille Miglia races and won the 1950 Targo Florio.**

Naturally, those with deep pockets and an enduring affection for beautiful Italian sports cars had to have one and told Alfa so – loudly. These heavy hints were taken and a production version was duly sanctioned in 2006. Construction began the following year, with a traditional steel chassis elegantly clothed in carbon-fibre bodywork finished in black, yellow, and Italian competition red or 8C red. Beneath the rear-hinged bonnet (more or less the only change from the prototype) a 4.7 litre Maserati V8 engine could be found. As Ferrari were assembling, this it boded well for the Competizione's performance – which was indeed so spectacular that the officially announced top speed is thought to be a politic underestimate.

The sporty driver will have great fun playing the gear-change game. The car features a six-speed transaxle gearbox with computerized selection. Using levers which are mounted behind the steering wheel, the driver chooses between the five modes – manual-normal, manual-sport, automatic-normal, automatic-sport and ice conditions. In sport mode, it can take as long as a microsecond to change gear. The 8C Competizione was assembled by Maserati at the Modena factory, with the chassis and bodies coming from different external suppliers.

**COUNTRY OF ORIGIN:**
Italy

**FIRST MANUFACTURED:**
2007 (until 2009)

**ENGINE:**
4,691 cc V8

**PERFORMANCE:**
Top speed of 182 mph (293 km/h); 0–60 mph (97 km/h) in 4 secs

**YOU SHOULD KNOW:**
The 8C Competizione came in a strictly limited edition of 500 cars which were all presold. Another opportunity to buy came in 2010, when 500 of the 8S Spider model were put on the market.

# ASTON MARTIN DBS V12

**COUNTRY OF ORIGIN:**
UK

**FIRST MANUFACTURED:**
2008 (until 2012)

**ENGINE:**
5,935 cc V12

**PERFORMANCE:**
Top speed of 188 mph
(302 km/h); 0–60 mph
(97 km/h) in 4.1 secs

**YOU SHOULD KNOW:**
The James Bond
connection was firmly
maintained by the DBS
V12. An original DBS
featured in the 1969 film
*On Her Majesty's Secret
Service*, a pre-production
DBS V12 greeted actor
Daniel Craig's first
appearance as 007 in
*Casino Royale* (2006) and
the car appeared again in
the sequel, *Quantum of
Solace* (2008).

Following the demise of the Vanquish S, Aston Martin's new leader of the pack was the DBS V12. Proudly reviving the iconic DBS designation of earlier years, this superb machine made a show-stopping inaugural appearance at the Pebble Beach Concours D'Elegance in 2007. The DBS V12 prototype was certainly an eye-catcher, shaped by the aerodynamic requirements of stable high-speed driving, flaunting impressive 10-spoke alloy wheels and finished in the striking new Casino Ice colour (graphite with a hint of blue). The interior was hand-crafted using the finest materials.

The first cars were delivered in 2008. They sported a potent V12 engine borrowed from the DBR9 racecar, coupled with six-speed manual or six-speed Touchtronic automatic transmission. The DBS was clearly based on the 2+2 DB9's design and platform but was an unashamed two-seater, with a lightweight bonded-aluminium chassis giving outstanding strength and rigidity. Ultra-light carbon-fibre body panels further reduced weight, as did a state-of-the-art braking system using vented carbon-ceramic discs front and back. Double-wishbone suspension featured adaptive damper control for instant adjustment of handling and ride characteristics.

No expense was spared in creating the ultimate touring car and the DBS V12 transferred the DBR9's race pedigree to Aston's flagship road car. The front mid-mounted engine was teamed with a rear mid-mounted transaxle to ensure near perfect weight distribution for stability, agility and an exhilarating driving experience. If the DB9 is a true grand tourer, the DBS V12 is an out-and-out sports car. It is better to drive than its GT sibling with more power and impressive cornering ability.

To Aston Martin's chagrin, in 2008 an Australian motoring website blew the whistle on what turned out to be the company worst-kept secret – the existence of a simply fabulous open-top DBS V12 Volante that was officially unveiled at the 2009 Geneva Motor Show.

# AUDI R8

**COUNTRY OF ORIGIN:**
Germany

**FIRST MANUFACTURED:**
2006

**ENGINE:**
4,163 cc V8; 5,204 cc V10

**PERFORMANCE:**
With 5.2 l engine –
top speed of 196 mph
(316 km/h); 0–60 mph
(97 km/h) in 3.9 secs

**YOU SHOULD KNOW:**
Serious students of the
sports car will note that
the Audi R8 shares a fifth
of its DNA with Audi-
owned Lamborghini's
Gallardo, for the R8
is built on a Gallardo
platform and the two
dashing sports cars have
several features, such as
transmission, in common.

Every ambitious car manufacturer in the heady pre-credit-crunch opening years of the 21st century aimed to put a supercar on the road, and Audi was no exception. By 2006 the German company had perfected its pitch to acquisitive city traders. The R8 was a mid-engined two-door sports coupe, which was based on the Le Mans quattro concept car presented in 2003. The new speedster was allowed to assume the hallowed name of Audi's R8 racing car.

The R8's styling was fairly typical of many a mid-sized sporting coupe, but no less pleasing for that. It was hand-built on the Audi Space Frame for lightness and the initial engine offering was an advanced FSI (Fuel-Stratified Injection) 4.2 litre V8 that developed 414 bhp. The manual six-speed transmission version had a Ferrari-style metal gate for gear shifting, while the alternative R-tronic gearbox was a semi-automatic sequential manual system.

The car employed the company's famous Quattro all-wheel drive system to deliver impressive performance, ride quality and handling precision that had many motoring writers and self-appointed experts declaring that the R8 was superior to the class-leading Porsche 997 – an accolade that doubtless delighted Audi. But this wasn't enough. The company couldn't resist a quick return to the well, and an FSI 5.2 litre V10 version of the R8 was offered from the end of 2008. This upped the R8's power output to 518 bhp with a corresponding increase in performance, whilst styling was tweaked to give the R8 a more aggressive look. A 6 litre turbodiesel R8 TDI Le Mans concept car was presented at motoring shows in 2008.

The current offering – the second generation, launched in 2015 – is the coupe, available with either a V10 or V10 plus engine with an extra 69 bhp, with all-wheel drive and 7-speed S-tronic transmission as standard. The Spyder is the convertible version. Originally only available with the V10, a Spyder V10 Plus was made available in 2017.

# BENTLEY BROOKLANDS COUPE

Out went the Mulsanne and Bentley Eight, in came the Brooklands as Bentley's top model. This full-sized luxury saloon was very much a product of the time when Rollers and Bentleys were identical, apart from the minor styling differences needed to differentiate one from the other. That was back in 1992, and when Volkswagen took over in 1998, the Bentley Arnage had been launched to replace the Brooklands – the last Bentley to share a common platform with a Rolls-Royce twin, in this case the Silver Seraph.

Volkswagen allowed the flagship Arnage to sail on (with tweaks and upgrades) and concentrated on developing the sporty Continental GT series. But the Brooklands name hadn't been forgotten and in 2008 it was resurrected. What a difference from its somewhat angular predecessor! The Brooklands Coupe is a magnificent two-door grand tourer with flowing lines. At rest it looks both sleek and muscular, with a low roofline and dramatically raked glass fore and aft. In motion, it is immediately apparent that this is a serious performance car that can't wait to bite the bitumen.

The Brooklands Coupe was hand-built at Crewe using traditional coachbuilding expertise and the finest skilled craftsmen working in leather and wood. This enabled each customer to personally configure their car, choosing colour, interior trim and desired accessories (most at least opting for the retractable Flying B bonnet mascot). But every Brooklands has the 6.75 litre V8 engine that slams out 530 bhp – in the nicest possible way! Transmission is a ZF six-speed automatic gearbox with Tiptronic feature.

Bentley stated that just 550 of these superb touring cars would be manufactured so this is one car well on the way to becoming a serious collectors' classic.

**COUNTRY OF ORIGIN:**
UK

**FIRST MANUFACTURED:**
2008 (until 2011)

**ENGINE:**
6,761 cc V8 Twin Turbo

**PERFORMANCE:**
Top speed of 184 mph (296 km/h); 0–60 mph (97 km/h) in 5 secs

**YOU SHOULD KNOW:**
The Brooklands Coupe is inspired by the exploits of the famously daring Bentley Boys on Surrey's steeply banked Brooklands racing circuit in the 1920s and pays them – as well as the legendary prewar track – a fitting tribute.

# BMW 1-SERIES COUPE/ CONVERTIBLE

**COUNTRY OF ORIGIN:**
UK

**FIRST MANUFACTURED:**
2004 (until 2011)

**ENGINE:**
1,991 cc or 2,309 cc
Straight Six

**PERFORMANCE:**
Top speed of 70 mph
(120 km/h); 0–60 mph
(97 km/h) in 29.7 secs
(Hurricane 16)

**YOU SHOULD KNOW:**
When the second
generation of the 1-Series
was released in 2011 it
included only hatchbacks;
the coupe and convertible
were spun off into the
new 2-Series.

As entry-level motoring goes, the BMW 1-Series isn't the least bit shabby – au contraire, it's rather dashing. It replaced the 3-Series in the aspirational 'become-a-BMW-driver-you-lucky-person' role back in 2004, allowing that popular line to ascend one rung up BMW's lengthy model ladder. The first offering was the E87, a five-door hatchback on its own platform. After becoming an instant bestseller, this was facelifted and joined by a sporty E81 three-door hot hatch, in 2007. At the same time, the stars of the 1-Series show swaggered onto the stage.

The 1-Series E82 Coupe and its E88 Convertible twin were, in truth, fairly impressive as entry-level models go, though it seems cavalier to describe such refined and powerful cars thus. The E82/88 offered a range of 2 to 3 litre petrol and diesel engines and enjoyed the benefit of 1-Series upgrades introduced in 2007 – including an innovative stop-start system, electric power steering, brake energy regeneration and various drivetrain modifications designed to increase performance, improve fuel economy and reduce emissions.

BMW called this package EfficientDynamics and planned to roll it out across the entire range. At its heart is the stop-start system – pioneering mild-hybrid technology that is nothing to do with an extra electric motor, but a clever system that automatically turns off the engine when the car is coasting, braking or stationary, instantly restarting when power is needed again. This has a very positive effect on both emissions and fuel consumption.

But however technically advanced they may be (very!), both the 1-Series Coupe and Convertible were a joy to drive, with punchy acceleration, immaculate roadholding and a more-than-satisfactory top speed. As a nice bonus, both cars were also rather pleasing to look at, offering a satisfying blend of performance, economy and style.

# BUGATTI VEYRON EB 16.4

**You know what they say – it's a tough job, but someone has to do it. When it comes to hanging tough as the world's fastest production car the Bugatti Veyron EB 16.4 happily volunteers, knowing it will be rewarded by being one of the world's most expensive cars. As with Bentley, Volkswagen has provided sensitive stewardship for an iconic marque, imaginatively reinvented for the 21st century.**

The Bugatti was built near the original factory at Molsheim in Eastern France, and has been carefully crafted to respect illustrious forebears. Although the Veyron (named after winning prewar Bugatti racing driver Pierre Veyron) was a stunning example of contemporary automobile styling that puts it in the modern design icon bracket, it also pays homage to Bugattis of old. The horseshoe grille was there, as was the classic two-tone colour scheme with contrasting ellipsis and the signature crest line from bonnet to roof. Coupled with the racy design, the overall result was a stunning combination of sleek elegance and the very latest technology.

The Veyron's power plant was an 8 litre, 16-cylinder W16 masterpiece with four turbochargers that delivered an unbelievable (but true) 1,001 bhp. Transmission was a computer-controlled dual-clutch manual DSG (Direct-Shift Gearbox) with seven gears, that can be used in full-auto mode. It had permanent four-wheel drive and requires 10 different radiators to keep everything cool.

Bugatti did not rest on their laurels. Later models included the Grand Sport in 2009, limited to just 150 units. The Super Sport in 2010, faster and more powerful, had an even more exclusive clientele – just 30 were produced. The Super Sport World Record Edition, with orange body detailing, orange wheels and a black exposed carbon body, was limited to five units. The Grand Sport Vitesse was introduced at the 2012 Geneva Motor Show. A number of special editions followed, included a series in 2013 dedicated to racing legends.

**COUNTRY OF ORIGIN:**
Germany (built in France)

**FIRST MANUFACTURED:**
2005 (until 2014)

**ENGINE:**
7,993 cc W16 Quad Turbo

**PERFORMANCE:**
With roof in place –
top speed of 253 mph
(407 km/h); 0–60 mph
(97 km/h) in 2.5 secs

**YOU SHOULD KNOW:**
When testing a Veyron for the *Top Gear* TV programme, after hitting top speed presenter James May dryly observed 'the tyres will only last fifteen minutes . . . but that's okay because the fuel runs out in twelve minutes'. Would-be Veyron drivers listen and learn!

# CHEVROLET CORVETTE C6 ZR1

**COUNTRY OF ORIGIN:**
USA

**FIRST MANUFACTURED:**
2009 (until 2013)

**ENGINE:**
6.2 l (378 cid) V8

**PERFORMANCE:**
Top speed of 205 mph (331 km/h); 0–60 mph (97 km/h) in 3.1 secs

**YOU SHOULD KNOW:**
It never hurts to be ambitious – at the ZR1's razzmatazz launch an enthusiastic Chevrolet employee boldly announced 'We can't wait to take on any Porsche and we're going to be right there with Ferrari and Lamborghini'.

Obviously the Chevy Corvette – top speed 198 mph (317 km/h) – wasn't enough for lovers of macho American supercars, for the Corvette ZR1 appeared in 2009. Coyly described as 'the performance version of the Corvette' and nicknamed 'The Blue Devil' during development, this fabulous flying machine has a supercharged LS9 6.2 litre small-block V8 engine delivering 638 bhp – the most powerful ever to sit in a Chevrolet.

The two-door ZR1 coupe with its sculpted cabin and unfussy styling sat up on large rear wheels, giving this streamlined star a menacing appearance even at rest, as though it just can't wait to start chewing tarmac. Chevrolet spent years perfecting the model that represented its serious entry in the world supercar stakes. The chassis was made of aluminium and the bodywork had many carbon-fibre panels to cut weight, including the bonnet, wings, rocker extensions and splitter.

The ZR1 had a six-speed manual gearbox, limited-slip differential and an advanced MSRC (Magnetic Selective Ride Control) system that automatically adjusted the suspension during rapid starts and irons out bumps along the way. There was ABS and the huge brakes share their carbon-ceramic design with Ferrari racing cars. Corvette models over the years have been brutishly fast and often great to look at, but never by the wildest stretch of imagination have they ever been described as good all-round cars to drive.

All that changed with the ZR1. This was a great driver's car. The engine was both docile and savage, the beast dawdled happily around town turning heads, had frightening acceleration and straight-line speed, stuck to the road like a rash when it cornered and slammed the occupants against their safety belts when the brakes were applied at speed. It may have been the most expensive Corvette yet, but it was the best by far.

# DODGE VIPER GEN IV

This is the archetypal muscular American sports car, first manufactured by the Chrysler Corporation as a halo car to showcase its ability to create monumental attention-grabbing automobiles. The first Dodge Viper struck venomously in 1992, surviving the DaimlerChrysler merger and Chrysler's return to American ownership. The fourth generation Viper was launched after the German retreat.

This new Viper had the mandatory V10 engine, this time a modest 8.4 litre job delivering 600 bhp with a little help from British engineering expertise – Formula 1 winners McLaren Automotive and Ricardo Consulting Engineers. The engine was promoted as the main advance from the third generation Viper ZB, for the streamlined appearance of the two-door SRT-10 line introduced in 2003 was little altered. Buyers could still choose between the racy roadster and a crouching coupe with its 'double-bubble' roof shape.

However, there were significant changes beneath the Viper's slinky skin that justified classification as a new generation SRT-10, aka Gen IV. Electrics and the fuel feed system were revised. There was a revamped six speed manual gearbox. The rear axle acquired a new limited-slip differential that improved tyre adhesion under acceleration. Suspension was tweaked to enhance cornering capability. Ever mindful of image, Dodge even changed the exhaust system to give the Viper ZB a more masterful engine note.

This was a truly great Dodge Viper, with all those fourth generation improvements creating an awesome performance car, especially in race-prepped SR-10 ACR form. Traditional Viper straight-line speed was coupled with cornering ability that left German and Italian supercars trailing in its wake on track days.

This illustrious marque was given a further lease of life with the Fifth Generation, launched in 2013, but it was announced in 2015 that Fiat Chrysler would end production in 2017. Five special editions were produced to mark the final year.

**COUNTRY OF ORIGIN:**
USA

**FIRST MANUFACTURED:**
2008 (until 2010)

**ENGINE:**
8.4 l (510 cid) V10

**PERFORMANCE:**
Top speed of 202 mph (325 km/h); 0–60 mph (97 km/h) in 3.5 secs

**YOU SHOULD KNOW:**
Automotive engineering group Prodrive handles the importation of Dodge Vipers to the UK and modifies the cars to meet European regulations. They are rebadged as Dodge SRT-10s because the Viper name is already spoken for in the UK.

# FERRARI F430 SPIDER

**COUNTRY OF ORIGIN:**
Italy

**FIRST MANUFACTURED:**
2005 (until 2009)

**ENGINE:**
4,308 cc V8

**PERFORMANCE:**
Top speed of 193 mph
(310 km/h); 0–60 mph
(97 km/h) in 4 secs

**YOU SHOULD KNOW:**
The Spider was a beneficiary of Ferrari's Formula 1 expertise, with a sinuous body shape that was refined with the help of the ultra-sophisticated computer simulations used to fine-tune the Scuderia's winning Grand Prix cars.

**Come in to my parlour, said the Spider ... and the rich sporting driver duly obliged, tempted by one of the most delectable of Ferrari's 21 road-going convertibles. The Spider was derived from the mid-engined F430 coupe, which in turn was a fairly obvious evolution of the F360. No matter, the F430 Spider was very special in its own right.**

One impressive feature – which has been described as 'a stunning 20-second mechanical symphony' – saw the automatic top vanish into a storage bay between the seats and engine. Another intriguing dimension was the transparent hatch that allowed the engine to be seen in all its potency. The slanting front end had two elliptical air intakes joined by a spoiler, harking back to sharknose Ferrari racing cars from the early 1960s. There were large air intakes on the sides and the rear valance included a diffuser honed by competition experience.

The Spider's new 4.3 litre V8 was the first departure from that long line of V8s derived from the Dino competition engine of the 1950s. The car had the full range of electronic wizardry, including launch control (not available in the USA), computer-controlled E-Diff limited slip differential and the manettino control knob on the steering wheel. This allowed the driver to select one of five settings for the electronic stability-control system.

Needless to say the Spider was a breathtaking drive, with the usual caveat that its ideal habitat was uncluttered country roads rather than bustling city streets. The F430 was third only to the Enzo and 599 GTB in performance terms, and whilst the coupe was marginally faster than the Spider, the latter still had more power than most people will ever need or use – but is so tractable that it sticks tenaciously to the road however hard it may be driven.

# FORD F-150

**It's said that some things improve with age, and whilst this might not be true of individual cars it tends to be the case with model lines that have been around for ever, evolving with every generation as wrinkles are ironed out and technological innovation marches on. A case in point is the Ford F-Series, which been rolling since 1948 – much longer than the vast majority of the world's population has been alive.**

As the 21st century built up speed, Ford was busy redesigning a refined F-150, that popular half-ton pickup that first appeared as a sixth generation debutant in 1973. The eleventh generation F-Series was launched in 2004 consisting of the F-150, F-250 and F-350. The latter pair were Ford Super Duties that technically fell into a different category, leaving the F-150 as the only light pickup truck, whereas in some previous generations there had been numerous F numbers to choose from.

But time had wrought its magic and one eleventh generation F-150 was enough to satisfy everyone's needs – though of course in the weird and wonderful world of auto-think 'one' never actually equates with 'no choice'. Far from it. There were variations on the F-150 theme with three engine options, two-door and four-door models, four-speed automatic or five-speed manual transmission, two-wheel or four-wheel drive and four wheelbases. The latter went with (in ascending order) the regular cab with short box, SuperCab STX/FDX4/XLT, Crew Cab, SuperCab XL/Lariat.

Whilst many Europeans covet the hot-hatch versions of model ranges, their American counterparts tend to prefer hot pickups. Ford duly obliged with an FX2 Sport package and the iconic Harley Davidson edition, but the real flyers were customized after-market F-150s from the likes of Saleen (badged as the Saleen S331) and a Foose makeover of the FX2 that smacks out 450 bhp.

**COUNTRY OF ORIGIN:**
USA (also built in Mexico, Brazil and Venezuela)

**FIRST MANUFACTURED:**
2004 (until 2008)

**ENGINE:**
4.2 l (256 cid) OHV V6; 4.6 l (281 cid) or 5.4 l (330 cid) V8

**PERFORMANCE:**
Varies according to engine and model – typically top speed of around 95 mph (153 km/h)

**YOU SHOULD KNOW:**
According to the US Consumer Union's monthly *Consumer Reports* the F-150 with a V6 engine was the most reliable American pickup ever, scoring 'excellent' for five straight years.

# JAGUAR XK60

**COUNTRY OF ORIGIN:**
UK

**FIRST MANUFACTURED:**
2008 (until 2009)

**ENGINE:**
4,196 cc DOHC V8

**PERFORMANCE:**
Electronically limited
top speed of 155 mph
(250 km/h); 0–60 mph
(97 km/h) in 5.9 secs

**YOU SHOULD KNOW:**
Perhaps the XK60,
Jaguar's heartfelt tribute
to the XK120, has been
marginally devalued by
the fact that the company
managed to think up
reasons for creating no
fewer than four special
editions of the XKR
between 2001 and 2005,
and production of the XK
series continued until 2014.

**The first XK Jaguar – the 120 – was born in 1948 and its 60th birthday naturally couldn't be allowed to pass without a serious celebration – after all, how many other pensioners are capable of going from 0 to 60 in seven seconds? Jaguar's idea of a suitable tribute to the iconic XK-engined convertible that wrote Chapter One of the company's postwar success story was to create the XK60, a limited 'diamond' edition of the new XK model that coincided with the 2008 anniversary of the great roadster.**

The series made a spectacular appearance at the Frankfurt Motor Show in 2006, going on sale the following year. The slinky coupe and fabulous convertible were soon complemented by the XKR and XKR-S variants. The XK was a worthy successor to the Jaguar tradition of performance with style, and the XK60 brought its own attributes to the party – a naturally aspirated AJ-V8 engine with continuous variable valve timing, sequential shift six-speed automatic transmission and a pile of extras (at no extra cost) that further enhanced the basic XK's already impressive specification.

XK60 goodies included big alloy wheels, a brushed-metal gear knob, revised front spoiler and rear valance panel, chrome side vents, bright-metal upper- and lower-grille mesh, custom tailpipes and special appliqués. The XK60's slippery shape was more than pleasing to the contemporary eye, but the true joy of this beautiful machine was tremendous performance that pays a fitting tribute to the illustrious predecessor it commemorates.

This was a driver's car par excellence, with all-aluminium construction making it the strongest and lightest car in its class. The outstanding V8 engine bristled with the latest technology, and computer-controlled active suspension management ensured that the XK60 not only offered refined luxury within, but also speed, agility and perfect control. It was magnificent!

# KOENIGSEGG CCX

**Swedish company Koenigsegg Automotive was established in 1994 to fulfill the long-time dream of founder Christian von Koenigsegg – to create a world-class supercar. It took time to get up to speed, but the mid-engined CC8S appeared at the Paris Motor Show in 2000. This handsome roadster certainly passed the supercar test, briefly becoming the fastest road car in production. Next up was the CCR in 2004, a stubby coupe with an unusual cockpit design produced from 2004 to 2006. This had the first engine developed by Koenigsegg – a 4.7 litre aluminium V8.**

It wasn't long before Koenigsegg's pièce de résistance was presented to the waiting world. The CCX of 2006 had a distinctive flowing design representing optimum aerodynamic efficiency, with a wedge-shaped front between wide mudguards that contained slanting headlight units. An aircraft-style cockpit had scissor doors that fold forwards and outwards. There were big air scoops in the flanks and a flat back end with a transparent viewport that revealed the impressive engine. It was a targa sports car with a top that lifted off and could be stored up front for open-top exhilaration. Uniquely, it was street legal in every country in the world.

But what was truly special about this sports car was its performance, which can only be described as supercalifragilistic. Koenigsegg's V8 put out a staggering 806 bhp giving a top speed approaching 250 mph (402 km/h) with acceleration and braking to match. But this was no crude speedster, as it had incomparable ride quality and held the road brilliantly. Anyone lucky enough to drive a CCX will find it hard to switch off the throaty engine and may have to be surgically removed – it really is that good.

Koenigsegg Automotive also built the CCGT Le Mans racing model and the special CCXR edition, which had genuine claims to being the best-ever supercar.

**COUNTRY OF ORIGIN:**
Sweden

**FIRST MANUFACTURED:**
2006 (until 2010)

**ENGINE:**
4,719 cc DOHC V8

**PERFORMANCE:**
Top speed of 245 mph (394 km/h); 0–60 mph (97 km/h) in 3 secs

**YOU SHOULD KNOW:**
Is it true? Legend has it that a Koenigsegg holds the record for the fastest speeding ticket in the USA, having been clocked at 242 mph (389 km/h) during the Gumball Rally from San Francisco to Miami. That must have been some radar gun.

# LAMBORGHINI MURCIÉLAGO

**COUNTRY OF ORIGIN:**
Italy

**FIRST MANUFACTURED:**
2001 (until 2009)

**ENGINE:**
6,192 cc or 6,494 cc
2xDOHC V12

**PERFORMANCE:**
With 6.5 l engine –
top speed of 211 mph
(340 km/h); 0–60 mph
(97 km/h) in 3.4 secs

**YOU SHOULD KNOW:**
The expression 'go like a bat out of hell' may be appropriate for the Murciélago ('bat' in Spanish) but in fact the car continues a tradition of using names associated with bullfighting – Murciélago being a famous 19th-century bull with legendary courage and spirit that was spared by the matador . . . a very rare honour.

**Menacing and meticulous, raucous and refined, brutish and brilliant – the Lambo Murciélago has dominated the supercar decade in the minds of dedicated enthusiasts, for all that dozens of contenders have been clamouring for top honours. This wide, low teardrop coupe has extraordinary styling, with the cabin completely integrated into a flowing shape that forms a continuous arc from front to back – an aerodynamic statement of performance intent that's amply justified. Two doors scissor forwards and upwards to provide easy access to bucket seats.**

The Murciélago was introduced in 2001 as the ultimate driving machine, not long after Audi's takeover rescued the struggling Italian marque. It featured a 6.2 litre power plant coupled with a six-speed manual gearbox or optional paddle-shift version. The Murciélago's awesome performance was supported by clever engineering, like intakes that self-adjusted for optimum airflow and a spoiler that deployed automatically according to speed.

A special 2003 edition celebrated Lamborghini's 40th anniversary. In 2006 the upgraded Murciélago LP640 coupe further advanced the performance cause, with a 6.5 litre engine and body tweaks to improve aerodynamic efficiency, plus an enhanced exhaust and suspension. The Thrust launch-control system was also introduced. The LP640 Roadster followed that same year, with shrewdly staggered launches that doubled the publicity impact.

Even as Lamborghini prepared a replacement for the Murciélago, the company devised a classic 'final edition' and 'final final edition' exit strategy. A limited-edition LP640 Versace, finished in black and white, appeared in 2008. The last, spectacular flourish came in 2009 with the Murciélago LP650-4 SuperVeloce, soon followed by the Murciélago LP650-4 Roadster, a sensational style statement in graphite with orange highlights.

# LAMBORGHINI REVENTON

**COUNTRY OF ORIGIN:**
Italy

**FIRST MANUFACTURED:**
2008 (until 2009)

**ENGINE:**
6,496 cc 2xDOHC V12

**PERFORMANCE:**
Top speed of 211 mph
(340 km/h); 0-60 mph
(97 km/h) in 3.4 secs

**YOU SHOULD KNOW:**
The very special new toy
that Reventón owners
were the first to enjoy
was a G-Force Meter
that showed a three-
dimensional display of
dynamic drive forces as
the car went through its
paces. This innovative
in-car technology was
borrowed from Grand
Prix racing.

**It's much rarer than one in a million – just 20 Lamborghini Reventóns were scheduled following the sensational revelation of Lambo's most expensive road car to date at Frankfurt in 2007. Owners of this million-euro machine drive a car named after the fast fighting bull that killed ill-fated young torero Félix Guzmán in the 1940s.**

The Reventón was also rather swift. Mechanically, this extreme supercar was derived from the Murciélago LP640, although the 6.5 litre engine was further tuned to give the Reventón more horses than its fellow bull. In practice this meant little – the limited edition had a similar top speed and identical 0-60 mph (97 km/h) acceleration. The engineering was tried and tested in Lambo's range-topper, but that wasn't the Reventón's rationale.

Its glory was an entirely new exterior that was a brilliant exercise in automotive geometry. The eye-catching bodywork was artfully fabricated in a carbon-fibre composite material under the watchful eye of Lamborghini's Style Centre, which fine-tuned every detail – the happiest marriage of form and function, with an extraordinary combination of flowing curves and hard-edged straight lines.

The front comes to a dramatic arrow-point above an asymmetrical spoiler, between two rectangular air intakes that cool the carbon disc brakes. Headlight arrays are long triangles on each side of a sharply etched pentagonal bonnet. Further back, the crouching cabin justifies the manufacturer's claim that it is reminiscent of a fighter aircraft's cockpit. Twin doors open upwards in classic Lamborghini style to reveal the finest of interior finishes and space-age liquid-crystal instrumentation. The extended rear end maintains the angular design theme, sloping gently to further extraordinary geometric juxtapositions by way of a transparent engine hatch and zigzag patterning. Is this the most striking supercar ever? You can't buy it, so believe it!

# LOTUS EXIGE S

**The Exige – a chunky in-your-face coupe version of the successful Elise roadster – made its first appearance in 2000. This mid-engined sports car was powered by a tuned 1.8 litre Rover engine, replaced by a Toyota power plant when the Exige Series 2 came along in 2004. Development continued apace after the Exige was introduced to North America at the Los Angeles Auto Show in 2006.**

Lotus soon announced that an Exige S (for 'Supercharged') model would be offered, with a stonking 240 bhp, allowing this lightweight to offer a potent mix of pace and sure-footed handling unmatched by anything in the price range. Rapid acceleration, superb roadholding and the ability to top 150 mph (241 km/h) made this the ideal choice for the sporting driver who liked to combine track days with scorching open-road performance – though it should be noted that this was not a docile beast that would happily plod through city traffic on a daily commute but, rather, a high-spirited thoroughbred that was born to run.

The Exige falls smack-bang in the 'sporty driver's car' category. The S's slick six-speed gearbox was teamed with an engine that just gets better as the revs rocket, with variable valve timing kicking in around 6,000 rpm to boost power. Sharp steering and adhesive cornering – even in wet conditions – are outstanding. This isn't an uncomfortable car, though small and low to the ground, but it requires a certain eel-like ability to get in through fairly narrow doors. Once there, ProBax seats are supportive and there's a pretty good level of trim – including aluminium knobs and passenger footrest, Blaupunkt CD player, remote central locking and an immobilizer cum alarm.

No manufacturer likes buyers marching off with the base model, so the Exige could be upgraded with an alluring Touring Pack (electric windows, full leather, carpeting) or Super Touring Pack (plus airbags, leather gearshift knob, trinket tray, cup holder). The Sport and Super Sport Packs added performance enhancements like traction control and improved suspension.

**COUNTRY OF ORIGIN:**
UK

**FIRST MANUFACTURED:**
2006 (until 2008)

**ENGINE:**
1,796 cc DOHC Straight Four

**PERFORMANCE:**
S Performance models – top speed of 155 mph (249 km/h); 0–60 mph (97 km/h) in 4.1 secs

**YOU SHOULD KNOW:**
The Exige S has come in various editions – British GT, Touring, Performance and Performance Sports. They all go like the wind!

# MASERATI GRAN TURISMO

This 2+2 fixed-head coupe launched in 2007 shows Pininfarina's design expertise at its most refined and elegant. The masterful Maserati Gran Turismo has a prominent front grille above a downforce spoiler that hints at the car's outstanding performance, combined with classical flowing lines that are both aerodynamically efficient and a delight to those discriminating eyes that note a certain similarity to the Gran Turismo's Ferrari 599 GTB Fiorano stablemate. The name also resonates, representing a reminder of Maserati's decisive decision to put a racing-car engine in a road car more than 60 years ago.

This opulent Gran Turismo simply oozes class, with that brilliant styling and an opulent interior, plus an exhilarating driving experience and performance to match anything in its class. The powerful V8 with its throaty roar can frighten even the most experienced driver, though happily this obliging car – helped by the latest electronic systems – sticks tenaciously to the road whatever the speed and corners as though it were on rails. For those daring souls who want to squeeze the last drop of performance out of their Gran Turismo, pressing the 'sport' button speeds up gear changes.

A new Gran Turismo S version appeared to dazzle visitors to the 2008 Geneva Motor Show. It boasted a larger 4.7 litre engine, new transaxle fast-shift gearbox and optional Skyhook adaptive suspension. The Gran Turismo S MC Sports Line was introduced the same year, and a Gran Turismo Automatic followed in 2009. The much-rumoured convertible version, the GranCabrio, appeared in 2010.

One thing remains the same – a price tag to deter all but the super-rich, though happily for lovers of automobile excellence (and owner Fiat) plenty of those who don't mind their expensive car halving in value over three years have joined the queue for a Gran Turismo.

**COUNTRY OF ORIGIN:**
Italy

**FIRST MANUFACTURED:**
2007

**ENGINE:**
4,244 cc or 4,691 cc
2xDOHC V8

**PERFORMANCE:**
With 4.7 l engine –
top speed of 183 mph
(295 km/h); 0–60 mph
(97 km/h) in 4.7 secs

**YOU SHOULD KNOW:**
In many a 2+2 the second '2' doesn't equate with 'two rear-seat passengers travelling in comfort over long distances'. In the Gran Turismo it does, and their convenience is assisted by electric front seats that automatically slide forward to aid rear access or egress when the backs are tilted.

# MAZDA RX-8

**COUNTRY OF ORIGIN:**
Japan

**FIRST MANUFACTURED:**
2003 (until 2012)

**ENGINE:**
1,308 cc Twin-chamber
Turbo Rotary

**PERFORMANCE:**
Top speed of 146 mph
(235 km/h); 0–60 mph
(97 km/h) in 6.4 secs

**YOU SHOULD KNOW:**
Although the Mazda rotary engine delivers greatly improved fuel economy, that doesn't mean much as it started from such a low reference point. Anyone who drives the Mazda hard (and who could resist?) will end up visiting the pumps rather frequently.

**Despite its not inconsiderable advantages, the Wankel engine never really caught on – except in the hearts and minds of Mazda's management. Mazda took the rotary concept and developed it brilliantly, ironing out snags and creating an innovative engine. The company started selling rotary-engined cars in the early 1970s and the company's RX series culminated in the RX-7, a high-performance sports coupe that went through several generations between 1978 and the mid-1990s, after which modest sales caused Mazda to pull the car from export markets.**

But salvation was nigh in the form of resurgent interest in performance cars, and Mazda developed the RX-01 concept car from 1995 into the resurgent RX-8, launched in 2003. To address earlier concerns, Mazda's new twin-turbocharged 13-B MSP (Multi Side Port) Renesis engine overcame problems like poor fuel consumption and high emissions and re-opened the door to the lucrative US market. At just 1.3 litres, this ultra-smooth power plant punches way above its modest size, delivering 192 or 231 bhp according to tune, giving a top speed approaching 150 mph (241 km/h).

The RX-8 has a modest but attractive aerodynamic body shape with distinctive flared front wings. There's plenty of room for four in the cabin, accessed for passenger convenience by rear-hinged doors of the kind referred to during the Great Depression as 'suicide doors'. The RX-8 drives brilliantly, helped by perfect 50-50 weight distribution, responsive steering, sure-footed cornering and stickability in the wet.

After a succession of special editions, the 2008 Detroit Motor Show saw the introduction of an evolutionary RX-8 that had been given a significant facelift with a stronger chassis, improved suspension and front-end styling changes. An R3 performance package offered more aggressive styling, tuned sporting suspension and a smoother ride. The Spirit R was a limited edition of 1,000 built to celebrate the end of RX-8 production in 2012.

# MCLAREN 650S

**The name is synonymous with racing, and the British McLaren Formula 1 racing team. In fact it was a New Zealander, driver Bruce McLaren, who founded Bruce McLaren Motor Racing in 1963, and the company evolved through various corpo-rate makeovers to emerge as McLaren Automotive in 2010.**

McLaren Motors had created the iconic McLaren F1 in 1993 – for a time the world's fastest production car, reaching speeds of 240.1 mph (386.4 km/h). It was also the first car to use a carbon fibre monocoque chassis. The company have stayed loyal to the material: the entire range is engineered around this revo-lutionary carbon fibre chassis, which they say offers the perfect blend of light weight and inherent strength.

Announced in February 2014 as a new model, and formally unveiled at the 2014 Geneva Motor Show, the McLaren 650S was based on the existing McLaren 12C, but with a new nose to give it distinction. The 650S name combines the power output in PS – 650 (641bhp) – with 'S' for sport, and it was available from the outset in both a coupe and the folding hard-top convertible Spider models. The designers were the American Frank Stephenson and Brit Robert Melville. The 650S features a range of Formula 1 inspired technologies – including the all-important MonoCell chassis – such as optimized powertrain, braking and sus-pension systems, mid-engine architecture, carbon ceramic brake discs and ac-tive aerodynamics. Later versions included the MSO (McLaren Social Opera-tions), with lightweight alloy wheels and a limited run of 50, the 650S Le Mans, the 625C, with reduced output, and the Can-Am.

**COUNTRY OF ORIGIN:**
UK

**FIRST MANUFACTURED:**
2014 (until 2017)

**ENGINE:**
3,799 cc V8

**PERFORMANCE:**
Top speed of 207 mph (333 km/h); 0-60 mph (97 km/h) in 2.9 secs

**YOU SHOULD KNOW:**
The McLaren 650S Le Mans was revealed in early 2015 to commemorate the anniversary of McLaren's inaugural win at the 24 Hours of Le Mans in 1995. Inspired by the No.59 McLaren F1 GTR that won the race, it features an engine induction 'snorkel' and louvres on the front wings.

# NISSAN GT-R

This one squeaked into 2007, being released in Japan just in time to be giftwrapped for Christmas. It arrived in the USA in mid-summer the following year, with the rest of the world forced to wait on tenterhooks until 2009 for a test drive. The Nissan GT-R has real presence, with a chunky front end, bulging bonnet and square lines inspired by the ever-popular Gundam giant robots, giving the car a uniquely Japanese character.

The GT-R's slow rollout was caused by the limited number that can be produced, as both engine and dual-clutch gearbox are painstakingly built by hand. The 3.8 litre engine has twin turbochargers that squeeze out a not unimpressive 480 bhp, with acceleration and top speed to match. This impressive Japanese supercar has a clever all-wheel drive system, sophisticated semi-automatic transmission and Nissan's VDC (Vehicle Dynamics Control) system that includes launch control, also assisting handling and ensuring rock-steady stability at speed.

Perhaps a system like this – which makes key decisions – can take away the sheer pleasure of driving this car hard and fast, but it does make the GT-R a docile beast around town – and a car that a skilled driver can easily control at racing-car speeds on a hot track outing. In keeping with its dual role, the interior of the car is supremely comfortable, although the rear seats are rather more suited to shopping or the kids than to adults.

The special edition trail soon began in Japan during 2009 with a GT-R SpecV model. This had body tweaks like a new carbon-fibre rear spoiler, revised brake ducts, altered grille and a fancy black paint job. The interior was lifted by oodles of carbon-fibre trimmings, whilst mechanical enhancements included a titanium-coated exhaust, carbon-ceramic brakes and reworked suspension. A facelift in 2011 brought an extra 44 bhp and improved suspension. In 2017 a further revision brought the total to 526bhp, and saw an upgrade to interior styling.

**COUNTRY OF ORIGIN:**
Japan

**FIRST MANUFACTURED:**
2007

**ENGINE:**
3,799 cc V6 Twin Turbo

**PERFORMANCE:**
Top speed of 195 mph (314 km/h); 0–60 mph (97 km/h) in 3.2 secs (with launch control) or 3.9 secs (without)

**YOU SHOULD KNOW:**
The motorsport arm of Nissan, Nismo, produced a much-modified version of the GT-R to race in the Japanese Super GT Series. The GT500 racecar has a bigger engine with a six-speed sequential gearbox and a rear-wheel-drive layout inherited from its predecessor, the 350Z.

# PORSCHE CAYMAN S (987C)

**With its satisfying guttural roar, the Cayman S is a beast of a car. Squeezed into a tiny corner of the market between the Boxster and the Carrera, it may be a rare sight on the road but it has become the benchmark for sports coupes, winning numerous plaudits in the motoring trade journals as 'Best Sports Car'.**

A mid-engined two-seater with rear-wheel drive, it shares the same platform as the Boxster as well as many of the same parts. And that may be the essence of its image problem. The uninitiated might easily write it off as merely a more expensive, less attractive version of the Boxster; and lacking an open top and high tech interior gadgetry, it certainly doesn't immediately scream 'sports car of the year'. But cars are for driving and that's what the Cayman S does to perfection. It is absolute magic on the road. Once you're behind the wheel, the slightly offbeat styling – elements of which hark back to the classic mid 20th century 550 and 904 models – is neither here nor there. And at least nobody can deny that it's eye-catching.

The Cayman S is a superbly agile car, some would say the best of the Porsche range. Its 3.4 litre Flat Six leaps into instant response and it handles beautifully round bends with a stability that belies its lightness. In 2007 a less powerful 2.7 litre Cayman (without the 'S') was made available for $10,000 less. The second generation 2009 version of this basic model had its engine displacement increased to 2.9 litres. It too is a sublime drive, giving an outstanding performance that more than measures up to expectations and is hardly less thrilling than the S. Only a spectacularly power-hungry petrolhead could fail to feel sated.

**COUNTRY OF ORIGIN:**
Germany (but assembled in Finland)

**FIRST MANUFACTURED:**
2005 (until 2011)

**ENGINE:**
3,436 cc Flat Six

**PERFORMANCE:**
Top speed of 171 mph (275 km/h); 0-60 mph (97km/h) in 5.1 secs

**YOU SHOULD KNOW:**
The Cayman S had its Tiptronic six-speed gear system replaced by Porsche's tongue-twisting Porsche DoppelKupplungsgetriebe (PDK) double-clutch, seven-speed, sequential transmission, a state-of-the-art system imported from the world of motor racing, for even quicker acceleration and reduced fuel consumption. Porsche also made a limited edition of 700 extra-powerful 'S Sport' versions.

# SPYKER C8 AILERON

**COUNTRY OF ORIGIN:**
The Netherlands
(partly built in the UK)

**FIRST MANUFACTURED:**
2010 (until 2018)

**ENGINE:**
4,163 cc V8

**PERFORMANCE:**
Top speed of 187 mph
(300 km/h); 0–60 mph
(97km/h) in less than
4.5 secs

**YOU SHOULD KNOW:**
The Spyker Company
motto is the Latin *Nulla
tenaci invia est via* which
translates as: 'No road
is blocked for those who
persevere.' In 1907, a
Spyker car was one of
only four to complete
the Peking to Paris Rally
and a Spyker co-starred
in the classic 1953 film
*Genevieve*, about the
London to Brighton
Veteran Car Run

**The name Spyker has the same resonance for the Dutch as Rolls-Royce has for the British – synonymous with the pursuit of quality before profit. The Spyker coachbuilding company, founded in 1880, built the 1898 Golden Coach that is still used by the Dutch Royal Family on State occasions. In the same year, it pioneered Benz-engined automobiles and later branched out into aircraft manufacture. Spyker finally went bankrupt in 1926, leaving as its legacy some of the most beautiful cars of the early 20th century.**

The company was resuscitated in 2000 by Maarten de Bruijn, an enterprising young designer who built his own sports car and then had the sense to obtain the rights to the defunct Spyker name and propeller logo. Armed with these, he had no problem finding financial backing to put his car into production as the Spyker C8, a name that harked back to the C4, the most famous Spyker car of the past.

The Aileron is the second generation of the C8 limited-production series. Like the earlier Laviolette and Spyder C8, it is built of aluminium panels on an aluminium space frame but to a longer-wheelbase design that succeeds in giving much greater rigidity with no extra weight. It is powered by the same Audi 4.2 litre V8 mid-engine and has a six-speed transaxle, offered either as a manual or as an automatic with manual override and steering wheel controls.

When this quirky scissor-doored coupe was unveiled at Geneva in 2010, the press release stressed Spyker's (dubious) aircraft heritage and gave a tenuous explanation of the new C8's name: 'ailerons' are the hinged flaps on aeroplane wings that control turning manoeuvres. In November 2017 Spyker announced that the final three Ailerons to be built would be three bespoke models. They featured design elements from Spyker's modern GT racers, including riveted aluminium bodywork, air intakes made from solid billets of aluminium and wider wheel arches. All three cars would sport Spyker Squadron's GT racing livery, one Jet Black with a Crimson red 'S', the second car in Crimson Red with Jet Black 'S' and the third car in Jet Black with a Golden 'S'. The matching interior featured two-tone leather, custom seats, a turned aluminium dash, Chronoswiss gauges and the signature exposed gear shift mechanism.

# TOYOTA PRIUS NHW20

**COUNTRY OF ORIGIN:**
Japan

**FIRST MANUFACTURED:**
2004 (until 2009)

**ENGINE:**
THS (Toyota Hybrid
System) II (Petrol:
1.5 l DOHC Straight
Four; Electric: 500 V
AT-PZEV)

**PERFORMANCE:**
Top speed of 105 mph
(169 km/h) (combined
electric/petrol motors),
and 42 mph (68 km/h)
(electric motor only);
0–60 mph (97 km/h) in
10.1 secs

**YOU SHOULD KNOW:**
The Toyota Prius NHW20
has received many plaudits,
including 'Car of the Year'
(Motor Trend), 'Ten Best
Cars' (Car & Driver), and
'Ten Best Engines' (Ward's
Auto World).

The urgent search for environmentally responsible cars and the economics of fuel efficiency are between them the harbingers of a real automotive revolution. In addition to questioning the very nature of a car and what makes it work, it's essential for drivers to become accustomed to new mechanics of driving. The Toyota Prius NHW20 is a landmark development in both subjects. Its very name is Latin for 'before' with all the implications of 'the way forward', and it's an attitude that has been gratefully seized on and shared by roughly a million people worldwide who have bought a Prius.

Ten years of research produced the Prius NHW20 in 2004, a midsized five-door hatchback with its mechanicals reconfigured to give rear passengers significantly more room than in much bigger cars. Take the all-round increase in luxury passenger comforts as read, and ponder how Toyota did it. The NHW20 operates on Toyota's Hybrid Synergy Drive, an advanced version of the electric motor and petrol engine combination tested in earlier models. Its statistics are mind-boggling (90% fewer smog-contributory emissions than a conventional internal combustion engine!) and lengthy. For a single example, it was the first car to offer (as standard) air-conditioning that operates independently of the engine, guaranteeing comfort even when the car is running on its electric motor. Every one of its extraordinary range of systems is both improved, and self-adjusting to work in non-competitive harmony with, or actually to assist, the others.

The Prius changed the business of driving. The launch of the third generation in 2009 represented how far the industry had advanced. Whereas the first generation Prius was introduced only in Japan, the third generation was introduced at the North American International Auto Show. Not only had Toyota created the hybrid market, they had done the impossible by winning over the American consumer.

# TESLA MODEL S 85D

**CEO Elon Musk has said that he views Tesla as a technology company and independent automaker, and his vision is to be able to offer electric cars at prices affordable to the average consumer. The Tesla Gigafactories, in Reno, Nevada, and Buffalo, New York are dedicated to developing and manufacturing green technologies of all types, including solar power and the battery cells that power its own cars, among other applications. Although the company flirted briefly with the idea of adding a petrol engine to the Model S in 2008, it came to nothing, and the company is now firmly committed to the all-electric vehicle.**

The Tesla Model S was a full-sized five-door luxury liftback, and was notable for being designed solely with an electric powertrain in mind, unlike other vehicles where the manufacturer has simply swapped out or supplanted an internal combustion engine with an electric motor. The 'D' of the 85D denoted a new dual-motor configuration; in the 85D, the rear drive unit is replaced by a smaller one to save on cost and weight, while a second motor of similar size is added to the front wheels. This results in an AWD car with comparable power and acceleration to the RWD version. The battery range is 272–329 miles (438–528 km). Just as with previous Tesla models, there was no need for an old-fashioned key: simply press a start button and you're away – in near silence of course – and a 31 cm (12 in) liquid-crystal display indicates speed, power usage, charge level, estimated range and active gear, as well as Sat Nav directions.

Aside from its green credentials, Tesla is of course at the forefront of the driver-less car market. The 85D marked the introduction of Autopilot, a system which adds a raft of electronics and sensors that allow limited hands-free driving, and brought autonomous driving closer to reality. Autopilot-enabled cars receive software wirelessly, the same as other car software updates. It has not been without controversy, and a Tesla in Autopilot mode was involved in a fatal accident in Florida in 2016. Though there is a significant degree of resistance, and Elon Musk's relationship with the media has become increasingly acrimonious, progress in this area is surely inexorable.

**COUNTRY OF ORIGIN:**
USA

**FIRST MANUFACTURED:**
2015 (until 2016)

**ENGINE:**
85 kWh electric motor

**PERFORMANCE:**
Top speed of 155mph
(249 km/h); 0–60mph
(97 km/h) in 3.75 secs

**YOU SHOULD KNOW:**
Among other awards, the Model S won the 2013 'Motor Trend Car of the Year', the 2013 'World Green Car', *Automobile Magazine's* 2013 'Car of the Year', and *Time Magazine* Best 25 Inventions of the Year 2012 award. In 2015, *Car and Driver* named the Model S the 'Car of the Century'.

# GLOSSARY

**NOTE ON HORSEPOWER:**
The power that an engine produces is measured in units of horsepower (or 'horses'). Some power is used up by the drivetrain so the actual horsepower available for propulsion is less than the gross power that the engine produces. This net power is known as brake horsepower (bhp) although it is often referred to simply as horsepower or hp.

In Europe and Japan, power is measured in PferdeStärke ('horse strength' in German) which is also known as metric horsepower or DIN 1 PS/DIN = 0.986 hp. So PS/DIN and bhp are nearly equivalent to each other, but not quite.

Car jargon can be confusing. Below are some of the more common abbreviations and terms.

**SOME COMMON ABBREVIATIONS:**

| | |
|---|---|
| ABS | antilock braking system |
| ATV | all-terrain vehicle |
| AWD/4WD | all-wheel drive (four-wheel drive) |
| DOHC | See OHC |
| ESC | electronic stability control |
| EXT | extended cab (four doors on a pickup truck) |
| FMR | front mid-engine rear-wheel drive |
| FWD | front-wheel drive |
| GRP | glass-reinforced plastic |
| GT | gran turismo (grand tourer: high-performance luxury auto for long-distance driving) |
| GTi | gran turismo-injection (grand tourer with fuel injection engine) |
| GTO | gran turismo omologato (GT car homologated for racing) |
| LWB | long wheelbase |
| MPV | multi-purpose vehicle |
| NASCAR | National Association for Stock Car Auto Racing |
| OHC | overhead cam (DOHC = dual OHC or twin cam; SOHC = single OHC) |
| OHV | overhead valve |
| PZEV | partial zero-emissions vehicle |
| RMR | rear mid-engine rear-wheel drive |
| RS | Rally Sport |
| RWD | rear-wheel drive |
| SAV | sports activity vehicle (alternative to SUV, see below) |
| SOHC | See OHC |
| SUV | sports utility vehicle (minivan/truck, usually AWD for on- and off-road driving) |
| SWB | short wheelbase |

**CAR TERMS:**

| | |
|---|---|
| cabriolet | car with a removable/retractable soft top; convertible; drophead coupe |
| coupe | two-door car with hard top |
| crossover | vehicle built on a car platform with characteristics of van or SUV |
| drivetrain | See powertrain |
| drophead | See cabriolet |

doors:

| | |
|---|---|
| butterfly | slide upwards and move outwards (similar to scissor) |
| gullwing | hinged at the top to lift upwards |
| scissor | slide upwards from single fixed hinge at end of windscreen |
| suicide | hinged at the rear rather than the front (also known as coach doors) |

| | |
|---|---|
| estate car | station wagon; shooting brake |
| flathead | See sidevalve |
| hardtop | a car design that has no central roof struts (B-pillars) |
| homologated | certified (or approved) as meeting the standard requirements for a particular class of car when taking part in racing |
| inline | See straight |
| monocoque | a way of manufacturing a car as an integrated piece (unibody) instead of a body mounted onto a separately built chassis |
| muscle car | large, fast gas-guzzler with supercharged V8 engine |
| pickup | truck-like vehicle (either two- or four-door) with open load bed at back |
| pillars | the struts that hold up the car roof |
| A-pillars | struts at either side of front windscreen |
| B-pillars | centre struts behind the front doors |
| C-pillars | struts at either side of rear window |
| pony car | compact performance car of the late 1950s to 1970, inspired by Ford Mustang design |
| pushrod | an engine with an overhead valve (OHV) design |
| powertrain | parts of the car that deliver power to the road – engine, transmission, differential, driveshafts, drive wheels; drivetrain |
| roadster | two-seater convertible sports car |
| running gear | 1. suspension, shock absorbers and steering  or 2. transmission, driveshaft and wheels |
| saloon | four-door (family) hardtop car; sedan |
| sedan | See saloon |
| sidevalve | engine design in which valves are positioned at the side of the combustion chamber instead of at the cylinderhead – hence also known as 'flathead' |
| straight or inline | arrangement of cylinders in an engine. Cylinders are either in a line or a V (with variations such as staggered or W) |
| supercar | car with high horsepower engine for high speed and fast acceleration |
| woodie | estate car with a wooden body |
| ute | Australian utility vehicle; See pickup |

**NOTE ON ENGINE DISPLACEMENT (CAPACITY)**

In Europe and Japan, manufacturers normally give displacement data in cubic centimetres (cc). In the USA, it is conventionally given in litres or cubic inches. Throughout this book the data is given in cc except for cars manufactured in the USA for which it is given in litres (l) with the equivalent cubic inch displacement (cid) in brackets. 1 cu in = 16.387 cc.

# INDEX

page numbers in *italics* refer to photographs

# PICTURE CREDITS